FREE Study Skills Videos/DV

Dear Customer,

Thank you for your purchase from Mometrix! We consider it an honor and a privilege that you have purchased our product and we want to ensure your satisfaction.

As part of our ongoing effort to meet the needs of test takers, we have developed a set of Study Skills Videos that we would like to give you for <u>FREE</u>. These videos cover our *best practices* for getting ready for your exam, from how to use our study materials to how to best prepare for the day of the test.

All that we ask is that you email us with feedback that would describe your experience so far with our product. Good, bad, or indifferent, we want to know what you think!

To get your FREE Study Skills Videos, you can use the **QR code** below, or send us an **email** at studyvideos@mometrix.com with *FREE VIDEOS* in the subject line and the following information in the body of the email:

- The name of the product you purchased.
- Your product rating on a scale of 1-5, with 5 being the highest rating.
- Your feedback. It can be long, short, or anything in between. We just want to know your impressions and experience so far with our product. (Good feedback might include how our study material met your needs and ways we might be able to make it even better. You could highlight features that you found helpful or features that you think we should add.)

If you have any questions or concerns, please don't hesitate to contact me directly.

Thanks again!

Sincerely,

Jay Willis
Vice President
jay.willis@mometrix.com
1-800-673-8175

SSAT

Middle Level Prep Book 2021-2022

SSAT Secrets Study Guide

Full-Length Practice Test

Video Tutorials

Covers Quantitative (Math), Verbal (Vocabulary), and Reading

3rd Edition

Written and edited by Mometrix Test Prep

Printed in the United States of America

This paper meets the requirements of ANSI/NISO Z39.48-1992 (Permanence of Paper).

Mometrix offers volume discount pricing to institutions. For more information or a price quote, please contact our sales department at sales@mometrix.com or 888-248-1219.

Mometrix Media LLC is not affiliated with or endorsed by any official testing organization. All organizational and test names are trademarks of their respective owners.

Paperback
ISBN 13: 978-1-5167-1916-7
ISBN 10: 1-5167-1916-6

DEAR FUTURE EXAM SUCCESS STORY

First of all, **THANK YOU** for purchasing Mometrix study materials!

Second, congratulations! You are one of the few determined test-takers who are committed to doing whatever it takes to excel on your exam. **You have come to the right place.** We developed these study materials with one goal in mind: to deliver you the information you need in a format that's concise and easy to use.

In addition to optimizing your guide for the content of the test, we've outlined our recommended steps for breaking down the preparation process into small, attainable goals so you can make sure you stay on track.

We've also analyzed the entire test-taking process, identifying the most common pitfalls and showing how you can overcome them and be ready for any curveball the test throws you.

Standardized testing is one of the biggest obstacles on your road to success, which only increases the importance of doing well in the high-pressure, high-stakes environment of test day. Your results on this test could have a significant impact on your future, and this guide provides the information and practical advice to help you achieve your full potential on test day.

Your success is our success

We would love to hear from you! If you would like to share the story of your exam success or if you have any questions or comments in regard to our products, please contact us at **800-673-8175** or **support@mometrix.com**.

Thanks again for your business and we wish you continued success!

Sincerely,
The Mometrix Test Preparation Team

> **Need more help? Check out our flashcards at:**
> **http://mometrixflashcards.com/SSAT**

TABLE OF CONTENTS

Introduction

Thank you for purchasing this resource! You have made the choice to prepare yourself for a test that could have a huge impact on your future, and this guide is designed to help you be fully ready for test day. Obviously, it's important to have a solid understanding of the test material, but you also need to be prepared for the unique environment and stressors of the test, so that you can perform to the best of your abilities.

For this purpose, the first section that appears in this guide is the **Secret Keys**. We've devoted countless hours to meticulously researching what works and what doesn't, and we've boiled down our findings to the five most impactful steps you can take to improve your performance on the test. We start at the beginning with study planning and move through the preparation process, all the way to the testing strategies that will help you get the most out of what you know when you're finally sitting in front of the test.

We recommend that you start preparing for your test as far in advance as possible. However, if you've bought this guide as a last-minute study resource and only have a few days before your test, we recommend that you skip over the first two Secret Keys since they address a long-term study plan.

If you struggle with **test anxiety**, we strongly encourage you to check out our recommendations for how you can overcome it. Test anxiety is a formidable foe, but it can be beaten, and we want to make sure you have the tools you need to defeat it.

Secret Key #1 – Plan Big, Study Small

There's a lot riding on your performance. If you want to ace this test, you're going to need to keep your skills sharp and the material fresh in your mind. You need a plan that lets you review everything you need to know while still fitting in your schedule. We'll break this strategy down into three categories.

Information Organization

Start with the information you already have: the official test outline. From this, you can make a complete list of all the concepts you need to cover before the test. Organize these concepts into groups that can be studied together, and create a list of any related vocabulary you need to learn so you can brush up on any difficult terms. You'll want to keep this vocabulary list handy once you actually start studying since you may need to add to it along the way.

Time Management

Once you have your set of study concepts, decide how to spread them out over the time you have left before the test. Break your study plan into small, clear goals so you have a manageable task for each day and know exactly what you're doing. Then just focus on one small step at a time. When you manage your time this way, you don't need to spend hours at a time studying. Studying a small block of content for a short period each day helps you retain information better and avoid stressing over how much you have left to do. You can relax knowing that you have a plan to cover everything in time. In order for this strategy to be effective though, you have to start studying early and stick to your schedule. Avoid the exhaustion and futility that comes from last-minute cramming!

Study Environment

The environment you study in has a big impact on your learning. Studying in a coffee shop, while probably more enjoyable, is not likely to be as fruitful as studying in a quiet room. It's important to keep distractions to a minimum. You're only planning to study for a short block of time, so make the most of it. Don't pause to check your phone or get up to find a snack. It's also important to **avoid multitasking**. Research has consistently shown that multitasking will make your studying dramatically less effective. Your study area should also be comfortable and well-lit so you don't have the distraction of straining your eyes or sitting on an uncomfortable chair.

 The time of day you study is also important. You want to be rested and alert. Don't wait until just before bedtime. Study when you'll be most likely to comprehend and remember. Even better, if you know what time of day your test will be, set that time aside for study. That way your brain will be used to working on that subject at that specific time and you'll have a better chance of recalling information.

Finally, it can be helpful to team up with others who are studying for the same test. Your actual studying should be done in as isolated an environment as possible, but the work of organizing the information and setting up the study plan can be divided up. In between study sessions, you can discuss with your teammates the concepts that you're all studying and quiz each other on the details. Just be sure that your teammates are as serious about the test as you are. If you find that your study time is being replaced with social time, you might need to find a new team.

Secret Key #2 – Make Your Studying Count

You're devoting a lot of time and effort to preparing for this test, so you want to be absolutely certain it will pay off. This means doing more than just reading the content and hoping you can remember it on test day. It's important to make every minute of study count. There are two main areas you can focus on to make your studying count.

Retention

It doesn't matter how much time you study if you can't remember the material. You need to make sure you are retaining the concepts. To check your retention of the information you're learning, try recalling it at later times with minimal prompting. Try carrying around flashcards and glance at one or two from time to time or ask a friend who's also studying for the test to quiz you.

To enhance your retention, look for ways to put the information into practice so that you can apply it rather than simply recalling it. If you're using the information in practical ways, it will be much easier to remember. Similarly, it helps to solidify a concept in your mind if you're not only reading it to yourself but also explaining it to someone else. Ask a friend to let you teach them about a concept you're a little shaky on (or speak aloud to an imaginary audience if necessary). As you try to summarize, define, give examples, and answer your friend's questions, you'll understand the concepts better and they will stay with you longer. Finally, step back for a big picture view and ask yourself how each piece of information fits with the whole subject. When you link the different concepts together and see them working together as a whole, it's easier to remember the individual components.

Finally, practice showing your work on any multi-step problems, even if you're just studying. Writing out each step you take to solve a problem will help solidify the process in your mind, and you'll be more likely to remember it during the test.

Modality

Modality simply refers to the means or method by which you study. Choosing a study modality that fits your own individual learning style is crucial. No two people learn best in exactly the same way, so it's important to know your strengths and use them to your advantage.

For example, if you learn best by visualization, focus on visualizing a concept in your mind and draw an image or a diagram. Try color-coding your notes, illustrating them, or creating symbols that will trigger your mind to recall a learned concept. If you learn best by hearing or discussing information, find a study partner who learns the same way or read aloud to yourself. Think about how to put the information in your own words. Imagine that you are giving a lecture on the topic and record yourself so you can listen to it later.

For any learning style, flashcards can be helpful. Organize the information so you can take advantage of spare moments to review. Underline key words or phrases. Use different colors for different categories. Mnemonic devices (such as creating a short list in which every item starts with the same letter) can also help with retention. Find what works best for you and use it to store the information in your mind most effectively and easily.

3

Secret Key #3 – Practice the Right Way

Your success on test day depends not only on how many hours you put into preparing, but also on whether you prepared the right way. It's good to check along the way to see if your studying is paying off. One of the most effective ways to do this is by taking practice tests to evaluate your progress. Practice tests are useful because they show exactly where you need to improve. Every time you take a practice test, pay special attention to these three groups of questions:

- The questions you got wrong
- The questions you had to guess on, even if you guessed right
- The questions you found difficult or slow to work through

This will show you exactly what your weak areas are, and where you need to devote more study time. Ask yourself why each of these questions gave you trouble. Was it because you didn't understand the material? Was it because you didn't remember the vocabulary? Do you need more repetitions on this type of question to build speed and confidence? Dig into those questions and figure out how you can strengthen your weak areas as you go back to review the material.

 Additionally, many practice tests have a section explaining the answer choices. It can be tempting to read the explanation and think that you now have a good understanding of the concept. However, an explanation likely only covers part of the question's broader context. Even if the explanation makes perfect sense, **go back and investigate** every concept related to the question until you're positive you have a thorough understanding.

As you go along, keep in mind that the practice test is just that: practice. Memorizing these questions and answers will not be very helpful on the actual test because it is unlikely to have any of the same exact questions. If you only know the right answers to the sample questions, you won't be prepared for the real thing. **Study the concepts** until you understand them fully, and then you'll be able to answer any question that shows up on the test.

It's important to wait on the practice tests until you're ready. If you take a test on your first day of study, you may be overwhelmed by the amount of material covered and how much you need to learn. Work up to it gradually.

On test day, you'll need to be prepared for answering questions, managing your time, and using the test-taking strategies you've learned. It's a lot to balance, like a mental marathon that will have a big impact on your future. Like training for a marathon, you'll need to start slowly and work your way up. When test day arrives, you'll be ready.

Start with the strategies you've read in the first two Secret Keys—plan your course and study in the way that works best for you. If you have time, consider using multiple study resources to get different approaches to the same concepts. It can be helpful to see difficult concepts from more than one angle. Then find a good source for practice tests. Many times, the test website will suggest potential study resources or provide sample tests.

Practice Test Strategy

If you're able to find at least three practice tests, we recommend this strategy:

UNTIMED AND OPEN-BOOK PRACTICE

Take the first test with no time constraints and with your notes and study guide handy. Take your time and focus on applying the strategies you've learned.

TIMED AND OPEN-BOOK PRACTICE

Take the second practice test open-book as well, but set a timer and practice pacing yourself to finish in time.

TIMED AND CLOSED-BOOK PRACTICE

Take any other practice tests as if it were test day. Set a timer and put away your study materials. Sit at a table or desk in a quiet room, imagine yourself at the testing center, and answer questions as quickly and accurately as possible.

Keep repeating timed and closed-book tests on a regular basis until you run out of practice tests or it's time for the actual test. Your mind will be ready for the schedule and stress of test day, and you'll be able to focus on recalling the material you've learned.

Secret Key #4 – Pace Yourself

Once you're fully prepared for the material on the test, your biggest challenge on test day will be managing your time. Just knowing that the clock is ticking can make you panic even if you have plenty of time left. Work on pacing yourself so you can build confidence against the time constraints of the exam. Pacing is a difficult skill to master, especially in a high-pressure environment, so **practice is vital**.

Set time expectations for your pace based on how much time is available. For example, if a section has 60 questions and the time limit is 30 minutes, you know you have to average 30 seconds or less per question in order to answer them all. Although 30 seconds is the hard limit, set 25 seconds per question as your goal, so you reserve extra time to spend on harder questions. When you budget extra time for the harder questions, you no longer have any reason to stress when those questions take longer to answer.

Don't let this time expectation distract you from working through the test at a calm, steady pace, but keep it in mind so you don't spend too much time on any one question. Recognize that taking extra time on one question you don't understand may keep you from answering two that you do understand later in the test. If your time limit for a question is up and you're still not sure of the answer, mark it and move on, and come back to it later if the time and the test format allow. If the testing format doesn't allow you to return to earlier questions, just make an educated guess; then put it out of your mind and move on.

On the easier questions, be careful not to rush. It may seem wise to hurry through them so you have more time for the challenging ones, but it's not worth missing one if you know the concept and just didn't take the time to read the question fully. Work efficiently but make sure you understand the question and have looked at all of the answer choices, since more than one may seem right at first.

Even if you're paying attention to the time, you may find yourself a little behind at some point. You should speed up to get back on track, but do so wisely. Don't panic; just take a few seconds less on each question until you're caught up. Don't guess without thinking, but do look through the answer choices and eliminate any you know are wrong. If you can get down to two choices, it is often worthwhile to guess from those. Once you've chosen an answer, move on and don't dwell on any that you skipped or had to hurry through. If a question was taking too long, chances are it was one of the harder ones, so you weren't as likely to get it right anyway.

On the other hand, if you find yourself getting ahead of schedule, it may be beneficial to slow down a little. The more quickly you work, the more likely you are to make a careless mistake that will affect your score. You've budgeted time for each question, so don't be afraid to spend that time. Practice an efficient but careful pace to get the most out of the time you have.

6

Secret Key #5 – Have a Plan for Guessing

When you're taking the test, you may find yourself stuck on a question. Some of the answer choices seem better than others, but you don't see the one answer choice that is obviously correct. What do you do?

The scenario described above is very common, yet most test takers have not effectively prepared for it. Developing and practicing a plan for guessing may be one of the single most effective uses of your time as you get ready for the exam.

In developing your plan for guessing, there are three questions to address:

- When should you start the guessing process?
- How should you narrow down the choices?
- Which answer should you choose?

When to Start the Guessing Process

Unless your plan for guessing is to select C every time (which, despite its merits, is not what we recommend), you need to leave yourself enough time to apply your answer elimination strategies. Since you have a limited amount of time for each question, that means that if you're going to give yourself the best shot at guessing correctly, you have to decide quickly whether or not you will guess.

Of course, the best-case scenario is that you don't have to guess at all, so first, see if you can answer the question based on your knowledge of the subject and basic reasoning skills. Focus on the key words in the question and try to jog your memory of related topics. Give yourself a chance to bring the knowledge to mind, but once you realize that you don't have (or you can't access) the knowledge you need to answer the question, it's time to start the guessing process.

It's almost always better to start the guessing process too early than too late. It only takes a few seconds to remember something and answer the question from knowledge. Carefully eliminating wrong answer choices takes longer. Plus, going through the process of eliminating answer choices can actually help jog your memory.

Summary: Start the guessing process as soon as you decide that you can't answer the question based on your knowledge.

7

How to Narrow Down the Choices

The next chapter in this book (**Test-Taking Strategies**) includes a wide range of strategies for how to approach questions and how to look for answer choices to eliminate. You will definitely want to read those carefully, practice them, and figure out which ones work best for you. Here though, we're going to address a mindset rather than a particular strategy.

Your odds of guessing an answer correctly depend on how many options you are choosing from.

Number of options left	5	4	3	2	1
Odds of guessing correctly	20%	25%	33%	50%	100%

You can see from this chart just how valuable it is to be able to eliminate incorrect answers and make an educated guess, but there are two things that many test takers do that cause them to miss out on the benefits of guessing:

- Accidentally eliminating the correct answer
- Selecting an answer based on an impression

We'll look at the first one here, and the second one in the next section.

To avoid accidentally eliminating the correct answer, we recommend a thought exercise called **the $5 challenge**. In this challenge, you only eliminate an answer choice from contention if you are willing to bet $5 on it being wrong. Why $5? Five dollars is a small but not insignificant amount of money. It's an amount you could afford to lose but wouldn't want to throw away. And while losing

$5 once might not hurt too much, doing it twenty times will set you back $100. In the same way, each small decision you make—eliminating a choice here, guessing on a question there—won't by itself impact your score very much, but when you put them all together, they can make a big difference. By holding each answer choice elimination decision to a higher standard, you can reduce the risk of accidentally eliminating the correct answer.

The $5 challenge can also be applied in a positive sense: If you are willing to bet $5 that an answer choice *is* correct, go ahead and mark it as correct.

Summary: Only eliminate an answer choice if you are willing to bet $5 that it is wrong.

8

Which Answer to Choose

You're taking the test. You've run into a hard question and decided you'll have to guess. You've eliminated all the answer choices you're willing to bet $5 on. Now you have to pick an answer. Why do we even need to talk about this? Why can't you just pick whichever one you feel like when the time comes?

The answer to these questions is that if you don't come into the test with a plan, you'll rely on your impression to select an answer choice, and if you do that, you risk falling into a trap. The test writers know that everyone who takes their test will be guessing on some of the questions, so they intentionally write wrong answer choices to seem plausible. You still have to pick an answer though, and if the wrong answer choices are designed to look right, how can you ever be sure that you're not falling for their trap? The best solution we've found to this dilemma is to take the decision out of your hands entirely. Here is the process we recommend:

Once you've eliminated any choices that you are confident (willing to bet $5) are wrong, select the first remaining choice as your answer.

Whether you choose to select the first remaining choice, the second, or the last, the important thing is that you use some preselected standard. Using this approach guarantees that you will not be enticed into selecting an answer choice that looks right, because you are not basing your decision on how the answer choices look.

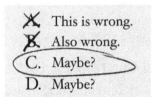

This is not meant to make you question your knowledge. Instead, it is to help you recognize the difference between your knowledge and your impressions. There's a huge difference between thinking an answer is right because of what you know, and thinking an answer is right because it looks or sounds like it should be right.

Summary: To ensure that your selection is appropriately random, make a predetermined selection from among all answer choices you have not eliminated.

Test-Taking Strategies

This section contains a list of test-taking strategies that you may find helpful as you work through the test. By taking what you know and applying logical thought, you can maximize your chances of answering any question correctly!

It is very important to realize that every question is different and every person is different: no single strategy will work on every question, and no single strategy will work for every person. That's why we've included all of them here, so you can try them out and determine which ones work best for different types of questions and which ones work best for you.

Question Strategies

⊘ READ CAREFULLY

Read the question and the answer choices carefully. Don't miss the question because you misread the terms. You have plenty of time to read each question thoroughly and make sure you understand what is being asked. Yet a happy medium must be attained, so don't waste too much time. You must read carefully and efficiently.

⊘ CONTEXTUAL CLUES

Look for contextual clues. If the question includes a word you are not familiar with, look at the immediate context for some indication of what the word might mean. Contextual clues can often give you all the information you need to decipher the meaning of an unfamiliar word. Even if you can't determine the meaning, you may be able to narrow down the possibilities enough to make a solid guess at the answer to the question.

⊘ PREFIXES

If you're having trouble with a word in the question or answer choices, try dissecting it. Take advantage of every clue that the word might include. Prefixes can be a huge help. Usually, they allow you to determine a basic meaning. *Pre-* means before, *post-* means after, *pro-* is positive, *de-* is negative. From prefixes, you can get an idea of the general meaning of the word and try to put it into context.

⊘ HEDGE WORDS

Watch out for critical hedge words, such as *likely, may, can, sometimes, often, almost, mostly, usually, generally, rarely,* and *sometimes*. Question writers insert these hedge phrases to cover every possibility. Often an answer choice will be wrong simply because it leaves no room for exception. Be on guard for answer choices that have definitive words such as *exactly* and *always*.

⊘ SWITCHBACK WORDS

Stay alert for *switchbacks*. These are the words and phrases frequently used to alert you to shifts in thought. The most common switchback words are *but, although,* and *however*. Others include *nevertheless, on the other hand, even though, while, in spite of, despite,* and *regardless of*. Switchback words are important to catch because they can change the direction of the question or an answer choice.

⊘ Face Value

When in doubt, use common sense. Accept the situation in the problem at face value. Don't read too much into it. These problems will not require you to make wild assumptions. If you have to go beyond creativity and warp time or space in order to have an answer choice fit the question, then you should move on and consider the other answer choices. These are normal problems rooted in reality. The applicable relationship or explanation may not be readily apparent, but it is there for you to figure out. Use your common sense to interpret anything that isn't clear.

Answer Choice Strategies

⊘ Answer Selection

The most thorough way to pick an answer choice is to identify and eliminate wrong answers until only one is left, then confirm it is the correct answer. Sometimes an answer choice may immediately seem right, but be careful. The test writers will usually put more than one reasonable answer choice on each question, so take a second to read all of them and make sure that the other choices are not equally obvious. As long as you have time left, it is better to read every answer choice than to pick the first one that looks right without checking the others.

⊘ Answer Choice Families

An answer choice family consists of two (in rare cases, three) answer choices that are very similar in construction and cannot all be true at the same time. If you see two answer choices that are direct opposites or parallels, one of them is usually the correct answer. For instance, if one answer choice says that quantity x increases and another either says that quantity x decreases (opposite) or says that quantity y increases (parallel), then those answer choices would fall into the same family. An answer choice that doesn't match the construction of the answer choice family is more likely to be incorrect. Most questions will not have answer choice families, but when they do appear, you should be prepared to recognize them.

⊘ Eliminate Answers

Eliminate answer choices as soon as you realize they are wrong, but make sure you consider all possibilities. If you are eliminating answer choices and realize that the last one you are left with is also wrong, don't panic. Start over and consider each choice again. There may be something you missed the first time that you will realize on the second pass.

⊘ Avoid Fact Traps

Don't be distracted by an answer choice that is factually true but doesn't answer the question. You are looking for the choice that answers the question. Stay focused on what the question is asking for so you don't accidentally pick an answer that is true but incorrect. Always go back to the question and make sure the answer choice you've selected actually answers the question and is not merely a true statement.

⊘ Extreme Statements

In general, you should avoid answers that put forth extreme actions as standard practice or proclaim controversial ideas as established fact. An answer choice that states the "process should be used in certain situations, if..." is much more likely to be correct than one that states the "process should be discontinued completely." The first is a calm rational statement and doesn't even make a definitive, uncompromising stance, using a hedge word *if* to provide wiggle room, whereas the second choice is far more extreme.

11

⊘ Benchmark

As you read through the answer choices and you come across one that seems to answer the question well, mentally select that answer choice. This is not your final answer, but it's the one that will help you evaluate the other answer choices. The one that you selected is your benchmark or standard for judging each of the other answer choices. Every other answer choice must be compared to your benchmark. That choice is correct until proven otherwise by another answer choice beating it. If you find a better answer, then that one becomes your new benchmark. Once you've decided that no other choice answers the question as well as your benchmark, you have your final answer.

⊘ Predict the Answer

Before you even start looking at the answer choices, it is often best to try to predict the answer. When you come up with the answer on your own, it is easier to avoid distractions and traps because you will know exactly what to look for. The right answer choice is unlikely to be word-for-word what you came up with, but it should be a close match. Even if you are confident that you have the right answer, you should still take the time to read each option before moving on.

General Strategies

⊘ Tough Questions

If you are stumped on a problem or it appears too hard or too difficult, don't waste time. Move on! Remember though, if you can quickly check for obviously incorrect answer choices, your chances of guessing correctly are greatly improved. Before you completely give up, at least try to knock out a couple of possible answers. Eliminate what you can and then guess at the remaining answer choices before moving on.

⊘ Check Your Work

Since you will probably not know every term listed and the answer to every question, it is important that you get credit for the ones that you do know. Don't miss any questions through careless mistakes. If at all possible, try to take a second to look back over your answer selection and make sure you've selected the correct answer choice and haven't made a costly careless mistake (such as marking an answer choice that you didn't mean to mark). This quick double check should more than pay for itself in caught mistakes for the time it costs.

⊘ Pace Yourself

It's easy to be overwhelmed when you're looking at a page full of questions; your mind is confused and full of random thoughts, and the clock is ticking down faster than you would like. Calm down and maintain the pace that you have set for yourself. Especially as you get down to the last few minutes of the test, don't let the small numbers on the clock make you panic. As long as you are on track by monitoring your pace, you are guaranteed to have time for each question.

⊘ Don't Rush

It is very easy to make errors when you are in a hurry. Maintaining a fast pace in answering questions is pointless if it makes you miss questions that you would have gotten right otherwise. Test writers like to include distracting information and wrong answers that seem right. Taking a little extra time to avoid careless mistakes can make all the difference in your test score. Find a pace that allows you to be confident in the answers that you select.

⊘ KEEP MOVING

Panicking will not help you pass the test, so do your best to stay calm and keep moving. Taking deep breaths and going through the answer elimination steps you practiced can help to break through a stress barrier and keep your pace.

Final Notes

The combination of a solid foundation of content knowledge and the confidence that comes from practicing your plan for applying that knowledge is the key to maximizing your performance on test day. As your foundation of content knowledge is built up and strengthened, you'll find that the strategies included in this chapter become more and more effective in helping you quickly sift through the distractions and traps of the test to isolate the correct answer.

Now that you're preparing to move forward into the test content chapters of this book, be sure to keep your goal in mind. As you read, think about how you will be able to apply this information on the test. If you've already seen sample questions for the test and you have an idea of the question format and style, try to come up with questions of your own that you can answer based on what you're reading. This will give you valuable practice applying your knowledge in the same ways you can expect to on test day.

Good luck and good studying!

Quantitative

Number Sense

NUMBERS AND THEIR CLASSIFICATIONS

There are several different kinds of numbers. When you learn to count as a child, you start with *Natural Numbers*. You may know them as counting numbers. These numbers begin with 1, 2, 3, and so on. *Whole Numbers* are all natural numbers and zero. *Integers* are all whole numbers and their related negative values (...-2, -1, 0, 1, 2...).

Aside from the number 1, all natural numbers are known as prime or composite. *Prime Numbers* are natural numbers that are greater than 1 and have factors that are 1 and itself (e.g., 3). On the other hand, *Composite Numbers* are natural numbers that are greater than 1 and are not prime numbers. The number 1 is a special case because it is not a prime number or composite number. *Rational numbers* include all integers, decimals, and fractions. Any terminating or repeating decimal number is a rational number.

Numbers are the basic building blocks of mathematics. These terms show some elements of numbers:

Integers – The set of positive and negative numbers. This set includes zero. Integers do not include fractions $\left(\frac{1}{3}\right)$, decimals (0.56), or mixed numbers $\left(7\frac{3}{4}\right)$.

Even number – Any integer that can be divided by 2 and does not leave a remainder.

Example: 2, 4, 6, 8, etc.

Odd number – Any integer that cannot be divided evenly by 2. For example: 3, 5, 7, 9, and so on.

Decimal number – a number that uses a decimal point to show the part of the number that is less than one. Example: 1.234.

Decimal point – a symbol used to separate the ones place from the tenths place in decimals. This symbol is used to separate dollars from cents in currency.

Decimal place – the position of a number to the right of the decimal point. In the decimal 0.123, the 1 is in the first place to the right of the decimal point. This is the place for tenths. The 2 is in the second place. This is the place for hundredths. The 3 is in the third place. This is the place for thousandths.

The decimal, or base 10, system is a number system that uses ten different digits (0, 1, 2, 3, 4, 5, 6, 7, 8, 9). Another system is the binary, or base 2, number system. This system is used by computers and uses the numbers 0 and 1. Some think that the base 10 system started because people had only their 10 fingers for counting.

PLACE VALUE

Write the Place Value of Each Digit in the Following Number: 14,059.826

1: ten thousands

4: thousands

0: hundreds

5: tens

9: ones

8: tenths

2: hundredths

6: thousandths

WRITING NUMBERS IN WORD FORM

Example 1

Write Each Number in Words.

29: twenty-nine

478: four hundred seventy-eight

9,435: nine thousand four hundred thirty-five

98,542: ninety-eight thousand five hundred forty-two

302876: three hundred two thousand eight hundred seventy-six

Example 2

Write each decimal in words.

0.06: six hundredths

0.6: six tenths

6.0: six

0.009: nine thousandths

0.113: one hundred thirteen thousandths

0.901: nine hundred and one thousandths

THE NUMBER LINE

A number line is a graph to see the distance between numbers. Basically, this graph shows the relationship between numbers. So a number line may have a point for zero and may show negative numbers on the left side of the line. Any positive numbers are placed on the right side of the line. For example, consider the points labeled on the following number line:

Example

Name each point on the number line below:

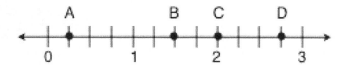

Use the dashed lines on the number line to identify each point. Each dashed line between two whole numbers is $\frac{1}{4}$. The line halfway between two numbers is $\frac{1}{2}$.

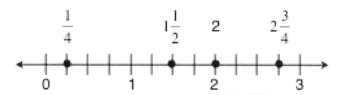

> **Review Video: Classification of Numbers**
> Visit mometrix.com/academy and enter code: 461071

LISTING NUMBERS: LEAST TO GREATEST

Example 1

4,002; 280; 108,511; 9

Answer: 9; 280; 4,002; 108,511

Example 2

5,075,000,600; 190,800,330; 7,000,300,001

Answer: 190,800,330; 5,075,000,600; 7,000,300,001

ROUNDING

Rounding is lowering the digits in a number and keeping the value similar. The result will be less accurate. However, this will be in a simpler form and will be easier to use. Whole numbers can be rounded to the nearest ten, hundred or thousand. Also, fractions and decimals can be rounded to the nearest whole number.

Example 1

Round each number to the nearest ten: 11 | 47 | 118.

When rounding to the nearest ten, anything ending in 5 or greater rounds up.

So, 11 rounds to 10 | 47 rounds to 50 | 118 rounds to 120.

Example 2

Round each number to the nearest hundred: 78 | 980 | 248.

When rounding to the nearest hundred, anything ending in 50 or greater rounds up.

So, 78 rounds to 100 | 980 rounds to 1000 | 248 rounds down to 200.

Example 3

Round each number to the nearest thousand: 302 | 1274 | 3756.

When rounding to the nearest thousand, anything ending in 500 or greater rounds up.

So, 302 rounds to 0 | 1274 rounds to 1000 | 3756 rounds to 4000.

Example 4

Round each number to the nearest whole number: $\frac{5}{8}$ | 2.12 | $\frac{14}{3}$.

When rounding fractions and decimals, anything half or higher rounds up.

So, $\frac{5}{8}$ rounds to 1 | 2.12 rounds to 2 | $\frac{14}{3}$ rounds to 5.

Decimals, Fractions, and Percents

DECIMALS

DECIMAL ILLUSTRATION

Use a model to represent the decimal: 0.24. Write 0.24 as a fraction.

The decimal 0.24 is twenty four hundredths. One possible model to represent this fraction is to draw 100 pennies, since each penny is worth 1 one hundredth of a dollar. Draw one hundred circles to represent one hundred pennies. Shade 24 of the pennies to represent the decimal twenty four hundredths.

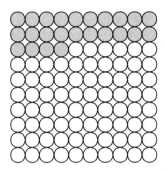

To write the decimal as a fraction, write a fraction: $\frac{\#\ shaded\ spaces}{\#\ total\ spaces}$. The number of shaded spaces is 24, and the total number of spaces is 100, so as a fraction 0.24 equals $\frac{24}{100}$. $\frac{24}{100}$ can then be reduced to $\frac{6}{25}$.

18

ADDING AND SUBTRACTING DECIMALS

When adding and subtracting decimals, the decimal points must always be aligned. Adding decimals is just like adding regular whole numbers.

Example: 4.5 + 2 = 6.5.

If the problem-solver does not properly align the decimal points, an incorrect answer of 4.7 may result. An easy way to add decimals is to align all of the decimal points in a vertical column visually. This will allow you to see exactly where the decimal should be placed in the final answer. Begin adding from right to left. Add each column in turn, making sure to carry the number to the left if a column adds up to more than 9. The same rules apply to the subtraction of decimals.

> **Review Video: Adding and Subtracting Decimals**
> Visit mometrix.com/academy and enter code: 381101

MULTIPLYING DECIMALS

A simple multiplication problem has two components: a multiplicand and a multiplier. When multiplying decimals, work as though the numbers were whole rather than decimals. Once the final product is calculated, count the number of places to the right of the decimal in both the multiplicand and the multiplier. Then, count that number of places from the right of the product and place the decimal in that position. For example, 12.3 x 2.56 has three places to the right of the respective decimals. Multiply 123 x 256 to get 31488. Now, beginning on the right, count three places to the left and insert the decimal. The final product will be 31.488.

> **Review Video: Multiplying Decimals**
> Visit mometrix.com/academy and enter code: 731574

DIVIDING DECIMALS

Every division problem has a divisor and a dividend. The dividend is the number that is being divided. In the problem 14 ÷ 7, 14 is the dividend and 7 is the divisor. In a division problem with decimals, the divisor must be converted into a whole number. Begin by moving the decimal in the divisor to the right until a whole number is created. Next, move the decimal in the dividend the same number of spaces to the right. For example, 4.9 into 24.5 would become 49 into 245. The decimal was moved one space to the right to create a whole number in the divisor, and then the same was done for the dividend. Once the whole numbers are created, the problem is carried out normally: 245 ÷ 49 = 5.

> **Review Video: Dividing Decimals**
> Visit mometrix.com/academy and enter code: 560690

FRACTIONS

A fraction has one integer that is written above another integer with a dividing line between them ($\frac{x}{y}$). It represents the quotient of the two numbers "x divided by y." Also, this can be thought of as x out of y equal parts. The x and y in this fraction are known as variables. When the value for a symbol can change, a variable is given to that value. So, a number like 3 is a constant. A value that does not change is a constant.

The top number of a fraction is called the numerator. This number stands for the number of parts. The 1 in $\frac{1}{4}$ means that this is one part out of the whole. The bottom number of a fraction is called the

19

denominator. This stands for the total number of equal parts. The 4 in $\frac{1}{4}$ means that the whole has four equal parts. A fraction cannot have a denominator of zero. This fraction is known as "undefined." The reverse of a fraction is known as the reciprocal. For example, the reciprocal of 1/2 is 2, and the reciprocal of 3 is 1/3.

Fractions can be changed by multiplying or dividing the numerator and denominator by the same number. This will not change the value of the fraction. You cannot do this with addition or subtraction. If you divide both numbers by a common factor, you will reduce or simplify the fraction. Two fractions that have the same value but are given in different ways are known as equivalent fractions. For example, $\frac{2}{10}, \frac{3}{15}, \frac{4}{20}$, and $\frac{5}{25}$ are equivalent fractions. Also, they can be reduced or simplified to $\frac{1}{5}$.

Two fractions can be changed to have the same denominator. This is known as finding a common denominator. The number for the common denominator should be the least common multiple of the original denominators. Example: $\frac{3}{4}$ and $\frac{5}{6}$; the least common multiple of 4 and 6 is 12. So, you can change these fractions to have a common denominator: $\frac{3}{4} = \frac{9}{12}$ and $\frac{5}{6} = \frac{10}{12}$.

If two fractions have a common denominator, you can add or subtract the fractions with the two numerators. Example: $\frac{1}{2} + \frac{1}{4} = \frac{2}{4} + \frac{1}{4} = \frac{3}{4}$. If the two fractions do not have the same denominator, one or both of them must be changed to have a common denominator. This needs to be done before they can be added or subtracted.

Two fractions can be multiplied. The two numerators need to be multiplied to find the new numerator. Also, the two denominators need to be multiplied to find the new denominator. Example: $\frac{1}{3} \times \frac{2}{3} = \frac{1 \times 2}{3 \times 3} = \frac{2}{9}$. Two fractions can be divided. First, flip the numerator and denominator of the second fraction. Then multiply the numerators and denominators.

Example: $\frac{2}{3} \div \frac{3}{4}$ becomes $\frac{2}{3} \times \frac{4}{3}$. Now, $\frac{8}{9}$ is your answer.

A fraction with a denominator that is greater than the numerator is known as a proper fraction. A fraction with a numerator that is greater than the denominator is known as an improper fraction. Proper fractions have values less than one. Improper fractions have values greater than one.

A mixed number is a number that has an integer and a fraction. Any improper fraction can be rewritten as a mixed number. Example: $\frac{8}{3} = \frac{6}{3} + \frac{2}{3} = 2 + \frac{2}{3} = 2\frac{2}{3}$.

Also, any mixed number can be rewritten as an improper fraction. Example: $1\frac{3}{5} = 1 + \frac{3}{5} = \frac{5}{5} + \frac{3}{5} = \frac{8}{5}$.

A fraction that has a fraction in the numerator, denominator, or both is called a *Complex Fraction*. These can be solved in many ways. The easiest way to solve the equation is to use order of operations.

For example, $\dfrac{\left(\frac{4}{7}\right)}{\left(\frac{5}{8}\right)} = {}^{0.571}/_{0.625} = 0.914$. Another way to solve this problem is to multiply the fraction in the numerator by the reciprocal of the fraction in the denominator. For example, $\dfrac{\left(\frac{4}{7}\right)}{\left(\frac{5}{8}\right)} = \dfrac{4}{7} \times \dfrac{8}{5} = \dfrac{32}{35} = 0.914$.

Review Video: Overview of Fractions
Visit mometrix.com/academy and enter code: 262335

PERCENTAGES

You can think of percentages as fractions that are based on a whole of 100. In other words, one whole is equal to 100%. The word percent means "per hundred." Fractions can be given as percents by using equivalent fractions with an amount of 100. Example: $\dfrac{7}{10} = \dfrac{70}{100} = 70\%$; Another example is $\dfrac{1}{4} = \dfrac{25}{100} = 25\%$. To give a percentage as a fraction, divide the percentage by 100. Then, reduce the fraction to its simplest possible terms. Example: $60\% = \dfrac{60}{100} = \dfrac{3}{5}$; $96\% = \dfrac{96}{100} = \dfrac{24}{25}$.

Converting decimals to percentages and percentages to decimals is as simple as moving the decimal point. To convert from a decimal to a percent, move the decimal point two places to the right. To convert from a percent to a decimal, move the decimal two places to the left.

Example: 0.23 = 23%; 5.34 = 534%; 0.007 = 0.7%; 700% = 7.00; 86% = 0.86; 0.15% = 0.0015.

A percentage problem can come in three main ways.

- Type 1: What percentage of 40 is 8?
- Type 2: What number is 20% of 40?
- Type 3: What number is 8 20% of?

The three parts in these examples are the same: a whole (W), a part (P), and a percentage (%).

To solve type (1), use the equation % = P/W.

To solve type (2), use the equation: P = W × %.

To solve type (3), use the equation W = P/%.

PERCENTAGE PROBLEMS

Percentage problems can be difficult because many are word problems. So, a main part of solving them is to know which quantities to use.

<u>Example 1</u>

In a school cafeteria, 7 students choose pizza, 9 choose hamburgers, and 4 choose tacos. Find the percentage that chose tacos.

To find the whole, you must add all of the parts: 7 + 9 + 4 = 20. Then, the percentage can be found by dividing the part by the whole (% = P/W): $\dfrac{4}{20} = \dfrac{20}{100} = 20\%$.

Example 2

At a hospital, 40% of the nurses work in labor and delivery. If 20 nurses work in labor and delivery, how many nurses work at the hospital?

To answer this problem, first think about the number of nurses that work at the hospital. Will it be more or less than the number of nurses who work in a specific department such as labor and delivery? More nurses work at the hospital, so the number you find to answer this question will be greater than 20.

40% of the nurses are labor and delivery nurses. "Of" indicates multiplication, and words like "is" and "are" indicate equivalence. Translating the problem into a mathematical sentence gives $40\% \cdot n = 20$, where n represents the total number of nurses. Solving for n gives $n = \frac{20}{40\%} = \frac{20}{0.40} = 50$.

Fifty nurses work at the hospital.

Example 3

A patient was given 40 mg of a certain medicine. Later, the patient's dosage was increased to 45 mg. What was the percent increase in his medication?

To find the percent increase, first compare the original and increased amounts. The original amount was 40 mg, and the increased amount is 45 mg, so the dosage of medication was increased by 5 mg (45 – 40 = 5). Note, however, that the question asks not by how much the dosage increased but by what percentage it increased. Percent increase = $\frac{\text{new amount} - \text{original amount}}{\text{original amount}} \cdot 100\%$.

So, $\frac{45 \text{ mg} - 40 \text{ mg}}{40 \text{ mg}} \cdot 100\% = \frac{5}{40} \cdot 100\% = 0.125 \cdot 100\% \approx 12.5\%$

The percent increase is approximately 12.5%.

CONVERTING DECIMALS TO FRACTIONS

A fraction can be turned into a decimal and vice versa. In order to convert a fraction into a decimal, simply divide the numerator by the denominator. For example, the fraction $\frac{5}{4}$ becomes 1.25. This is done by dividing 5 by 4. The fraction $\frac{4}{8}$ becomes 0.5 when 4 is divided by 8. This remains true even if the fraction $\frac{4}{8}$ is first reduced to $\frac{1}{2}$. The decimal conversion will still be 0.5. In order to convert a decimal into a fraction, count the number of places to the right of the decimal. This will be the number of zeros in the denominator. The numbers to the right of the decimal will become the whole number in the numerator.

Example 1:

$0.45 = \frac{45}{100}$

$\frac{45}{100}$ reduces to $\frac{9}{20}$

Example 2:

$0.237 = \frac{237}{1000}$

Example 3:

$$0.2121 = \frac{2121}{10000}$$

Operations

There are four basic operations in math: addition, subtraction, multiplication, and division.

Addition increases the value of one number by the value of another number.

Example: 2 + 4 = 6; 8 + 9 = 17. The result is called the sum. With addition, the order does not matter. 4 + 2 or 2 + 4 equals 6. This is the commutative property for addition.

Subtraction decreases the value of one number by the value of another number. The result is called the difference. Example: 6 – 4 = 2 and 17 – 8 = 9. Note for subtraction that the order does matter. For example, 6 – 4 and 4 – 6 do not have the same difference.

Multiplication is like repeated addition. This operation tells how many times one number needs to be added to the other number. Example: 3 × 2 (three times two) = 2 + 2 + 2 = 6. With multiplication, the order does not matter. 2 × 3 (or 3 + 3) = 3 × 2 (or 2 + 2 + 2). This is the commutative property for multiplication.

Division is the opposite operation to multiplication. This operation shows how much of a number is in another number. The first number is known as the dividend. The second number is known as the divisor. The answer to the division problem is known as the quotient.

Example: 20 ÷ 4 = 5. If 20 is split into 4 equal parts, then each part is 5. With division, the order of the numbers does matter. 20 ÷ 4 and 4 ÷ 20 do not give the same result. Note that you cannot divide a number by zero. If you try to divide a number by zero, then the answer is known as undefined.

WORKING WITH POSITIVE & NEGATIVE NUMBERS

Addition: If the signs are the same, then add the absolute values of the addends and use the original sign with the sum. The addends are the numbers that will be added to have the sum. For example, $(+4) + (+8) = +12$ and $(-4) + (-8) = -12$. When the signs are different, take the absolute values of the addends and subtract the smaller value from the larger value. Then, put the original sign of the larger value on the difference. For example, $(+4) + (-8) = -4$ and $(-4) + (+8) = +4$.

Subtraction: For signed numbers, change the sign of the number after the minus symbol. Then, follow the same rules for addition. For example, $(+4)-(+8)$ becomes $(+4) + (-8) = -4$.

Multiplication: If the signs are the same, then the product is positive. For example, $(+4) \times (+8) = +32$ and $(-4) \times (-8) = +32$. If the signs are different, then the product is negative. For example, $(+4) \times (-8) = -32$ and $(-4) \times (+8) = -32$. When more than two factors are multiplied together, the sign of the product is decided by how many negative factors are in the equation. If there are an odd number of negative factors, then the product is negative. An even number of negative factors gives a positive product. For example, $(+4) \times (-8) \times (-2) = +64$ and $(-4) \times (-8) \times (-2) = -64$.

Division: The rules for dividing signed numbers are similar to multiplying signed numbers. If the dividend and divisor have the same sign, the quotient is positive. If the dividend and divisor have opposite signs, the quotient is negative. For example, $(-4) \div (+8) = -0.5$.

ORDER OF OPERATIONS

Order of Operations is a list of rules that gives the order of doing each operation in an expression. If you have an expression that with many different operations, Order of Operations tells you which operations to do first. An easy way to remember Order of Operations is PEMDAS.

This is written out as "Please Excuse My Dear Aunt Sally." PEMDAS stands for Parentheses, Exponents, Multiplication, Division, Addition, Subtraction. You need to understand that multiplication and division are equal as steps. Also, addition and subtraction are equal as steps. So, those pairs of operations are worked from left to right.

Example: Use order of operations for the expression $5 + 20 \div 4 \times (2 + 3)^2 - 6$.

P: Work on the operations inside the parentheses, $(2 + 3) = 5$.

E: Simplify the exponents, $(5)^2 = 25$.

The equation now looks like this: $5 + 20 \div 4 \times 25 - 6$.

MD: Work on multiplication and division from left to right, $20 \div 4 = 5$; then $5 \times 25 = 125$.

The equation now looks like this: $5 + 125 - 6$.

AS: Work on addition and subtraction from left to right, $5 + 125 = 130$; then $130 - 6 = 124$.

Review Video: Order of Operations
Visit mometrix.com/academy and enter code: 259675

ESTIMATION

Estimation is the process of finding an approximate answer to a problem. Estimation may involve rounding to the nearest whole number to make addition or subtraction easier.

Example 1

There are 24 people in an English class. Miss Foster decides to order three exam books for each student, plus 6 extras. She estimates that she should order 90 exam books. Identify if her solution is reasonable.

Write an expression to determine the total number of exam books to order. Since three books are ordered for each student, first multiply the number of books per student by the number of students: 3 books per student · 24 students = 72 books. Next, add the six extra exam books that Miss Foster would like to order. The total number of books to order is: 72 + 6 = 78 books. Her original estimate of 90 exam books is too large.

Example 2

The following food items are available in a school cafeteria for lunch:

Sandwich: $3.15; Soup: $1.84

Salad: $2.62; Pretzels: $0.95

Milk: $0.40

Daniel has $4.00 and wants to purchase a milk, sandwich, and soup. Emily has $4.00 and wants to purchase a salad, pretzels, and milk. Estimate the cost of each student's lunch and determine if they have enough money to purchase the food they would like for lunch.

Daniel wants to purchase a milk, sandwich, and soup. Rounded to the nearest fifty cents, the cost of his items is $0.50, $3.00, and $2.00. The total for his three items would be approximately:

$$0.50 + 3.00 + 2.00 = 5.50$$

It will cost Daniel approximately $5.50 for his lunch. He does not have enough money to purchase the items he has selected.

Emily wants to purchase a salad, pretzels, and milk. Rounded to the nearest fifty cents, the cost of her items is $2.50, $1.00, and $0.50. The total for her three items would be approximately:

$$2.50 + 1.00 + 0.50 = 4.00$$

It will cost Emily approximately $4.00 for her lunch. She has approximately enough money to purchase the items she has selected.

Factors and Multiples

FACTORS AND MULTIPLES

Factors are numbers that are multiplied for a product. An example is the equation $2 \times 3 = 6$. The numbers 2 and 3 are factors. A prime number has only two factors: 1 and itself. Other numbers can have many factors.

> **Review Video: Factors**
> Visit mometrix.com/academy and enter code: 920086

A common factor is a number that divides exactly into two or more numbers. For example, the factors of 12 are 1, 2, 3, 4, 6, and 12. The factors of 15 are 1, 3, 5, and 15. So, the common factors of 12 and 15 are 1 and 3. A prime factor is a factor that is a prime number. Thus, the prime factors of 12 are 2 and 3. For 15, the prime factors are 3 and 5.

The greatest common factor (GCF) is the largest number that is a factor of two or more numbers. For example, the factors of 15 are 1, 3, 5, and 15. The factors of 35 are 1, 5, 7, and 35. So, the greatest common factor of 15 and 35 is 5.

A multiple of a number is the product of the number and some other integer. Common multiples are multiples that are shared by two numbers. The least common multiple (LCM) is the smallest number that is a multiple of two or more numbers. For example, the multiples of 3 are 3, 6, 9, 12, 15, etc. The multiples of 5 are 5, 10, 15, 20, etc. Therefore, the least common multiple of 3 and 5 is 15.

> **Review Video: Multiples**
> Visit mometrix.com/academy and enter code: 626738

Ratios, Proportions, and Scale Drawings

RATIOS

A ratio is a comparison of two numbers in a certain order. Example: There are 14 computers in a lab, and the class has 20 students. So, there is a student to computer ratio of 20 to 14. Normally, this is written as 20:14.

Ratios can be listed as *a to b*, *a:b*, or *a/b*. Examples of ratios are miles per hour (miles/hour), meters per second (meters/second), and miles per gallon (miles/gallon).

> **Review Video: Ratios**
> Visit mometrix.com/academy and enter code: 996914

PROPORTIONS AND CROSS PRODUCTS

A proportion is a relationship between two numbers. This relationship shows how one changes when the other changes. A direct proportion is a relationship where a number increases by a set amount with every increase in the other number.

Another way is for the number to decrease by that same amount for every decrease in the other quantity. Example: For every 1 sheet cake, 18 people can have cake. The number of sheet cakes and the number of people that can be served from them is a direct proportion.

Inverse proportion is a relationship where an increase in one number has a decrease in the other. This can work the other way where a decrease in a number has an increase in the other.

Example: The time needed for a car trip decreases as the speed increases. Also, the time for the trip increases as the speed decreases. So, the time needed for the trip is inversely proportional to the speed of the car.

Two equal ratios have cross products that are equal. This can be written as $\frac{m}{b} = \frac{w}{z}$. For example, Fred travels 2 miles in 1 hour, and Jane travels 4 miles in 2 hours. So, their speeds are proportional because $\frac{2}{1} = \frac{4}{2}$.

In a proportion, the product of the numerator of the first ratio and the denominator of the second ratio is equal to the product of the denominator of the first ratio and the numerator of the second ratio. In other words, you can see that $m \times z = b \times w$. So, $2 \times 2 = 1 \times 4$.

> **Review Video: Proportions**
> Visit mometrix.com/academy and enter code: 505355

ACTUAL DRAWINGS AND SCALE DRAWINGS

A map has a key for measurements to compare real distances with a scale distance.

Example: The key on one map says that 2 inches on the map is 12 real miles. Find the distance of a route that is 5 inches long on the map.

A proportion is needed to show the map measurements and real distances. First, write a ratio that has the information in the key. The map measurement can be in the numerator, and the real distance can be in the denominator.

$$\frac{2 \text{ inches}}{12 \text{ miles}}$$

Next, write a ratio with the known map distance and the unknown real distance. The unknown number for miles can be represented with the letter m.

$$\frac{5 \text{ inches}}{m \text{ miles}}$$

Then, write out the ratios in a proportion and solve it for m.

$$\frac{2 \text{ inches}}{12 \text{ miles}} = \frac{5 \text{ inches}}{m \text{ miles}}$$

Now, you have $2m = 60$. So you are left with $m = 30$. Thus, the route is 30 miles long.

Algebra, Functions, and Patterns

TRANSLATING
WORDS TO MATHEMATICAL EXPRESSION

Write "four less than twice x" as a mathematical expression.

Remember that an expression does not have an equals sign. "Less" indicates subtraction, and "twice" indicates multiplication by two. Four less than $2x$ is $2x - 4$. Notice how this is different than $4 - 2x$. You can plug in values for x to see how these expressions would yield different values.

WORDS TO MATHEMATICAL EQUATION

Translate "three hundred twenty-five increased by six times $3x$ equals three hundred forty-three" into a mathematical equation.

The key words and phrases are "increased by," "times," and "equals."

Three hundred twenty-five increased by six times $3x$ equals three hundred forty-three:

$$325 + 6(3x) = 343$$

The mathematical sentence is $325 + 6(3x) = 343$.

MATHEMATICAL EXPRESSION TO A PHRASE

Write a phrase which represents this mathematical expression: $75 - 3t + 14^2$.

Because there are many words which indicate various operations, there are several ways to write this expression, including "seventy-five minus three times t plus fourteen squared."

ROOTS AND SQUARE ROOTS

A root, or *Square Root*, is a number that when multiplied by itself gives a real number. For example, $\sqrt{4} = +2$ and -2 because $(-2) \times (-2) = 4$ and $(2) \times (2) = 4$. Now, $\sqrt{9} = +3$ and -3 because $(-3) \times (-3) = 9$ and $(3) \times (3) = 9$. So, +2 and -2 are square roots of 4. Also, +3 and -3 are square roots of 9.

Instead of using a superscript (e.g., a^x), roots use the radical symbol (e.g., $\sqrt{}$) for the operation. A radical will have a number underneath the bar (i.e., radical symbol). Also, a number can be placed in the index. This is the upper left where n is placed: $\sqrt[n]{a}$. So, this is read as *the nth root of a*. There are two special cases for the use of n. When n = 2, this is a square root. When n = 3, this is a cube root.

If there is no number to the upper left, it is understood to be a square root (n = 2). Almost all of the roots that you will face will be square roots. A square root is the same as a number raised to the $\frac{1}{2}$ power. When we say that a is the square root of b (a = $\sqrt{b}$), we mean that the variable multiplied by itself equals b: (a × a = b).

A perfect square is a number that has an integer for its square root. There are 10 perfect squares from 1 to 100: 1, 4, 9, 16, 25, 36, 49, 64, 81, 100. These are the squares for integers: 1, 2, 3, 4, 5, 6, 7, 8, 9, and 10.

EXPONENTS AND PARENTHESES

A number like 7, 23, or 97 is a base number. A number that is connected to the base number like 7^3, 23^4, or 97^2 is a superscript number. An exponent is a superscript number placed at the top right of a base number. Exponents are a short form of a longer math operation. This superscript number shows how many times the base number is to be multiplied by itself.

Example: $a^2 = a \times a$ or $2^4 = 2 \times 2 \times 2 \times 2$. A number with an exponent of 2 is said to be *squared*. A number with an exponent of 3 is said to be *cubed*. The value of a number raised to an exponent is called its power. So, 8^4 is read as *8 to the 4th power* or *8 raised to the power of 4*. A negative exponent can be written as a fraction to have a positive exponent. Example: $a^{-2} = 1/a^2$.

LAWS OF EXPONENTS

The laws of exponents are as follows:

1. Any number to the power of 1 is equal to itself: $a^1 = a$.
   Examples: $2^1=2$ | $-3^1=-3$
2. The number 1 raised to any power is equal to 1: $1^n = 1$.
   Examples: $1^3=1$ | $1^{30}=1$
3. Any number raised to the power of 0 is equal to 1: $a^0 = 1$.
   Examples: $8^0=1$ | $(-10)^0=1$ | $(1/2)^0=1$
4. Add exponents to multiply powers of the same base number: $a^n \times a^m = a^{n+m}$.
   Example: $2^3 \times 2^4 = 2^{3+4} = 2^7 = 128$
5. Subtract exponents to divide powers of the same base number: $a^n \div a^m = a^{n-m}$.
   Example: $\frac{2^5}{2^3} = 2^{5-3} = 2^2 = 4$
6. When a power is raised to a power, the exponents are multiplied: $(a^n)^m = a^{n \times m}$.
   Example: $(3^2)^3 = 3^2 \times 3^2 \times 3^2 = 3^6 = 729$
7. Multiplication and division operations that are inside parentheses can be raised to a power. This is the same as each term being raised to that power: $(a \times b)^n = a^n \times b^n$; $(a \div b)^n = a^n \div b^n$.
   Multiplication: $(2 \times 3)^2 = 2^2 \times 3^2 = 4 \times 9 = 36$
   Division: $(4 \div 3)^3 = 4^3 \div 3^3 = 64 \div 27 = 2.37$

Note: Exponents do not have to be integers. Fractional or decimal exponents follow all the rules above as well. Example: $5^{\frac{1}{4}} \times 5^{\frac{3}{4}} = 5^{\frac{1}{4}+\frac{3}{4}} = 5^1 = 5$.

> **Review Video: Laws of Exponents**
> Visit mometrix.com/academy and enter code: 532558

Parentheses are used to show which operation should be done first when there is more than one operation. Example: $4 - (2 + 1) = 1$. So, the first step for this problem is to add 2 and 1. Then, subtract the sum from 4.

PROPERTIES

The Commutative Property of Addition is shown here, which states that you can add terms in any order.

$$2x + y = y + 2x$$

The Distributive Property is shown here, which states that a number multiplied to an expression in parentheses must be multiplied to every term in the parentheses.

$$5 \times (x + 1) = (5 \times x) + (5 \times 1)$$

The Identity Property of Multiplication is shown here, which states that multiplying a number or term by 1 does not change its value.

$$3 \times 1 = 3$$

The Commutative Property of Multiplication is shown here, which states that you can multiply terms in any order.

$$6 \times m \times n = m \times n \times 6$$

The Associative Property of Multiplication is shown here, which states that any group of numbers and/or variables can be grouped together in parentheses to be multiplied first before multiplying by the remaining numbers and/or variables.

$$4 \times (5a) = (4a) \times 5$$

The Identity Property of Addition is shown here, which states that adding 0 to any number or term does not change the value of that number or term.

$$s + 0 = s$$

The Associative Property of Addition is shown here, which states that any group of numbers and/or variables can be grouped together in parentheses to be added first before adding the remaining numbers and/or variables.

$$10 + (6 + 1) = (10 + 6) + 1$$

COEFFICIENTS AND THE DISTRIBUTIVE PROPERTY

COEFFICIENTS

A coefficient is a number or symbol that is multiplied by a variable. For example, in the expression 2(ab), the number 2 is the coefficient of (ab). The expression can be written in other ways to have a different coefficient. For example, the expression can be 2a(b). This means that 2a is the coefficient of (b).

DISTRIBUTIVE PROPERTY

The distributive property can be used to multiply each addend in parentheses. Then, the products are added to reach the result. The formula for the distributive property looks like this:

$$a(b + c) = ab + ac$$

Example: 6(2+4)

First, multiply 6 and 2. The answer is 12.

Then, multiply 6 and 4. The answer is 24.

Last, we add 12 and 24. So, the final answer is 36.

SOLVING FOR A VARIABLE

Similar to order of operation rules, algebraic rules must be obeyed to ensure a correct answer. Begin by locating all parentheses and brackets, and then solving the equations within them. Then, perform the operations necessary to remove all parentheses and brackets. Next, convert all fractions into whole numbers and combine common terms on each side of the equation.

Beginning on the left side of the expression, solve operations involving multiplication and division. Then, work left to right solving operations involving addition and subtraction. Finally, cross-multiply if necessary, to reach the final solution.

Example 1:

$4a$-10=10

Constants are the numbers in equations that do not change. The variable in this equation is a. Variables are most commonly presented as either x or y, but they can be any letter. Every variable is equal to a number; one must solve the equation to determine what that number is. In an algebraic expression, the answer will usually be the number represented by the variable. In order to solve this equation, keep in mind that what is done to one side must be done to the other side as well. The first step will be to remove 10 from the left side by adding 10 to both sides. This will be expressed as $4a$-10+10=10+10, which simplifies to $4a$=20. Next, remove the 4 by dividing both sides by 4. This step will be expressed as $4a$÷4=20÷4. The expression now becomes a=5.

Since variables are the letters that represent an unknown number, you must solve for that unknown number in single variable problems. The main thing to remember is that you can do anything to one side of an equation as long as you do it to the other.

Example 2:

Solve for x in the equation 2x + 3 = 5.

Answer: First you want to get the "2x" isolated by itself on one side. To do that, first get rid of the 3. Subtract 3 from both sides of the equation 2x + 3 – 3 = 5 – 3 or 2x = 2. Now since the x is being multiplied by the 2 in "2x", you must divide by 2 to get rid of it. So, divide both sides by 2, which gives 2x / 2 = 2 / 2 or x = 1.

MANIPULATING EQUATIONS

Sometimes you will have variables missing in equations. So, you need to find the missing variable. To do this, you need to remember one important thing: whatever you do to one side of an equation, you need to do to the other side. If you subtract 100 from one side of an equation, you need to subtract 100 from the other side of the equation. This will allow you to change the form of the equation to find missing values.

Example

Ray earns $10 an hour. This can be given with the expression $10x$, where x is equal to the number of hours that Ray works. This is the independent variable. The independent variable is the amount that can change. The money that Ray earns is in y hours. So, you would write the equation: $10x = y$. The variable y is the dependent variable. This depends on x and cannot be changed. Now, let's say that Ray makes $360. How many hours did he work to make $360?

$$10x = 360$$

Now, you want to know how many hours that Ray worked. So, you want to get x by itself. To do that, you can divide both sides of the equation by 10.

$$\frac{10x}{10} = \frac{360}{10}$$

So, you have: $x = 36$. Now, you know that Ray worked 36 hours to make $360.

FUNCTIONS
Example 1

The table below is the value of each part of an ordered pair. An ordered pair is written as: (x, y)

x	y
2	6
4	12
6	18
8	24

You can find y if you know x. The number in the y column is three times the number in the x column. Multiply the x number by 3 to get the y number.

x	y
2	$2 \times 3 = 6$
4	$4 \times 3 = 12$
6	$6 \times 3 = 18$
8	$8 \times 3 = 24$

Example 2

The table shows some data points for a linear function. What is the missing value in the table?

x	y
0	?
3	50
5	80

The data in the table represent a linear function. For a linear function, the rate of change is equal to the slope. To find the slope, calculate the change in y divided by the change in x for the two given points from the table: $m = \frac{80-50}{5-3} = \frac{30}{2} = 15$

The rate of change of the linear function is 15. This means for each increase of 1 in the value of x, the value of y increases by 15. Similarly, each decrease of 1 in the value of x decreases the value of y by 15. The x-value 0 is 3 less than 3, so subtract $3 \cdot 15 = 45$ from 50 to get $y = 5$. This is the missing value in the table.

SEQUENCING

Example 1

Use the sequence to find each of the following.

6, 13, 20, 27, 34, 41, …

a) Find the position of 34.

b) Find the value of the term in position 7.

a) The position of a term is its place in the sequence. The sequence begins with 6, in position 1, 13 is position 2, etc. The term 34 has a position of 5.

b) The terms in positions 1 through 6 are given. To find the term in position 7, identify the difference between each term.

13 – 6 = 7

20 – 13 = 7

27 – 20 = 7

34 – 27 = 7

41 – 34 = 7

The terms are increasing by 7. To find the 7th term, add 7 to the sixth term, 41:

41 + 7 = 48

The term in position 7 is 48.

Example 2

The nth term of a sequence is: $4n - 6$. Find the terms in position: 1, 4, and 10.

To find the terms in each given position, evaluate the expression for the nth term at the given position values.

1st term: $4(1) - 6 = 4 - 6 = -2$

4th term: $4(4) - 6 = 16 - 6 = 10$

10th term: $4(10) - 6 = 40 - 6 = 34$

Example 3

Write an algebraic expression to determine the nth term of the arithmetic sequence:

31, 25, 19, 13, ...

To find the nth term, find the common difference between each pair of given terms.

2nd term – 1st term: 25 – 31 = –6

3rd term – 2nd term: 19 – 25 = –6

4th term – 3rd term: 13 – 19 = –6

The first term is 31, so when n = 1, the term is 31.

1st term: 31 + –6(n – 1)

Simplify this expression and check it for terms 2, 3, and 4 by evaluating the expression at n = 2, 3, and 4.

31 + –6(n – 1) = 31 – 6n + 6 = –6n + 37

2nd term: –6(2) + 37 = –12 + 37 = 25

3rd term: –6(3) + 37 = –18 + 37 = 19

4th term: –6(4) + 37 = –24 + 37 = 13

The nth term of the arithmetic sequence is –6n + 37.

Geometry

LINES AND PLANES

A point is a fixed location in space. This point has no size or dimensions. Commonly, this fixed location is a dot. A collinear point is a point which is on the line. A non-collinear point is a point that is not on a line.

A line is a set of points that go forever in two opposite directions. The line has length but no width or depth. A line can be named by any two points that are on the line. A line segment is a part of a line that has definite endpoints. A ray is a part of a line that goes from a single point and goes in one direction along the line. A ray has a definite beginning but no ending.

A plane is a two-dimensional flat surface that has three non-collinear points. A plane goes an unending distance in all directions in those two dimensions. This plane has an unending number of points, parallel lines and segments, intersecting lines and segments. Also, a plane can have an unending number of parallel or intersecting rays. A plane will never have a three-dimensional figure or skew lines. Two given planes will be parallel, or they will intersect to form a line. A plane may intersect a circular conic surface (e.g., a cone) to make conic sections (e.g., the parabola, hyperbola, circle, or ellipse).

Perpendicular lines are lines that intersect at right angles. The symbol ⊥ stands for perpendicular lines. The shortest distance from a line to a point that is not on the line is a perpendicular segment from the point to the line.

Parallel lines are lines in the same plane that have no points in common and never meet. The lines can be in different planes, have no points in common, and never meet. However, the lines will not be parallel because they are in different planes.

A bisector is a line or line segment that divides another line segment into two equal lengths. A perpendicular bisector of a line segment has points that are equidistant (i.e., equal distances) from the endpoints of the segment.

Intersecting lines are lines that have exactly one point in common. Concurrent lines are several lines that intersect at a single point. A transversal is a line that intersects at least two other lines. The lines may or may not be parallel to one another. A transversal that intersects parallel lines is common in geometry.

COORDINATE PLANE

Often, algebraic functions and equations are shown on a graph. This graph is known as the *Cartesian Coordinate Plane*. The Cartesian coordinate plane has two number lines that are perpendicular. These lines intersect at the zero point. This point is also known as the origin. The horizontal number line is known as the *x*-axis.

On the *x*-axis, there are positive values to the right of the origin and negative values to the left of the origin. The vertical number line is known as the *y*-axis. There are positive values above the origin and negative values below the origin. Any point on the plane can be found with an ordered pair.

This ordered pair comes in the form of (*x,y*). This pair is known as coordinates. The *x*-value of the coordinate is called the abscissa. The *y*-value of the coordinate is called the ordinate. The two number lines divide the plane into four parts. Each part is known as a quadrant. The quadrants are labeled as I, II, III, and IV.

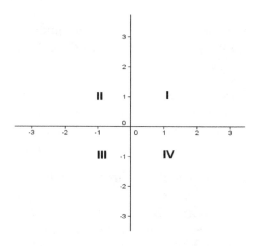

<u>Example</u>

The following points go on the coordinate plane:

A. (−4, −2) | B. (−1, 3) | C. (2, 2) | D. (3, −1)

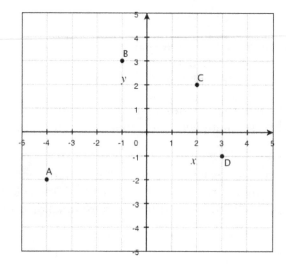

Before learning the different forms of equations for graphing, you need to know some definitions. A ratio of the change in the vertical distance to the change in horizontal distance is called the *Slope*.

On a graph with two points, (x_1, y_1) and (x_2, y_2), the **slope** is found with the formula $m = \frac{y_2 - y_1}{x_2 - x_1}$; where $x_1 \neq x_2$ and m stands for slope. If the value of the slope is **positive**, the line has an *upward direction* from left to right. If the value of the slope is **negative**, the line has a *downward direction* from left to right. The example of the graph below is a positive slope.

If the y-coordinates are the same for both points, the slope is zero. So, the line is a *Horizontal Line*. If the x-coordinates are the same for both points, there is no slope. So, the line is a *Vertical Line*. Two or more lines that have equal slopes are *Parallel Lines*. *Perpendicular Lines* have slopes that are negative reciprocals of each other. For example, $\frac{a}{b}$ and $\frac{-b}{a}$.

<u>Example</u>

With the graph below, write an equation in slope-intercept form that describes the line.

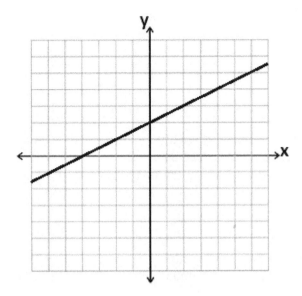

First, find several coordinates on the graph. Then, put them into a table:

x	y
-6	-1
-4	0
-2	1
0	2
2	3

Next, find a relationship between x and y. In this case, as x increases by 2, y increases by 1. This means that $m = 0.5$. The reason is that y changes by half the amount that x does. Also, you know that $b = 2$. The reason is that the graph crosses the y-axis at 2. So, the equation for this graph is $y = 0.5x + 2$.

This is a list of some forms of equations:

- Standard Form: $Ax + By = C$; the slope is $\frac{-A}{B}$ and the y-intercept is $\frac{C}{B}$
- *Slope Intercept Form*: $y = mx + b$, where m is the slope and b is the y-intercept
- Point-Slope Form: $y - y_1 = m(x - x_1)$, where m is the slope and (x_1, y_1) is a point on the line
- Two-Point Form: $\frac{y - y_1}{x - x_1} = \frac{y_2 - y_1}{x_2 - x_1}$, where (x_1, y_1) and (x_2, y_2) are two points on the given line
- *Intercept Form*: $\frac{x}{x_1} + \frac{y}{y_1} = 1$, where $(x_1, 0)$ is the point at which a line intersects the x-axis, and $(0, y_1)$ is the point at which the same line intersects the y-axis

UNIT RATE AS THE SLOPE

A new book goes on sale in book stores and online stores. In the first month, 5,000 copies of the book are sold. Over time, the book continues to grow in popularity. The data for the number of copies sold is in the table below.

# of Months on Sale	1	2	3	4	5
# of Copies Sold (In Thousands)	5	10	15	20	25

So, the number of copies that are sold and the time that the book is on sale is a proportional relationship. In this example, an equation can be used to show the data: y=5x, where x is the number of months that the book is on sale, and y is the number of copies sold. So, the slope is $\frac{rise}{run} = \frac{5}{1}$. This can be reduced to 5.

CALCULATIONS USING POINTS

Sometimes you need to do calculations by using points on a graph. With these points, you can find the midpoint and distance. If you know the equation for a line you can find the distance between the line and the point.

To find the *Midpoint* of two points (x_1, y_1) and (x_2, y_2), you need the average of the x-coordinates. This average will give you the x-coordinate of the midpoint. Then, take the average of the y-coordinates. This will give you the y-coordinate of the midpoint. The formula is $\left(\frac{x_1+x_2}{2}, \frac{y_1+y_2}{2}\right) = $ midpoint.

The *Distance* between two points is the same as the length of the hypotenuse of a right triangle. So, there is the length of the segment that is parallel to the x-axis. This segment is the difference between the x-coordinates of the two points. Also, there is the length of the segment parallel to the y-axis. This is the difference between the y-coordinates of the two points. Use the Pythagorean Theorem $a^2 + b^2 = c^2$ or $c = \sqrt{a^2 + b^2}$ to find the distance. The formula is $\sqrt{(x_2 - x_1)^2 + (y_2 - y_1)^2} = $ distance.

A line may be given as $Ax + By + C = 0$ where A, B, and C are coefficients. With this equation, you can use a point (x_1, y_1) not on the line and use the formula $d = \frac{|Ax_1 + By_1 + C|}{\sqrt{A^2 + B^2}}$. This formula will give the distance between the line and the point (x_1, y_1).

> **Review Video: <u>Calculations Using Points on a Graph</u>**
> Visit mometrix.com/academy and enter code: 883228

TRANSFORMATION

- Rotation: An object is rotated, or turned, between 0 and 360 degrees, around a fixed point. The size and shape of the object are unchanged.
- Reflection: An object is reflected, or flipped, across a line, so that the original object and reflected object are the same distance from the line of reflection. The size and shape of the object are unchanged.
- Translation: An object is translated, or shifted, horizontally and/or vertically to a new location. The orientation, size, and shape of the object are unchanged.

ROTATION

A line segment begins at (1, 4) and ends at (5, 4). Draw the line segment and rotate the line segment 90º about the point (3, 4).

The point about which the line segment is being rotated is on the line segment. This point should be on both the original and rotated line. The point (3, 4) is the center of the original line segment, and should still be the center of the rotated line segment. The dashed line is the rotated line segment.

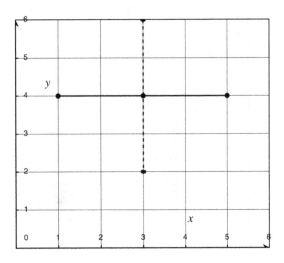

REFLECTION

Example 1: To create a congruent rectangle by reflecting, first draw a line of reflection. The line can be next to or on the figure. Then draw the image reflected across this line.

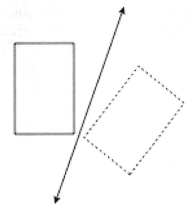

Example 2: A line segment begins at (1, 5) and ends at (5, 4). Draw the line segment, then reflect the line segment across the line *y* = 3.

To reflect a segment, consider folding a piece of paper at the line of reflection. The new image should line up exactly with the old image when the paper is folded. The dashed line is the reflected line segment.

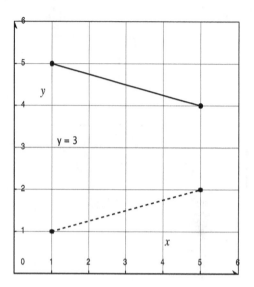

TRANSLATION

Example 1: A line segment on an x-y grid starts at (3, 2) and ends at (4, 1). Draw the line segment, and translate the segment up 2 units and left 2 units.

The solid line segment is the original line segment, and the dashed line is the translated line segment. The *y*-coordinate of each point has increased by 2, because the points moved two units away from 0. The *x*-coordinate of each point has decreased by 2, because the points moved two units closer to 0.

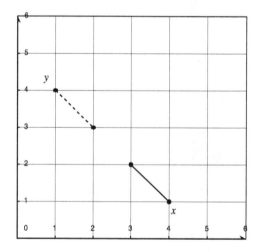

40

Example 2: Identify a transformation that could have been performed on the solid triangle to result in the dashed triangle.

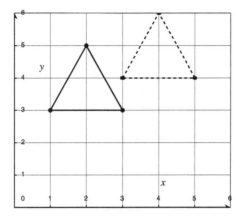

The transformed triangle has the same orientation as the original triangle. It has been shifted up one unit and two units to the right. Because the orientation of the figure has not changed, and its new position can be described using shifts up and to the right, the figure was translated.

ANGLES

An angle is made when two lines or line segments meet at a point. The angle may be a starting point for a pair of segments or rays. Also, angles come from the intersection of lines. The symbol ∠ stands for angles. Angles that are opposite to one another are called vertical angles, and their measures are equal. The vertex is the point where two segments or rays meet to make an angle. Angles that are made from intersecting rays, lines, and/or line segments have four angles at the vertex.

An acute angle is an angle with a degree measure less than 90°. A right angle is an angle with a degree measure of exactly 90°. An obtuse angle is an angle with a degree measure greater than 90° but less than 180°. A straight angle is an angle with a degree measure of exactly 180°. A reflex angle is an angle with a degree measure greater than 180° but less than 360°. A **full angle** is an angle with a degree measure of exactly 360°. This is also a circle.

> **Review Video: <u>Angles</u>**
> Visit mometrix.com/academy and enter code: 264624

Two angles with a sum of exactly 90° are known as complementary. The two angles may or may not be adjacent (i.e., *next to* or *beside*). In a right triangle, the two acute angles are complementary.

Two angles with a sum that is exactly 180° are known as supplementary. The two angles may or may not be adjacent. Two intersecting lines always make two pairs of supplementary angles. Adjacent supplementary angles will always make a straight line.

TRIANGLES

An equilateral triangle is a triangle with three congruent sides. Also, an equilateral triangle will have three congruent angles and each angle will be 60°. All equilateral triangles are acute triangles.

41

An isosceles triangle is a triangle with two congruent sides. An isosceles triangle will have two congruent angles as well.

A scalene triangle is a triangle with no congruent sides. Also, a scalene triangle will have three angles of different measures. The angle with the largest measure is opposite from the longest side. The angle with the smallest measure is opposite from the shortest side.

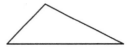

An acute triangle is a triangle whose three angles are all less than 90°. If two of the angles are equal, the acute triangle is also an isosceles triangle. If the three angles are all equal, the acute triangle is also an equilateral triangle.

A right triangle is a triangle with exactly one angle equal to 90°. A right triangle can never be acute or obtuse.

An obtuse triangle is a triangle with one angle greater than 90°. The other two angles may or may not be equal. If the two remaining angles are equal, the obtuse triangle is also an isosceles triangle.

CONGRUENCY, SIMILARITY, AND SYMMETRY

Congruent figures are geometric figures that have the same size and shape. All corresponding angles are equal, and all corresponding sides are equal. Congruence is shown by the symbol ≅.

Congruent polygons

Similar figures are geometric figures that have the same shape, but may not have the same size. All corresponding angles are equal, and all corresponding sides are proportional. However, they do not have to be equal. Similarity is shown by the symbol ~.

Similar polygons

Note that all congruent figures are also similar. However, not all similar figures are congruent.

Line of Symmetry: The line that divides a figure or object into equal parts. Each part is congruent to the other. An object may have no lines of symmetry, one line of symmetry, or multiple (i.e., more than one) lines of symmetry.

Lines of symmetry:

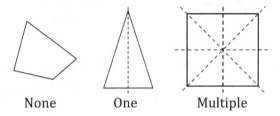

None   One   Multiple

POLYGONS

Each straight line segment of a polygon is called a side. The point at which two sides of a polygon intersect is called the vertex. In a polygon, the number of sides is always equal to the number of vertices. A polygon with all sides congruent and all angles equal is called a regular polygon.

A line segment from the center of a polygon that is perpendicular to a side of the polygon is called the apothem. A line segment from the center of a polygon to a vertex of the polygon is called a radius. In a regular polygon, the apothem can be used to find the area of the polygon using the formula $A = \frac{1}{2}ap$, where a is the apothem, and p is the perimeter.

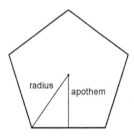

- Triangle – 3 sides
- Quadrilateral – 4 sides
- Pentagon – 5 sides
- Hexagon – 6 sides
- Heptagon – 7 sides
- Octagon – 8 sides
- Nonagon – 9 sides
- Decagon – 10 sides
- Dodecagon – 12 sides

Generally, an n-gon is a polygon that has more than 12 angles and sides. The space of n is for the number of sides. Also, an 11-sided polygon is known as an 11-gon.

Quadrilateral: A closed two-dimensional geometric figure that has four straight sides. The sum of the interior angles of any quadrilateral is 360°. A quadrilateral whose diagonals divide each other is a parallelogram.

A quadrilateral whose opposite sides are parallel (i.e., 2 pairs of parallel sides) is a parallelogram. A quadrilateral whose diagonals are perpendicular bisectors of each other is a rhombus. A quadrilateral with opposite sides (i.e., both pairs) that are parallel and congruent is a rhombus.

Parallelogram: A quadrilateral that has two pairs of opposite parallel sides. The sides that are parallel are also congruent. The opposite interior angles are always congruent, and the consecutive interior angles are supplementary. The diagonals of a parallelogram divide each other. Each diagonal divides the parallelogram into two congruent triangles.

A parallelogram that has a right angle is a rectangle. In the diagram below, the top left corner and the bottom left corner are consecutive angles. Consecutive angles of a parallelogram are supplementary. If there is one right angle in a parallelogram, there are four right angles in that parallelogram.

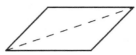

Trapezoid: Normally, a quadrilateral has one pair of parallel sides. Some define a trapezoid as a quadrilateral that has at least one pair of parallel sides. There are no rules for the second pair of sides. So, there are no rules for the diagonals of a trapezoid.

Rectangles, rhombuses, and squares are all special forms of parallelograms.

Rectangle: A parallelogram with four right angles. All rectangles are parallelograms, but not all parallelograms are rectangles. The diagonals of a rectangle are congruent.

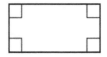

Rhombus: A parallelogram with four congruent sides. All rhombuses are parallelograms, but not all parallelograms are rhombuses. The diagonals of a rhombus are perpendicular to each other.

A rhombus with one right angle is a square. The rhombus is a special form of a parallelogram. So, the rules about the angles of a parallelogram are true for the rhombus.

44

Square: A parallelogram with four right angles and four congruent sides. All squares are also parallelograms, rhombuses, and rectangles. The diagonals of a square are congruent and perpendicular to each other.

THREE DIMENSIONAL FIGURES
RIGHT RECTANGULAR PRISM

A rectangular prism has six rectangular faces. The six faces give it 12 edges and eight vertices.

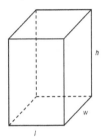

CUBE

A cube has six square faces. The six faces give it 12 edges and eight vertices.

SPHERE

A sphere is a perfectly round object that has no faces, edges, or vertices. This three-dimensional object is similar to the two-dimensional circle.

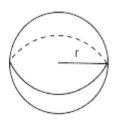

45

RIGHT TRIANGULAR PRISM

A triangular prism has five faces. Two faces are triangles, and three faces are rectangles. This prism has 9 edges and six vertices.

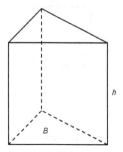

CYLINDER

The cylinder has two circular faces. In three dimensions, the cylinder has edges or vertices.

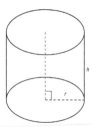

RIGHT RECTANGULAR PYRAMID

A rectangular pyramid has four triangular faces and one rectangular face. This pyramid has eight edges and five vertices.

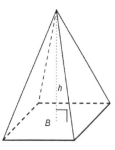

CONE

A cone has one circular face. Cones do not have any edges or vertices. The cones that you will encounter are right circular. This means that they have a circle for a base instead of a polygonal base. A pyramid is a cone with a polygonal base.

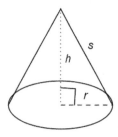

Measurement

AREA AND PERIMETER FORMULAS

The perimeter of any triangle is found by adding the three side lengths $P = a + b + c$. For an equilateral triangle, this is the same as $P = 3s$, where s is any side length. The reason is that the three sides are the same length.

Find the side of a triangle

You may have problems that give you the perimeter of a triangle. So, you are asked to find one of the sides.

Example: The perimeter of a triangle is 35 cm. One side length is 10 cm. Another side length is 20cm. Find the length of the missing side.

First: Set up the equation to set apart a side length.

Now, the equation is $35 = 10 + 20 + c$. So, you are left with $35 = 30 + c$.

Second: Subtract 30 from both sides: $35 - 30 = 30 - 30 + c$

Then, you are left with $5 = c$

The area of any triangle can be found by taking half of the base (i.e., b). Then, multiply that result by the height (i.e., h) of the triangle. So, the standard formula for the area of a triangle is $A = \frac{1}{2}bh$. For many triangles, it may be difficult to calculate h. So, other formulas are given here that may be easier.

Find the height or the area of the base

You may have problems that give you the area of a triangle. So, you are asked to find the height or the base.

Example: The area of a triangle is 70 cm², and the height is 10. Find the base.

First: Set up the equation to set apart the base.

The equation is $70 = \frac{1}{2}10b$.

Now, multiply both sides by 2: $70 \times 2 = \frac{1}{2}10b \times 2$.

So, you are left with: $140 = 10b$.

Second: Divide both sides by 10 to get the base: $\frac{140}{10} = \frac{10b}{10}$

Then, you have $14 = b$.

47

Note: When you need to find the height, you can follow the steps above to find it.

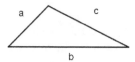

Another formula that works for any triangle is $A = \sqrt{s(s-a)(s-b)(s-c)}$, where A is the area, s is the semi-perimeter $s = \frac{a+b+c}{2}$, and a, b, and c are the lengths of the three sides. The area of an equilateral triangle can be found by the formula $A = \frac{\sqrt{3}}{4}s^2$, where A is the area and s is the length of a side. You could use the $30° - 60° - 90°$ ratios to find the height of the triangle. Then, use the standard triangle area formula.

The area of an isosceles triangle can be found by the formula, $A = \frac{1}{2}b\sqrt{a^2 - \frac{b^2}{4}}$, where A is the area, b is the base, and a is the length of one of the two congruent sides. If you do not remember this formula, you can use the Pythagorean Theorem to find the height. Then, you can use the standard formula for the area of a triangle.

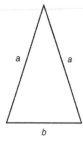

The area of a square is found by using the formula $A = s^2$, where A is the area and s is the length of one side.

Find the side of a square

You may have problems that give you the area of a square. So, you are asked to find the side.

Example: The area of a square is 9 cm². Find the side.

First: Set up the equation to set apart s.

The equation is $9 = s^2$.

Second: Now, you can take the square root of both sides: $\sqrt{9} = \sqrt{s^2}$.

So, you are left with: $3 = s$

The perimeter of a square is found by using the formula $P = 4s$, where P is the perimeter, and s is the length of one side. All four sides are equal in a square. So, you can multiply the length of one side by 4. This is faster than adding the same number four times.

Find the side of a square

You may have problems that give you the perimeter of a square. So, you are asked to find the side.

Example: The perimeter of a square is 60 cm. Find the side.

First: Set up the equation to set apart s.

The equation is $60 = 4s$.

Second: Now, you can divide both sides by 4: $\frac{60}{4} = \frac{4s}{4}$. You are left with $15 = s$

The area of a rectangle is found by the formula $A = lw$, where A is the area of the rectangle, l is the length and w is the width. Usually, the longer side is the length, and the shorter side is the width. However, the numbers for l and w can used be for one or the other.

Find the width or length of a rectangle

You may have problems that give you the area of a rectangle. So, you are asked to find the width.

Example: The area of a rectangle is 150cm², and the length is 10cm. Find the width.

First: Set up the equation to set apart width.

The equation is $150 = 10w$.

Second: Divide both sides by 10: $\frac{150}{10} = \frac{10w}{10}$. You are left with $15 = w$

Note: When you need to find the length, you can follow the steps above to find it.

The perimeter of a rectangle can be found with two formulas $P = 2l + 2w$ or $P = 2(l + w)$, where l is the length, and w is the width.

Find the width or length of a rectangle

You may have problems that give you the perimeter of a rectangle. So, you are asked to find the width.

Example: The perimeter of a rectangle is 100cm, and the length is 20cm. Find the width.

First: Set up the equation to set apart the width.

The equation is $100 = 2(20 + w)$

Second: Distribute the 2 across $(20 + w)$: $100 = 40 + 2w$

Then, subtract 40 from both sides: $100 - 40 = 40 + 2w - 40$

So, you are left with: $60 = 2w$. Then, divide both sides by 2: $\frac{60}{2} = \frac{2w}{2}$.

Now, you have $30 = w$.

Note: When you need to find the length, you can follow the steps above to find it.

The area of a parallelogram is found by the formula $A = bh$, where b is the length of the base, and h is the height. Note that the base and height match with the length and width in a rectangle. So, this formula can be used for rectangles as well. Do not confuse the height of a parallelogram with the length of the second side. They have the same measure only with rectangles.

Find the length of the base or the height of a parallelogram

You may have problems that give you the area of a parallelogram. So, you are asked to find the area of the base or the height.

Example: The area of the parallelogram is 84 cm². The base is 7cm. Find the height.

Set up the equation to set apart the height.

So, you have $84 = 7h$. Now, divide both sides by 7: $\frac{84}{7} = \frac{7h}{7}$.

Then, you are left with $12 = h$

The perimeter of a parallelogram is found by the formula $P = 2a + 2b$ or $P = 2(a + b)$, where a and b are the lengths of the two sides.

Find the missing side of a parallelogram

You may have problems that give you the perimeter of a parallelogram. So, you are asked to find one of the sides. Example: The perimeter of a parallelogram is 100cm, and one side is 20cm. Find the other side.

First: Set up the equation to set apart one of the side lengths.

The equation is $100 = 2(20 + b)$

Second: Distribute the 2 across $(20 + b)$: $100 = 40 + 2b$

Then, subtract 40 from both sides: $100 - 40 = 40 + 2b - 40$

So, you are left with: $60 = 2b$. Then, divide both sides by 2: $\frac{60}{2} = \frac{2b}{2}$

Now, you have $30 = b$.

> **Review Video: Area and Perimeter of a Parallelogram**
> Visit mometrix.com/academy and enter code: 718313

The area of a trapezoid is found by the formula $A = \frac{1}{2}h(b_1 + b_2)$, where h is the height, and b_1 and b_2 are the two parallel sides (i.e., bases). The height is the segment that joins the parallel bases.

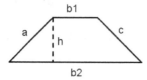

Find the height of a trapezoid

50

You may have problems that give you the area of a trapezoid. So, you are asked to find the height.

Example: The area of a trapezoid is 30cm². B_1 is 3cm, and B_2 is 9cm. Find the height.

First: Set up the equation to set apart the height.

The equation is $30 = \frac{1}{2}h(3 + 9)$.

Second: Now, multiply both sides by 2: $30 \times 2 = \frac{1}{2}(12)h \times 2$.

So, you are left with: $60 = (12)h$.

Third: Divide both sides by 12: $\frac{60}{12} = \frac{(12)h}{12}$. Now, you have $5 = h$

Find a base of a trapezoid

You may have problems that give you the area of a trapezoid and the height. So, you are asked to find one of the bases.

Example: The area of a trapezoid is 90cm². b_1 is 5cm, and the height is 12cm. Find b_2.

First: Set up the equation to set apart b_2.

The equation is $90 = \frac{1}{2}12(5 + b_2)$.

Second: Now, multiply the height by $\frac{1}{2}$: $90 = 6(5 + b_2)$.

So, you can distribute the 6 across $(5 + b_2)$: $90 = 30 + 6b_2$

Third: Subtract 30 from both sides $90 - 30 = 30 + 6b_2 - 30$.

Now, you have $60 = 6b_2$.

Then, divide both sides by 6: $\frac{60}{6} = \frac{6b_2}{6}$. So, $b_2 = 10$.

The perimeter of a trapezoid is found by the formula $P = a + b_1 + c + b_2$, where a, b_1, c, and b_2 are the four sides of the trapezoid.

Find the missing side of a trapezoid

Example: The perimeter of a trapezoid is 50cm. B_1 is 20cm, B_2 is 10cm, and a is 5cm. Find the length of side c.

First: Set up the equation to set apart the missing side.

The equation is $50 = 5 + 20 + c + 10$. So, you have $50 = 35 + c$

Second: Subtract 35 from both sides: $50 - 35 = 35 + c - 35$.

So, you are left with $15 = c$

Review Video: <u>Area and Perimeter of a Trapezoid</u>
Visit mometrix.com/academy and enter code: 587523

CIRCLES

The center is the single point inside the circle that is equidistant from every point on the circle. The point O is in the diagram below. The radius is a line segment that joins the center of the circle and any one point on the circle. All radii of a circle are equal. The segments OX, OY, and OZ are in the diagram below. The diameter is a line segment that passes through the center of the circle and has both endpoints inside the circle. The length of the diameter is twice the length of the radius. The segment XZ is in the diagram below. Concentric circles are circles that have the same center but not the same length of radii. A bulls-eye target is an example of concentric circles.

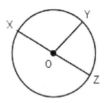

The **area of a circle** is found with the formula $A = \pi r^2$, where r is the length of the radius. If the diameter of the circle is given, divide it in half to get the radius before using the formula. (Note: In the following formulas, 3.14 is used for π.)

The **circumference of a circle** is found by the formula $C = 2\pi r$, where r is the radius.

SURFACE AREA AND VOLUME FORMULAS
PRISM

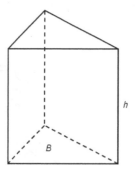

The **volume of any prism** is found with the formula $V = Bh$, where B is the area of the base, and h is the height. The perpendicular distance between the bases is the height.

Find the area of the base or the height of a prism

You may have problems that give you the volume of a prism. So, you are asked to find the area of the base or the height.

Example: The volume of the prism is 200 cm³. The area of the base is 10cm. Find the height.

First: Set up the equation to set apart the height.

So, you have $200 = 10h$.

Second: Now, divide both sides by 10: $\frac{200}{10} = \frac{10h}{10}$.

Then, you are left with $20 = h$

Note: When you need to find the area of the base, you can follow the steps above to solve for it.

The **surface area of any prism** is the sum of the areas of both bases and all sides. So, the formula for a sphere is $SA = 2B + Ph$, where B is the area of the base, P is the perimeter of the base, and h is the height of the prism.

Find the area of the base

You may have problems that give you the surface area of a prism. So, you are asked to find the area of the base.

Example: The surface area of the prism is 100 cm². The perimeter of the base is 10cm, and the height is 2cm. Find the area of the base.

First: Set up the equation to set apart the area of the base.

So, you have $100 = 2B + 20$.

Second: Subtract 20 from both sides: $100 - 20 = 2B + 20 - 20$.

Now, you are left with $80 = 2B$. So, divide both sides by 2.

Then, you have $40 = B$.

Find the perimeter of the base or the height of a prism

You may have problems that give you the surface area of a prism and the area of the base. So, you are asked to find the perimeter of the base or the height.

Example: The surface area of the prism is 280 cm². The area of the base is 15cm², and the perimeter of the base is 10cm. Find the height.

First: Set up the equation to set apart the height.

The equation is $280 = 2(15) + (10)h$. So, you have $250 = 30 + (10)h$

Second: Subtract 30 from both sides: $280 - 30 = 30 + (10)h - 30$.

Now, you are left with: $250 = (10)h$.

Then, divide both sides by 10.

$\frac{250}{10} = \frac{(10)h}{10} = 25$. So, the height of the prism is 25cm.

Note: When you need to find the perimeter of the base, you can follow the steps above to find it.

RECTANGULAR PRISM

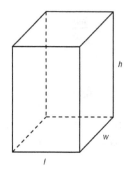

The **volume of a rectangular prism** can be found with the formula $V = lwh$, where V is the volume, l is the length, w is the width, and h is the height.

Find the length, width, or height of a rectangular prism

You may have problems that give you the volume of a rectangular prism. So, you are asked to find the length, width, or height.

Example: The volume of the rectangular prism is 200 cm³. The width is 10cm, and the height is 10cm. Find the length.

> First: Set up the equation to set apart the length.

> > So, you have $200 = l(10)(10)$ that becomes $200 = (100)l$.

> Second: Divide both sides by 100.

> > Now, you have $\frac{200}{100} = \frac{(100)l}{100}$. So, you are left with $2 = l$.

Note: When you need to find the width or height, you can follow the steps above to solve for either.

The **surface area of a rectangular prism** can be calculated as $SA = 2lw + 2hl + 2wh$ or $SA = 2(lw + hl + wh)$.

Find the length, width, or height of a rectangular prism

You may have problems that give you the surface area of a rectangular prism. So, you are asked to find the length, width, or height.

Example: The surface area of the rectangular prism is 200 cm². The width is 15cm, and the height is 5cm. Find the length.

> First: Set up the equation to set apart the length.

> > So, you have $200 = 2(15)l + 2(5)l + 2(15)(5)$ that becomes

> > > $$200 = (40)l + 150.$$

> Second: Subtract 150 from both sides.

> > So, $200 - 150 = (40)l + 150 - 150$ becomes $50 = (40)l$.

Then, divide both sides by 40 to set apart l: $\frac{50}{40} = \frac{(40)l}{40}$.

You are left with $1.25 = l$.

Note: When you need to find the width or height, you can follow the steps above to solve for either.

CUBE

The **volume of a cube** can be found with the formula $V = s^3$, where s is the length of a side.

The **surface area of a cube** is calculated as $SA = 6s^2$, where SA is the total surface area and s is the length of a side. These formulas are the same as the ones used for the volume and surface area of a rectangular prism. However, these are simple formulas because the three numbers (i.e., length, width, and height) are the same.

CONVERSION

When going from a larger unit to a smaller unit, multiply the number of the known amount by the equivalent amount. When going from a smaller unit to a larger unit, divide the number of the known amount by the equivalent amount.

> **Review Video: Metric System Conversions**
> Visit mometrix.com/academy and enter code: 163709

Also, you can set up conversion fractions. In these fractions, one fraction is the conversion factor. The other fraction has the unknown amount in the numerator. So, the known value is placed in the denominator. Sometimes the second fraction has the known value from the problem in the numerator, and the unknown in the denominator. Multiply the two fractions to get the converted measurement.

MEASUREMENT EQUIVALENTS
INCHES, YARDS, AND FEET
12 inches = 1 foot

1 yard = 3 feet

1 yard = 36 inches

1 MILE IN FEET AND YARDS
1 mile = 5280 feet

1 mile = 1760 yards

1 QUART IN PINTS AND CUPS
1 quart = 2 pints

1 quart = 4 cups

1 GALLON IN QUARTS, PINTS, AND CUPS
1 gallon = 4 quarts

1 gallon = 8 pints

1 gallon = 16 cups

1 POUND IN OUNCES

1 pound = 16 ounces

Don't think that because something weighs one pound that its volume is one pint. Ounces of weight are not equal to fluid ounces which measure volume.

1 TON IN POUNDS

1 ton = 2000 pounds

METRIC MEASUREMENTS
1 LITER IN MILLILITERS AND CUBIC CENTIMETERS

1 liter = 1000 milliliters

1 liter = 1000 cubic centimeters

Do not confuse *cubic centimeters* with *centiliters*. 1 liter = 1000 cubic cent*imeters*, but 1 liter = 100 centi*liters*.

1 METER IN MILLIMETERS AND CENTIMETERS

1 meter = 1000 millimeters

1 meter = 100 centimeters

1 GRAM IN MILLIGRAMS

1 gram = 1000 milligrams

1 KILOGRAM IN GRAMS

1 kilogram = 1000 grams

KILO, CENTI, AND MILLI

Kilo-: one thousand

Centi-: one hundredth

Milli-: one thousandth

EXAMPLE 1

There are 100 centimeters in 1 meter. Convert the measurements below.

a. Convert 1.4 m to cm

b. Convert 218 cm to m

Write a ratio with the conversion factor: $\frac{100\text{ cm}}{1\text{ m}}$. Use proportions to convert the given units.

a. $\frac{100\text{ cm}}{1\text{ m}} = \frac{x\text{ cm}}{1.4\text{ m}}$. Cross multiply to get $x = 140$. So, there are 1.4 m in 140 cm.

b. $\frac{100\text{ cm}}{1\text{ m}} = \frac{218\text{ cm}}{x\text{ m}}$. Cross multiply to get $100x = 218$, or $x = 2.18$. So, there are 218 cm in 2.18 m.

EXAMPLE 2

There are 12 inches in 1 foot. Also, there are 3 feet in 1 yard. Convert the following measurements.

a. 42 inches to feet

b. 15 feet to yards

Write ratios with the conversion factors: $\frac{12\text{ in}}{1\text{ ft}}$ and: $\frac{3\text{ ft}}{1\text{ yd}}$. Use proportions to convert the given units.

a. $\frac{12\text{ in}}{1\text{ ft}} = \frac{42\text{ in}}{x\text{ ft}}$. Cross multiply to get $12x = 42$, or $x = 3.5$. So, there are 42 inches in 3.5 feet.

b. $\frac{3\text{ ft}}{1\text{ yd}} = \frac{15\text{ ft}}{x\text{ yd}}$. Cross multiply to get $3x = 15$, or $x = 5$. So, there are 15 feet in 5 yards.

Data Analysis and Probability

MEASURES OF CENTRAL TENDENCY

The quantities of mean, median, and mode are known as measures of central tendency. Each can give a picture of what a whole set of data looks like with a single number. Knowing what each value stands for is important to understanding the information from these measures.

MEAN

The mean, or the arithmetic mean or average, of a data set is found by adding all of the values in the set. Then you divide the sum by how many values that you had in a set. For example, a data set has 6 numbers, and the sum of those 6 numbers is 30. So, the mean is 30/6 = 5. When you know the average, you may be asked to find a missing value. Look over the following steps for how this is done.

Example: You are given the values of 5, 10, 12, and 13. Also, you are told that the average is 9.6. So, what is the one missing value?

First: Add the known values together: 5 + 10 + 12 + 13 = 40.

Now, set up an equation with the sum of the known values in the divisor. Then, put the number of values in the dividend. For this example, you have 5 values. So, you have $\frac{40+?}{5} = 9.6$. Now, multiply both sides by 5: $5 \times \frac{40+?}{5} = 9.6 \times 5$

Second: You are left with 40+? = 48. Now, subtract 40 from both sides: 40 − 40+? = 48 − 40. So, you know that the missing value is 8.

MEDIAN

The median is the middle value of a data set. The median can be found by putting the data set in numerical order (e.g., 3, 7, 26, 28, 39). Then, you pick the value that is in the middle of the set. In the data set (1, 2, 3, 4, 5), there is an odd number of values. So, the median is 3. Sometimes, there is an even number of values in the set. So, the median can be found by taking the average of the two middle values. In the data set (1, 2, 3, 4, 5, 6), the median would be (3 + 4)/2 = 3.5.

MODE

The mode is the value that appears the most in a data set. In the data set (1, 2, 3, 4, 5, 5, 5), the number 5 appears more than the other numbers. So, the value 5 is the mode. If more than one value appears the same number of times, then there are multiple values for the mode. For example, a data set is (1, 2, 2, 3, 4, 4, 5, 5). So, the modes would be 2, 4, and 5. Now, if no value appears more than any other value in the data set, then there is no mode.

> **Review Video: Mean, Median, and Mode**
> Visit mometrix.com/academy and enter code: 286207

RANGE

The range is the difference between the greatest data point and the least data point in the set. In the set (12, 23, 1, 8, 45, 22), the greatest data point is 45. The least data point is 1. When you subtract 1 from 45, you have 44. So, 44 is the range of the data set.

FIRST AND THIRD QUARTILE

FIRST QUARTILE

The first quartile of a data set is the median of the front half of a data set. A simple way to find this is to set up the first quartile as the first half of the ordered data and find the median. Do not include the median of the full data set if there are an odd number of data points.

For example, you have the data set {3, 1, 12, 7, 17, 4, 10, 8, 9, 20, 4}. Put the data in order to get {1, 3, 4, 4, 7, 8, 9, 10, 12, 17, 20}. The front half that does not include the median of eight is {1, 3, 4, 4, 7}. This has a median of 4. So, the first quartile of this data set is 4.

THIRD QUARTILE

The third quartile of a data set is the median of the back half of a data set. A simple way to find this is to set up the third quartile as the back half of the ordered data and find the median. Do not include the median of the full data set if there are an odd number of data points.

For example, you have the data set {3, 1, 12, 7, 17, 4, 10, 8, 9, 20, 4}. Put the data in order to get {1, 3, 4, 4, 7, 8, 9, 10, 12, 17, 20}. The back half that does not include the median of eight is {9, 10, 12, 17, 20}. This has a median of 12. So, the third quartile of this data set is 12.

COMMON CHARTS AND GRAPHS

Charts and *Tables* are ways of organizing information into separate rows and columns. These rows and columns are labeled to find and to explain the information in them. Some charts and tables are organized horizontally with rows giving the details about the labeled information. Other charts and tables are organized vertically with columns giving the details about the labeled information.

A *Bar Graph* is one of the few graphs that can be drawn correctly in two ways: horizontally and vertically. A bar graph is similar to a line plot because of how the data is organized on the graph. Both axes must have their categories defined for the graph to be useful. A thick line is drawn from zero to the exact value of the data. This line can be used for a number, a percentage, or other numerical value. Longer bar lengths point to greater data values. To understand a bar graph, read the labels for the axes to know the units being reported. Then look where the bars end and match this to the scale on the other axis. This will show you the connection between the axes. This bar graph shows the responses from a survey about the favorite colors of a group.

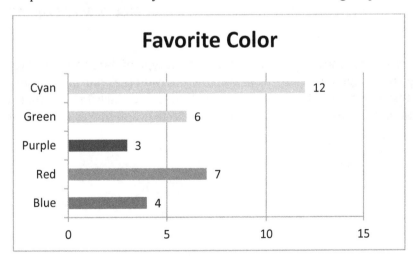

Line Graphs have one or more lines of different styles (e.g., solid or broken). These lines show the different values for a data set. Each point on the graph is shown as an ordered pair. This is similar to a Cartesian plane. In this case, the *x*- and *y*- axes are given certain units (e.g., dollars or time). Each point that is for one measurement is joined by line segments. Then, these lines show what the values are doing. The lines may be increasing (i.e., line sloping upward), decreasing (i.e., line sloping downward), or staying the same (i.e., horizontal line). More than one set of data can be put on the same line graph. This is done to compare more than one piece of data. An example of this would be graphing test scores for different groups of students over the same stretch of time. This allows you to see which group had the greatest increase or decrease in performance over a certain amount of years. This example is shown in the graph below.

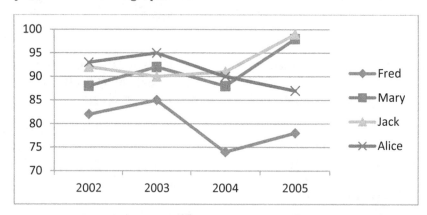

A *Line Plot*, or a *Dot Plot*, has plotted points that are NOT connected by line segments. In this graph, the horizontal axis lists the different possible values for the data. The vertical axis lists how many times one value happens. A single dot is graphed for each value. The dots in a line plot are connected. If the dots are connected, then this will not correctly represent the data.

A *Pictograph* is a graph that is given in the horizontal format. This graph uses pictures or symbols to show the data. Each pictograph must have a key that defines the picture or symbol. Also, this key should give the number that stands for each picture or symbol. The pictures or symbols on a pictograph are not always shown as whole elements.

In this case, the fraction of the picture or symbol stands for the same fraction of the quantity that a whole picture or symbol represents. For example, there is a row in the pictograph with $3\frac{1}{2}$ ears of corn. Each ear of corn represents 100 stalks of corn in a field. So, this would equal $3\frac{1}{2} \times 100 = 350$ stalks of corn in the field.

Circle Graphs, or *Pie Charts*, show the relationship of each type of data compared to the whole set of data. The circle graph is divided into sections by drawing radii (i.e., plural for radius) to make central angles. These angles stand for a percentage of the circle. Each 1% of data is equal to 3.6° in the graph. So, data that stands for a 90° section of the circle graph makes up 25% of the whole. The pie chart below shows the data from the frequency table where people were asked about their favorite color.

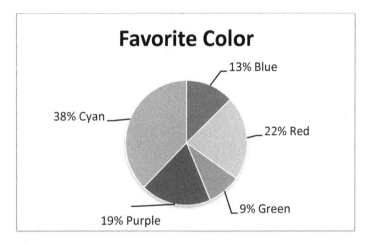

PROBABILITY

Probability is a branch of statistics that deals with the likelihood of something taking place. One classic example is a coin toss. There are only two possible results: heads or tails. The likelihood, or probability, that the coin will land as heads is 1 out of 2 (i.e., 1/2, 0.5, 50%). Tails has the same probability. Another common example is a 6-sided die roll. There are six possible results from rolling a single die. So, each side has an equal chance of happening. So, the probability of any number coming up is 1 out of 6.

> **Review Video: Intro to Probability**
> Visit mometrix.com/academy and enter code: 212374

Terms often used in probability:

Simple event – a situation that produces results of some sort (e.g., a coin toss)

Compound event – event that involves two or more items (e.g., rolling a pair of dice and taking the sum)

Outcome – a possible result in an experiment or event (e.g., heads and tails)

Desired outcome (or success) – an outcome that meets a particular set of requirements (e.g., a roll of 1 or 2 when we want a number that is less than 3)

Independent events – two or more events whose outcomes do not affect one another (e.g., two coins tossed at the same time)

Dependent events – two or more events whose outcomes affect one another (e.g., drawing two specific cards right after the other from the same deck)

Certain outcome—probability of outcome is 100% or 1

Impossible outcome—probability of outcome is 0% or 0

Mutually exclusive outcomes – two or more outcomes whose requirements cannot all be done in a single outcome. An example is a coin coming up heads and tails on the same toss.

Theoretical probability is the likelihood of a certain outcome happening for a given event. It can be known without actually doing the event.

Theoretical probability can be calculated as:

$$P(\text{probability of success}) = \frac{(\text{Desired Outcomes})}{(\text{Total Outcomes})}$$

Example:

There are 20 marbles in a bag and 5 are red. The theoretical probability of randomly selecting a red marble is 5 out of 20, (i.e., 5/20 = 1/4, 0.25, or 25%).

When we talk about probability, we mean theoretical probability most of the time. Experimental probability, or relative frequency, is the number of times an outcome happens in an experiment or a certain number of observed events.

Theoretical probability is based on what *should* happen. Experimental probability is based on what *has* happened. Experimental probability is calculated in the same way as theoretical. However, actual desired outcomes are used instead of possible desired outcomes.

Theoretical and experimental probability do not always line up with one another. Theoretical probability says that out of 20 coin tosses 10 should be heads. However, if we were actually to toss 20 coins, we might record just 5 heads. This doesn't mean that our theoretical probability is incorrect; it just means that this particular experiment had results that were different from what was predicted.

Verbal

The Verbal test of the SSAT consists of a total of 60 questions (30 Synonyms and 30 Analogies).

Synonyms

As part of your exam, you need to understand how words connect to each other. This is done with understanding words that mean the same thing or synonyms. For example, *dry* and *arid* are synonyms. There are pairs of words in English that can be called synonyms. Yet, they have somewhat different definitions.

For example, *wise* and *intelligent* can be used to describe someone who is very educated. So, you would be correct to call them synonyms. However, *wise* is used for good judgment. *Intelligent* is closer to good thinking.

Words should not be called synonyms when their differences are too great. For example, *hot* and *warm* are not synonyms because their meanings are too different. How do you know when two words are synonyms? First, try to replace one word for the other word. Then, be sure that the meaning of the sentence has not changed. Replacing *warm* for *hot* in a sentence gives a different meaning. *Warm* and *hot* may seem close in meaning. Yet, *warm* means that the temperature is normal. And, *hot* means that the temperature is very high.

> **Review Video: <u>Synonyms</u>**
> Visit mometrix.com/academy and enter code: 355036
>
> **Review Video: <u>What are Synonyms and Antonyms?</u>**
> Visit mometrix.com/academy and enter code: 105612

SYNONYMS

For the Synonyms section, you will have one word and four choices for a synonym of that word. Before you look at the choices, try to think of a few words that could be a synonym for your question. Then, check the choices for a synonym of the question. Some words may seem close to the question, but you are looking for the best choice of a synonym. So, don't let your first reaction be your final decision.

Example 1

Tranquil:

      A. Agitated
      B. Nervous
      C. Stable
      D. Thrive
      E. Violent

Example 2

Agile:

     A. Cultivated
     B. Dispirited
     C. Frustrate
     D. Rapid
     E. Sluggish

Example 3

Obstruction:

     A. Assistance
     B. Barrier
     C. Displace
     D. Exhibition
     E. Promotion

ANSWERS

Example 1: C, Stable

Example 2: A, Rapid

Example 3: D, Barrier

Analogies

DETERMINE THE RELATIONSHIP

As you try to decide on how the words in question are connected, don't jump to understand the meaning of the words. Instead, see if you can find the relationship between the two words. To understand the relationship, you can start by creating a sentence that links the two words and puts them into perspective. At first, try to use a simple sentence to find a connection.

Then, go through each answer choice and replace the words in the answer choices with the parts of your simple sentence. Depending on the question, you may need to make changes to your sentence to make it more specific.

Example:

Wood is to fire as

Simple Sentence: *Wood* feeds a *fire* as

Wood is to fire as

     A. Farmer is to cow
     B. Gasoline is to engine

Using the simple sentence, you would state "Farmer feeds a cow" which is correct. Yet, the next answer choice "Gasoline feeds an engine" is also true. So which is the correct answer? With this simple sentence, we need to be more specific.

Specific Sentences: "Wood feeds a fire and is consumed" / "Wood is burned in a fire"

These specific sentences show that answer choice (A) is incorrect and answer choice (B) is clearly correct. With the specific sentences, you have "Gasoline feeds an engine and is consumed" is correct. Also, "Farmer feeds a cow and is consumed" is clearly incorrect.

If your simple sentence seems correct with more than one answer choice, then keep making changes until only one answer choice makes sense.

ELIMINATING SIMILARITIES

This method works well in the Analogies section and the Synonyms section. You can start by looking over the answer choices and see what clues they provide. If there are any common relationships between the pairs of terms, then those answer choices have to be wrong.

Example:

Tough is to rugged as

> A. Soft is to hard
> B. Clear is to foggy
> C. Inhale is to exhale
> D. Throw is to catch
> E. Rigid is to taut

In this example, tough and rugged are synonyms. Also, the first four answer choices are antonyms. You may not realize that taut and rigid are synonyms. However, it has to be correct. The reason is that you know the other four answer choices all had the same relationship of being antonyms.

WORD TYPES

Example:

Gardener is to hedge as

> A. Wind is to rock
> B. Woodcarver is to stick

In this example, you could start with a simple sentence of "Gardener cuts away at hedges." Now, both answer choices seem correct with this sentence. For choice (A), you can say that "Wind cuts away at rocks" due to erosion. For choice (B), you can say that a "Woodcarver cuts away at sticks." The difference is that a gardener is a person, and a woodcarver is a person. However, the wind is a thing which makes answer choice (B) correct.

FACE VALUE

When you are not sure about an answer, you should try to accept the problem at face value. Don't read too much into it. These problems will not ask you to make impossible comparisons. Truly, the SSAT test writers are not trying to throw you off with cheap tricks. If you have to make a stretch of the question to make a connection between the two terms, then you should start over and find another relationship. Don't make the problem more difficult. These are normal questions with differences in difficulty. Sometimes the terms that go together and their relationships may not be very clear. So, you will want to read over the question and answer choices carefully.

Example:

Odor is to smell as flavor is to

> A. believe
> B. know
> C. feel
> D. taste
> E. punish

Would a flavor be "punished," "known", "felt", "tasted", or "believed"? The analogy is about a synonym. So, answer choice D which is "taste" is a synonym of flavor and is the best answer.

READ CAREFULLY

To understand the analogies, you need to read the terms and answer choices carefully. You can miss the question because you misread the terms. Each question here has only a few words, so you can spend time reading them carefully. Yet, you cannot forget your time limit of the section. So, don't spend too much time on one question. Just focus on reading carefully and be sure to read all of the choices. You may find an answer choice that seems correct. Yet, when you finish reading over the choices, you may find a better choice.

Reading Comprehension

Reading and Reasoning

TYPES OF PASSAGES

A **narrative** passage is a story that can be fiction or nonfiction (i.e., false or true). To be a narrative, the passage must have a few things. First, the text must have a plot (i.e., an order of events). Some narratives are written in a clear order, but this is not necessary. If the narrative is good, then you will find these events interesting. Second, a narrative has characters. These characters can be people, animals, or even lifeless items. As long as they play in the plot, they are a character. Third, a narrative passage often has figurative language. This is a tool that authors use to stir the imagination of readers with comparisons or comments. For example, a metaphor is a comparison between two things without using the words *like* or *as*. *He stood like a king* is not an example of a metaphor. *The moon was a frosty snowball* is an example of a metaphor. In reality, this is not true. Yet, the comparison gives a sense of calm to readers.

> **Review Video: <u>Narratives</u>**
> Visit mometrix.com/academy and enter code: 280100

An **expository** passage aims to inform or teach readers. The passage is nonfiction and usually centers around an easily explained topic. Often, an expository passage has helpful organizing words: *first, next, for example*, and *therefore*. These words let readers know where they are in the passage. While expository passages don't need to have difficult vocabulary and fancy writing, they are better with them. Yet, this can make it difficult to pay attention to an expository passage. Expository passages are not always about things that will interest you. Also, writers focus more on clearness and precision than with keeping the reader's interest. By careful reading, you will establish a good habit of focus when you read an expository passage.

> **Review Video: <u>Expository Passages</u>**
> Visit mometrix.com/academy and enter code: 256515

A **technical** passage is written to describe a complicated thing or action. Technical writing is common in medical and technology fields. In those fields, ideas of mathematics, science, and engineering need to be explained simply and clearly. A technical passage usually proceeds in a step-by-step order to help with understanding the passage. Technical passages often have clear headings and subheadings. These headings act like the organizing words in an expository passage: they let readers know where they are in a passage. Also, you will find that these passages divide sections up with numbers or letters.

Many technical passages look more like an outline than the paragraphs that you are reading right now. Depending on the audience, the amount of difficult vocabulary will change in a technical passage. Some technical passages try to stay away from language that readers will have to look up. However, some difficult vocabulary has to be used for writers to share their message.

> **Review Video: <u>Technical Passages</u>**
> Visit mometrix.com/academy and enter code: 478923

A **persuasive** passage is written to change the mind of readers so that they agree with the author. The purpose of the passage may be very clear or very difficult to find. A persuasive passage wants to make an acceptable argument and win the trust of the reader. In some cases, a persuasive passage will be similar to an informative passage. Both passages make an argument and offer supporting details. However, a persuasive passage is more likely to appeal to the reader's feelings and make arguments based on opinions. Persuasive passages may not describe other points of view. So, when they do show other points of view, they may show favoritism to one side.

Persuasive passages will focus on one main argument and make many minor arguments (i.e., arguments that help the main argument) along the way. If you are going to accept the main argument, then you need to accept the minor arguments. So, the main argument will only be as strong as the minor arguments. These arguments should be rooted in fact and experience, not opinions. The best persuasive passages give enough supporting detail to back up arguments without confusing readers. Remember that a fact must be open to independent verification (i.e., the fact must be something that can be backed up by someone else). Also, statistics (i.e., data or figures collected for study) are helpful only when they look at other choices. For example, a statistic on the number of bicycles sold would only be useful if it was taken over a limited time period and in a specific area. Good readers are careful with statistics because statistics can show what we want to see. Or, they can hide what we don't want to see. The writers of your test know that their passages will be met by questioning readers. So, your skill at questioning what you read will be a help in your exam.

> **Review Video: How to Write a Persuasive Essay**
> Visit mometrix.com/academy and enter code: 621428

Opinions come from how we feel and what we think. Persuasive writers try often to appeal to the emotions (i.e., use or influence someone's feelings) of readers to make their arguments. You should always ask questions about this approach. You should ask questions because an author can pull you into accepting something that you don't want to accept. Sometimes these appeals can be used in a fair way. For example, some subjects cannot be totally addressed without an appeal to a reader's feelings. Think about an article on drunk driving. Some examples in the article will alarm or sadden readers because of the terrible outcome.

On the other hand, appeals to feelings are unacceptable when they try to mislead readers. For example, a presidential candidate (i.e., someone running for president) says that they care about the country. The candidate pushes you to make a connection. You care about the country as well and have positive feelings about the country. The candidate wants you to connect your positive feelings about the country with your thoughts about him or her. If you make more connections with the candidate, then you are likely to vote for him or her. Also, the person running for president hints that other candidates do not care about the country.

Another common and unacceptable appeal to feelings is the use of loaded language. Calling a religious person a *fanatic* or a person interested in the environment a *tree hugger* are examples of loaded language.

ORGANIZATION OF THE PASSAGE

The way a passage is organized can help readers to understand the author's purpose and his or her conclusions. There are many ways to organize a passage, and each one has an important use.

Some nonfiction texts are organized to **present a problem** followed by a solution. For this type of passage, the problem is explained before the solution is given. When the problem is well known, the solution may be given in a few sentences at the beginning. Other passages may focus on the solution, and the problem will be talked about only a few times. Some passages will outline many

68

solutions to a problem. This will leave you to choose among the possible solutions. If authors have loyalty to one solution, they may not describe some of the other solutions. Be careful with the author's plan when reading a problem-solution passage. When you know the author's point of view, you can make a better judgment of the author's solution.

Sometimes authors will organize information clearly for you to follow and locate the information. However, this is not always the case with passages in an exam. Two common ways to order a passage are cause and effect and chronological order. When using **chronological order** (i.e., a plan that moves in order from the first step to the last), the author gives information in the order that the event happened. For example, biographies are written in chronological order. The person's birth and childhood are first. Their adult life is next. The events leading up to the person's death are last.

In **cause and effect** passages, an author shows one thing that makes something else happen. For example, if one were to go to bed very late and wake up very early, then they would be tired in the morning. The cause is a lack of sleep, with the effect of being tired the next day.

Finding the cause-and-effect relationships in a passage can be tricky. Often, these relationships come with certain words or terms. When authors use words like *because*, *since*, *in order*, and *so*, they are describing a cause and effect relationship. Think about the sentence: *He called her because he needed the homework*. This is a simple causal relationship. The cause was his need for the homework, and the effect was his phone call. Yet, not all cause and effect relationships are marked like this. Think about the sentences: *He called her. He needed the homework*. When the cause-and-effect relationship does not come with a keyword, the relationship can be known by asking why. For example, *He called her*. Why did he call her? The answer is in the next sentence: He needed the homework.

> **Review Video: Rhetorical Strategy of Cause-and-Effect Analysis**
> Visit mometrix.com/academy and enter code: 725944

When authors try to change the minds of readers, they may use cause-and-effect relationships. However, these relationships should not always be taken at face value. To read a persuasive essay well, you need to judge the cause-and-effect relationships. For example, imagine an author wrote the following: *The parking deck has not been making money because people want to ride their bikes.* The relationship is clear: the cause is that people want to ride their bikes. The effect is that the parking deck has not been making money. However, you should look at this argument again. Maybe there are other reasons that the parking deck was not a success: a bad economy, too many costs, etc.

Many passages follow the **compare-and-contrast** model. In this model, the similarities and differences between two ideas or things are reviewed. A review of the similarities between ideas is called comparison. In a perfect comparison, the author shows ideas or things in the same way. If authors want to show the similarities between football and baseball, then they can list the equipment and rules for each game. Think about the similarities as they appear in the passage and take note of any differences.

Careful thinking about ideas and conclusions can seem like a difficult task. You can make this task easy by understanding the basic parts of ideas and writing skills. Looking at the way that ideas link to others is a good way for you to begin. Sometimes authors will write about two ideas that are against each other. Other times, an author will support a topic, and another author will argue against the topic. The review of these rival ideas is known as **contrast**. In contrast, all ideas should

69

be presented clearly. If the author does favor a side, you need to read carefully to find where the author shows or hides this favoritism. Also, as you read the passage, you should write out how one side views the other.

PURPOSES FOR WRITING

To be a careful reader, pay attention to the author's **position** and purpose. Even passages that seem fair and equal--like textbooks--have a position or bias (i.e., the author is unfair or inaccurate with opposing ideas). Readers need to take these positions into account when considering the author's message. Authors who appeal to feelings or like one side of an argument make their position clear. Authors' positions may be found in what they write and in what they don't write. Normally, you would want to review other passages on the same topic to understand the author's position. However, you are in the middle of an exam. So, look for language and arguments that show a position.

> **Review Video: Author's Position**
> Visit mometrix.com/academy and enter code: 827954

Sometimes, finding the **purpose** of an author is easier than finding his or her position. In most cases, the author has no interest in hiding his or her purpose. A passage for entertainment will be written to please readers. Most stories are written to entertain. However, they can inform or persuade. Informative texts are easy to recognize. The most difficult purpose of a text to determine is persuasion. In persuasion, the author wants to make the purpose hard to find. When you learn that the author wants to persuade, you should be skeptical of the argument. Persuasive passages may try to establish an entertaining tone and hope to amuse you into agreement. On the other hand, an informative tone may be used to seem fair and equal to all sides.

An author's purpose is clear often in the organization of the text (e.g., section headings in bold font point to an informative passage). However, you may not have this organization in your passages. So, if authors make their main idea clear from the beginning, then their likely purpose is to inform. If the author makes a main argument and gives minor arguments for support, then the purpose is probably to persuade. If the author tells a story, then his or her purpose is most likely to entertain. If the author wants your attention more than to persuade or inform, then his or her purpose is most likely to entertain. You must judge authors on how well they reach their purpose. In other words, think about the type of passage (e.g., technical, persuasive, etc.) that the author has written and if the author has followed the demands of the passage type.

> **Review Video: Understanding the Author's Intent**
> Visit mometrix.com/academy and enter code: 511819

The author's purpose will influence his or her writing approach and the reader's reaction. In a persuasive essay, the author wants to prove something to readers. There are several important marks of persuasive writing. Opinion given as fact is one mark. When authors try to persuade readers, they give their opinions as if they were facts. Readers must be on guard for statements that sound like facts but cannot be tested. Another mark of persuasive writing is the appeal to feelings. An author will try to play with the feelings of readers by appealing to their ideas of what is right and wrong. When an author uses strong language to excite the reader's feelings, then the author may want to persuade. Many times, a persuasive passage will give an unfair explanation of other sides. Or, the other sides are not shown.

An **informative passage** is written to teach readers. Informative passages are almost always nonfiction. The purpose of an informative passage is to share information in the clearest way. In an

70

informative passage, you may have a thesis statement (i.e., an argument on the topic of a passage that is explained by proof). A thesis statement is a sentence that normally comes at end of the first paragraph. Authors of informative passages are likely to put more importance on being clear. Informative passages do not normally appeal to the feelings. They often contain facts and figures. Informative passages almost never include the opinion of the author. However, you should know that there can be a bias in the facts. Sometimes, a persuasive passage can be like an informative passage. This is true when authors give their ideas as if they were facts.

Entertainment passages describe real or imagined people, places, and events. Entertainment passages are often stories or poems. So, figurative language is a common part of these passages. Often, an entertainment passage appeals to the imagination and feelings. Authors may persuade or inform in an entertainment passage. Or, an entertainment passage may cause readers to think differently about a subject.

When authors want to **share feelings,** they may use strong language. Authors may share feelings about a moment of great pain or happiness. Other times, authors will try to persuade readers by sharing feelings. Some phrases like *I felt* and *I sense* hint that the author is sharing feelings. Authors may share a story of deep pain or great joy. You must not be influenced by these stories. You need to keep some distance to judge the author's argument.

Almost all writing is descriptive. In one way or another, authors try to describe events, ideas, or people. Some texts are concerned only with **description**. A descriptive passage focuses on a single subject and seeks to explain the subject clearly. Descriptive passages contain many adjectives and adverbs (i.e., words that give a complete picture for you to imagine). Normally, a descriptive passage is informative. Yet, the passage may be persuasive or entertaining.

WRITING DEVICES

Authors will use different writing devices to make their message clear for readers. One of those devices is comparison and contrast. When authors show how two things are alike, they are **comparing** them. When authors describe how two things are different, they are **contrasting** them. The compare and contrast passage is a common part of nonfiction. Comparisons are known by certain words or phrases: *both, same, like, too,* and *as well.* Yet, contrasts may have words or phrases like *but, however, on the other hand, instead,* and *yet.* Of course, comparisons and contrasts may be understood without using those words or phrases. A single sentence may compare and contrast. Think about the sentence *Brian and Sheila love ice cream, but Brian loves vanilla and Sheila loves strawberry.* In one sentence, the author has described both a similarity (e.g., love of ice cream) and a difference (e.g., favorite flavor).

> **Review Video: Compare and Contrast**
> Visit mometrix.com/academy and enter code: 798319

Another regular writing device is **cause and effect**. A cause is an act or event that makes something happen. An effect is what results from the cause. A cause and effect relationship is not always easy to find. So, there are some words and phrases that show causes: *since, because,* and *due to.* Words and phrases that show effects include *consequently, therefore, this lead(s) to, as a result.* For example, *Because the sky was clear, Ron did not bring an umbrella.* The cause is the clear sky, and the effect is that Ron did not bring an umbrella. Readers may find that the cause and effect relationship is not clear. For example, *He was late and missed the meeting.* This does not have any words that show cause or effect. Yet, the sentence still has a cause (e.g., he was late) and an effect (e.g., he missed the meeting).

Remember the chance for a single cause to have many effects. (e.g., *Single cause*: Because you left your homework on the table, your dog eats the homework. *Many effects*: (1) As a result, you fail your homework. (2) Your parents do not let you see your friends. (3) You miss out on the new movie. (4) You miss holding the hand of an important person.)

Also, there is a chance of a single effect to have many causes. (e.g., *Single effect*: Alan has a fever. *Many causes*: (1) An unexpected cold front came through the area, and (2) Alan forgot to take his multi-vitamin.)

Now, an effect can become the cause of another effect. This is known as a cause and effect chain. (e.g., As a result of her hatred for not doing work, Lynn got ready for her exam. This led to her passing her test with high marks. Hence, her resume was accepted, and her application was accepted.)

Point of view has an important influence on a passage. A passage's point of view is how the author or a character sees or thinks about things. A point of view influences the events of a passage, the meetings among characters, and the ending to the story. For example, two characters watch a child ride a bike. Character one watches outside. Character two watches from inside a house. Both see the same event, yet they are around different noises, sights, and smells. Character one may see different things that happen outside that character two cannot see from inside. Also, point of view can be influenced by past events and beliefs. For example, if character one loves bikes, then she will remember how proud she is of the child. If character two is afraid of riding bikes, then he may not remember the event or fear for the child's safety.

In fiction, the two main points of view are first person and third person. The narrator is the person who tells a story's events. The protagonist is the main character of a story. If the narrator is the protagonist in a story, then the story is written in first-person. In first person, the author writes from the view of *I*. Third-person point of view is the most common among stories. With third person, authors refer to each character by using *he* or *she* and the narrator is not involved in the story. In third-person omniscient, the narrator is not a character in the story and tells the story of all of the characters at the same time.

> **Review Video: Point of View**
> Visit mometrix.com/academy and enter code: 383336

Transitional words and phrases are devices that guide readers through a passage. You may know the common transitions. Though you may not have thought about how they are used. Some transitional phrases (*after, before, during, in the middle of*) give information about time. Some hint that an example is about to be given (*for example, in fact, for instance*). Writers use transitions to compare (*also, likewise*) and contrast (*however, but, yet*). Transitional words and phrases can point to addition (*and, also, furthermore, moreover*) and understood relationships (*if, then, therefore, as a result, since*). Finally, transitional words and phrases can separate the chronological steps (*first, second, last*).

> **Review Video: Transitional Words and Phrases**
> Visit mometrix.com/academy and enter code: 197796

UNDERSTANDING A PASSAGE

One of the most important skills in reading comprehension is finding **topics** and **main ideas.** There is a small difference between these two. The topic is the subject of a passage (i.e., what the passage is all about). The main idea is the most important argument being made by the author. The topic is

72

shared in a few words while the main idea needs a full sentence to be understood. As an example, a short passage might have the topic of penguins, and the main idea could be written as *Penguins are different from other birds in many ways.*

In most nonfiction writing, the topic and the main idea will be stated clearly. Sometimes, they will come in a sentence at the very beginning or end of the passage. When you want to know the topic, you may find it in the first sentence of each paragraph. A body paragraph's first sentence is often--but not always--the main topic sentence. The topic sentence gives you a summary of the ideas in the paragraph. You may find that the topic or main idea is not given clearly. So, you must read every sentence of the passage. Then, try to come up with an overall idea from each sentence.

Note: A thesis statement is not the same as the main idea. The main idea gives a brief, general summary of a text. The thesis statement gives a clear idea on an issue that is backed up with evidence.

> **Review Video: Topics and Main Ideas**
> Visit mometrix.com/academy and enter code: 407801

The main idea is the umbrella argument of a passage. So, **supporting details** back up the main idea. To show that a main idea is correct, authors add details that prove their idea. All passages contain details. However, they are referred to as supporting details when they help an argument in the passage. Supporting details are found in informative and persuasive texts. Sometimes they will come with terms like *for example* or *for instance.* Or, they will be numbered with terms like *first, second,* and *last.* You should think about how the author's supporting details back up his or her main idea. Supporting details can be correct, yet they may help the author's main idea. Sometimes supporting details can seem helpful. However, they may be useless when they are based on opinions.

> **Review Video: Supporting Details**
> Visit mometrix.com/academy and enter code: 396297

An example of a main idea: *Giraffes live in the Serengeti of Africa.* A supporting detail about giraffes could be: *A giraffe in the Serengeti benefits from a long neck by reaching twigs and leaves on tall trees.* The main idea gives the general idea that the text is about giraffes. The supporting detail gives a clear fact about how the giraffes eat.

A **theme** is an issue, an idea, or a question raised by a passage. For example, a theme of *Cinderella* is determination as Cinderella serves her step-sisters and step-mother. Passages may have many themes, and you must be sure to find only themes that you are asked to find. One common mark of themes is that they give more questions than answers. Authors try to push readers to consider themes in other ways. You can find themes by asking about the general problems that the passage is addressing. A good way to find a theme is to begin reading with a question in mind (e.g., How does this passage use the theme of love?) and to look for answers to that question.

> **Review Video: Themes in Literature**
> Visit mometrix.com/academy and enter code: 732074

EVALUATING A PASSAGE

When you read informational passages, you need to make a conclusion from the author's writing. You can **identify a logical conclusion** (i.e., find a conclusion that makes sense) to know whether you agree or disagree with an author. Coming to this conclusion is like making an inference. You combine the information from the passage with what you already know. From the passage's information and your knowledge, you can come to a conclusion that makes sense. One way to have a conclusion that makes sense is to take notes of all the author's points. When the notes are organized, they may point to the logical conclusion. Another way to reach conclusions is to ask if the author's passage raises any helpful questions. Sometimes you will be able to draw many conclusions from a passage. Yet, some of these may be conclusions that were never imagined by the author. Therefore, find reasons in the passage for the conclusions that you make.

Review Video: How to Support a Conclusion
Visit mometrix.com/academy and enter code: 281653

Text evidence is the information that supports a main argument or minor argument. This evidence, or proof, can lead you to a conclusion. Information used as text evidence is clear, descriptive, and full of facts. Supporting details give evidence to back-up an argument.

For example, a passage may state that winter occurs during opposite months in the Northern hemisphere (i.e., north of the equator) and Southern hemisphere (i.e., south of the equator). Text evidence for this claim may include a list of countries where winter occurs in opposite months. Also, you may be given reasons that winter occurs at different times of the year in these hemispheres (e.g., the tilt of the Earth as it rotates around the sun).

Review Video: Textual Evidence
Visit mometrix.com/academy and enter code: 486236

A reader should always draw conclusions from passages. Sometimes conclusions are implied (i.e., information that is assumed) from written information. Other times the information is **stated directly** within the passage. You should try to draw conclusions from information stated in a passage. Furthermore, you should always read through the entire passage before drawing conclusions. Many readers expect the author's conclusions at the beginning or the end of the passage. However, many texts do not follow this format.

Implications are things that the author does not say directly. Yet, you can assume from what the author does say. For example, *I stepped outside and opened my umbrella. By the time I got to work, the cuffs of my pants were soaked*. The author never says that it is raining. However, you can conclude that this information is implied. Conclusions from implications must be well supported by the passage. To draw a conclusion, you should have many pieces of proof. Yet, let's say that you have only one piece. Then, you need to be sure that there is no other possible explanation than your conclusion. Practice drawing conclusions from implications in real life events to improve your skills.

Outlining the information in a passage should be a well-known skill to readers. A good outline will show the pattern of the passage and lead to better conclusions. A common outline calls for the main ideas of the passage to be listed in the order that they come. Then, beneath each main idea, you can list the minor ideas and details. An outline does not need to include every detail from the passage. However, the outline should show everything that is important to the argument.

Review Video: Outlining as an Aid to Drawing Conclusions
Visit mometrix.com/academy and enter code: 584445

Another helpful tool is the skill of **summarizing** information. This process is similar to creating an outline. First, a summary should define the main idea of the passage. The summary should have the most important supporting details or arguments. Summaries can be unclear or wrong because they do not stay true to the information in the passage. A helpful summary should have the same message as the passage.

Ideas from a passage can be organized using **graphic organizers**. A graphic organizer reduces information to a few key points. A graphic organizer like a timeline may have an event listed for each date on the timeline. However, an outline may have an event listed under a key point that happens in the passage.

You need to make a graphic organizer that works best for you. Whatever helps you remember information from a passage is what you need to use. A spider-map is another example. This map takes a main idea from the story and places it in a bubble. From one main idea bubble, you put supporting points that connect to the main idea. A Venn diagram groups information as separate or connected with some overlap.

> **Review Video: Graphic Organizers**
> Visit mometrix.com/academy and enter code: 665513

Paraphrasing is another method that you can use to understand a passage. To paraphrase, you put what you have read into your own words. Or, you can *translate* what the author shared into your words by including as many details as you can.

RESPONDING TO A PASSAGE

One part of being a good reader is making predictions. A **prediction** is a guess about what will happen next. Readers make predictions from what they have read and what they already know. For example: *Staring at the computer screen in shock, Kim reached for the glass of water.* The sentence leaves you to think that she is not looking at the glass. So, you may guess that Kim is going to knock over the glass. Yet, in the next sentence, you may read that Kim does not knock over the glass. As you have more information, be ready for your predictions to change.

> **Review Video: Predictive Reading**
> Visit mometrix.com/academy and enter code: 437248

Test-taking tip: To respond to questions that ask about predictions, your answer should come from the passage.

You will be asked to understand text that gives ideas without stating them directly. An **inference** is something that is implied but not stated directly by the author. For example: *After the final out of the inning, the fans were filled with joy and rushed the field*. From this sentence, you can infer that the fans were watching baseball and their team won. You should not use information outside of the passage before making inferences. As you practice making inferences, you will find that they need all of your attention.

> **Review Video: Inference**
> Visit mometrix.com/academy and enter code: 379203

Test-taking tip: When asked about inferences, look for context clues. Context is what surrounds the words and sentences that add explanation or information to an unknown piece. An answer can be *true* but not *correct*. The context clues will help you find the answer that is best. When asked for the implied meaning of a statement, you should locate the statement first. Then, read the context around the statement. Finally, look for an answer with a similar phrase.

For your exam, you must be able to find a text's **sequence** (i.e., the order that things happen). When the sequence is very important to the author, the passage comes with signal words: *first, then, next,* and *last.* However, a sequence can be implied. For example, *He walked through the garden and gave water and fertilizer to the plants.* Clearly, the man did not walk through the garden at the beginning. First, he found water. Then, he collected fertilizer. Next, he walked through the garden. Finally, he gave water and fertilizer to the plants. Passages do not always come in a clear sequence. Sometimes they begin at the end. Or, they can start over at the beginning. You can strengthen your understanding of the passage by taking notes to understand the sequence.

Building a Vocabulary

There is more to a word than its dictionary definition. The **denotative** meaning of a word is the actual meaning found in a dictionary. For example, a house and a home are places where people live. The **connotative meaning** is what comes to mind when you think of a word. For example, a house may be a simple, solid building. Yet, a home may be a comfortable, welcoming place where a family lives. Most non-fiction is fact-based with no use of figurative language. So, you can assume that the writer will use denotative meanings. In fiction, drama, and poetry, the author may use the connotative meaning. Use context clues to know if the author is using the denotative or connotative meaning of a word.

> **Review Video: Connotation and Denotation**
> Visit mometrix.com/academy and enter code: 310092

Readers of all levels will find new words in passages. The best way to define a word in **context** is to think about the words that are around the unknown word. For example, nouns that you don't know may be followed by examples that give a definition. Think about this example: *Dave arrived at the party in hilarious garb: a leopard-print shirt, buckskin pants, and tennis shoes.* If you didn't know the meaning of garb, you could read the examples (i.e., a leopard-print shirt, buckskin pants, and tennis shoes) and know that *garb* means *clothing.* Examples will not always be this clear. Try another example: *Parsley, lemon, and flowers were just a few of the items he used as garnishes.* The word *garnishes* is explained by parsley, lemon, and flowers. From this one sentence, you may know that the items are used for decoration. Are they decorating a food plate or an ice table with meat? You would need the other sentences in the paragraph to know for sure.

> **Review Video: Context Clues**
> Visit mometrix.com/academy and enter code: 613660

Also, you can use contrasts to define an unfamiliar word in context. In many sentences, authors will not describe the unfamiliar word directly. Instead, they will describe the opposite of the unfamiliar word. So, you are given some information that will bring you closer to defining the word. For example: *Despite his intelligence, Hector's bad posture made him look obtuse.* Despite means that Hector's posture is at odds with his intelligence. The author explains that Hector's posture does not prove his intelligence. So, *obtuse* must mean *unintelligent.* Another example: *Even with the horrible weather, we were beatific about our trip to Alaska.* The weather is described as *horrible.* So, *beatific* must mean something positive.

Sometimes, there will be very few context clues to help you define an unknown word. When this happens, **substitution** is a helpful tool. First, try to think of some synonyms for the words. Then, use those synonyms in place of the unknown words. If the passage makes sense, then the substitution has given some information about the unknown word. For example: *Frank's* *admonition rang in her ears as she climbed the mountain.* Don't know the definition of *admonition*? Then, try some substitutions: *vow, promise, advice, complaint,* or *compliment.* These words hint that an *admonition* is some sort of message. Once in a while substitution can get you a precise definition.

Usually, you can define an unfamiliar word by looking at the descriptive words in context. For example: *Fred dragged the recalcitrant boy kicking and screaming up the stairs.* The words *dragged, kicking,* and *screaming* all hint that the boy hates going up the stairs. So, you may think that *recalcitrant* means something like unwilling or protesting. In this example, an unfamiliar adjective was identified.

Description is used more to define an unfamiliar noun than unfamiliar adjectives. For example: *Don's wrinkled frown and constantly shaking fist labeled him as a curmudgeon.* Don is described as having a *wrinkled frown* and *constantly shaking fist.* This hints that a *curmudgeon* must be a grumpy, old man. Contrasts do not always give detailed information about the unknown word. However, they do give you some clues to understand the word.

Many words have more than one definition. So, you may not know how the word is being used in a sentence. For example, the verb *cleave* can mean *join* or *separate.* When you see this word, you need to pick the definition that makes the most sense. For example: *The birds cleaved together as they flew from the oak tree.* The use of the word *together* hints that *cleave* is being used to mean *join.* Another example: *Hermione's knife cleaved the bread cleanly.* A knife cannot join bread together. So, the word must hint at separation. Learning the purpose of a word with many meanings needs the same tricks as defining an unknown word. Look for context clues and think about the substituted words.

Critical Thinking Skills

OPINIONS AND FACTS
Critical thinking skills are mastered by understanding the types of writing and the purposes of authors. Every author writes for a purpose. To know the purpose of authors and how they accomplish their purpose has two important steps. First, think carefully about their writing. Then, determine if you agree with their conclusions.

Readers must always be aware of the difference between fact and opinion. A **fact** can be proved or disproved. An **opinion** is the author's personal thoughts or feelings. So, an opinion cannot be proved or disproved.

For example, an author writes that the distance from New York City to Boston is about two hundred miles. The author is giving a fact. We can drive to Boston from New York City and find that it took about 200 miles. However, another author writes that New York City is too crowded. This author is giving an opinion. The reason that this is an opinion is that there is no independent measurement for overpopulation. You may think that where you live is overcrowded. Yet, someone else may say that more people can live in your area.

An opinion may come with words like *believe, think,* or *feel.* Know that an opinion can be backed up with facts. For example, someone may give the population density (i.e., the number of people living for each square mile) of New York City as a reason for an overcrowded population. An opinion backed up with facts can seem convincing. However, this does not mean that you should accept the argument.

Use these steps to know the difference between fact and opinion. First, think about the type of source that is presenting information (e.g., Is this information coming from someone or something that is trusted by me and others?). Next, think about the information that backs up a claim (e.g., Are the details for the argument opinions or facts?). Then, think about the author's motivation to have a certain point of view on a topic (e.g., Why does this person care about this issue?).

For example, a group of scientists tests the value of a product. The results are likely to be full of facts. Now, compare the group of scientists to a company. The company sells a product and says that their products are good. The company says this because they want to sell their product. Yet, the scientists use the scientific method (i.e. an independent way of proving ideas and questions) to prove the value of the product. The company's statements about the product may be true. But, the group of scientists *proves* the value of the product.

> **Review Video: Fact or Opinion**
> Visit mometrix.com/academy and enter code: 870899

When writers try to persuade, they often make mistakes in their thinking patterns and writing choices. These patterns and choices are important for making an informed decision. Authors show their bias when they ignore fair counterarguments or twist opposing points of view. A **bias** is obvious when the author is unfair or inaccurate with opposing ideas.

A **stereotype** is like a bias. Yet, a stereotype is used only with a group or place. Stereotyping is thought to be wrong because the practice pairs uninformed ideas with people or places. Be very careful with authors who stereotype. These uninformed ideas almost always show the author's ignorance and lack of curiosity.

> **Review Video: Bias and Stereotype**
> Visit mometrix.com/academy and enter code: 644829

Literature

LITERARY GENRES

Fiction is a general term for any type of narrative that is invented or imagined. Your exam will have a passage that was written for your test. Or, a passage may be taken from a published work. During your exam, you may recognize a passage that you have read. In this case, you still need to follow the rule of reading the passage once. Then, go to the test questions. This rule applies to the other genres as well. Now, let's start with fiction.

Review Video: <u>Best Tips for Effectively Reading Fiction</u>
Visit mometrix.com/academy and enter code: 391411

Fiction has many subgroups, but the genre can be put into three main subgroups:

- **Short stories**: a fictional passage that has fewer than 20,000 words. Short stories have only a few characters and normally have one important event. The short story began in magazines in the late 1800s.
- **Novels**: longer works of fiction that may have many characters and a far-reaching plot. The attention may be on an event, action, social problem, or an experience. Note: novels may be written like poetry.
- **Novellas**: a work of fiction that is longer than a short story, but shorter than a novel. Novellas may also be called short novels or novelettes. They come from the German tradition and have increased in popularity across the world.

Many elements influence a work of fiction. Some important ones are:

- **Speech and dialogue**: Dialogue is the communication among characters. These characters may speak for themselves. Or, the narrator may share what a character has spoken. This speech or dialogue may seem realistic or obviously imaginary. The choice depends on the author's purpose.
- **External and internal conflict**: External conflict is the action and events that are around the character. Internal conflict is the thoughts and feelings that bother a character. This conflict that happens inside a character is used to develop the plot. Or, the internal conflict can be used to show the growth or lack of growth in a character.
- **Dramatic involvement**: Some narrators want readers to join with the events of the story (e.g., Thornton Wilder's *Our Town*). Other authors try to separate themselves from readers with figurative language.
- **Action**: The events that continue the plot, such as interactions between characters and physical movement and conflict.
- **Duration**: The amount of time that passes in the passage may be long or short. If the author gives an amount of time (e.g., three days later), then that information is important to remember.
- **Setting and description**: Is the setting (i.e., time and place within the passage) important to the plot or characters? How are the action scenes described?
- **Themes**: This is any point of view or topic that is given constant attention.
- **Symbolism**: Authors may share what they mean through imagery and other figurative devices. For example, smoke can be a symbol of danger, and doves are often symbols of peace.

Plot lines are one way to show the information given in a story. Every plot line has the same stages. You can find each of these stages in every story that you read. These stages include the introduction, rising action, conflict, climax, falling action, and resolution. The introduction tells you the point of the story and sets up the plot. The rising action is the event that leads up to the conflict (i.e., an internal or external problem) with the climax at the peak. The falling action is the events that come after the climax of the conflict. The resolution is the conclusion and may have the final solution to the problem in the conflict. A plot line looks like this:

Review Video: Plot line Definition
Visit mometrix.com/academy and enter code: 944011

Most passages put events in chronological order. However, some authors may use an unusual order to have a particular influence on readers. For example, many of the Greek epics begin *in medias res* (i.e., in the middle of things). The passage begins with an introduction to the climax. Then, the author goes to the beginning and shares how events came to that climax. This order is found in many mystery novels. First, a crime is committed. Then, a detective must go back and piece together the events that led to the crime. As you read, try to keep in mind the cause-and-effect relationships that shape the story. A cause must come before an effect. So, use an outline of the different causes and effects in a passage. Be sure that this outline shows the correct chronological order. Remember that the order of events in a story is not always the order that they happened.

The **narrator** can give insight about the purpose of the work and the main themes and ideas. There are important questions to ask about understanding the voice and role of the narrator:

- Who is the narrator of the passage? What is the narrator's perspective: first person or third person? Is the narrator involved in the plot? Are there changes in narrators?
- Does the narrator explain things in the passage? Or, are things explained with the plot and events? Does the narrator give special description to one character or event and not to others? A narrator may express approval or disapproval about a character or events in the work.
- Tone is the attitude of a character through his or her words. If the narrator is involved in the story, how is the narrator addressing others? Is the tone casual or formal? Close or distant? Does the narrator's vocabulary give any information about the narrator?

Review Video: The Narrator
Visit mometrix.com/academy and enter code: 742528

A **character** is someone or something that is connected closely with the plot and growth of the passage. As characters grow in a story, they move along the plot line. Characters can be named as flat or round and static or dynamic. Flat characters are simple individuals that are known for one or two things. Often, they are supporting characters to round characters. Minor flat characters are stock characters that fill out the story without influencing the outcome. Round characters, usually protagonists, are crucial to the story. They are explored widely and explained in much detail. If characters change or develop, they can be known as static or dynamic. Static characters either do not change or change very little in a passage. In other words, who they are at the beginning is who they are at the end. However, dynamic characters change over the course of a passage. In other words, who they are at the beginning is not at all who they are at the end.

> ### Review Video: <u>What is the Definition of a Character in a Story</u>
> Visit mometrix.com/academy and enter code: 429493

Prose is ordinary spoken language as opposed to verse (i.e., language with metric patterns). The everyday, normal communication is known as prose and can be found in textbooks, memos, reports, articles, short stories, and novels. Distinguishing characteristics of prose include:

- Some sort of rhythm may be present, but there is no formal arrangement.
- The common unit of organization is the sentence which may include literary devices of repetition and balance.
- There must be coherent relationships among sentences.

Poetry, or verse, is the manipulation of language with respect to meaning, meter, sound, and rhythm. Lines of poetry vary in length and scope, and they may or may not rhyme. Related groups of lines are called stanzas and may be any length. Some poems are as short as a few lines, and some are as long as a book.

A line of poetry can be any length and can have any metrical pattern. A line is determined by the physical position of the words on a page. A line is one group of words that follows the next group in a stanza. Lines may or may not have punctuation at the end depending on the need for punctuation. Consider the following example from John Milton:

> "When I consider how my light is spent,
>
> E're half my days, in this dark world and wide,"

A stanza is a group of lines. The grouping denotes a relationship among the lines. A stanza can be any length, but the separation of lines into different stanzas indicates an intentional pattern created by the poet. The breaks between stanzas indicate a change of subject or thought. As a group of lines, the stanza is a melodic unit that can be analyzed for metrical patterns and rhyme patterns. Stanzas of a certain length have been named to indicate an author's purpose with a form of poetry. A few examples include the couplet (two lines), the tercet (three lines), and the quatrain (four lines).

Another important genre is **drama**: a play written to be spoken aloud. The drama is, in many ways, inseparable from performance. Ideally, reading drama involves using imagination to visualize and re-create the play with characters and settings. Readers stage the play in their imagination and watch characters interact and developments unfold. Sometimes this involves simulating a theatrical presentation, while other times you need to imagine the events. In either case, you are imagining the unwritten to recreate the dramatic experience. Novels present some of the same problems, but a narrator will provide much more information about the setting, characters, inner dialogues, and many other supporting details. In drama, much of this is missing, and you are required to use your powers of projection and imagination to understand the dramatic work. There are many empty spaces in dramatic texts that must be filled by the reader to appreciate the work.

Review Video: Dramas
Visit mometrix.com/academy and enter code: 216060

Figurative Language

When authors want to share their message in a creative way, they use figurative language devices. Learning these devices will help you understand what you read. **Figurative language** is communication that goes beyond the actual meaning of a word or phrase. **Descriptive language** that awakens imagery in the reader's mind is one type of figurative language. Exaggeration is another type of figurative language. Also, when you compare two things, you are using figurative language. Similes and metaphors are the two main ways of comparing things. An example of a simile: *The child howled like a coyote when her mother told her to pick up the toys.* In this example, the child's howling is compared to a coyote. This helps the reader understand the sound being made by the child.

A **figure of speech** is a word or phrase that is not a part of straightforward, everyday language. Figures of speech are used for emphasis, fresh expression, or clearness. However, clearness of a passage may be incomplete with the use of these devices. For example: *I am going to crown you.*

The author may mean:

1. I am going to place a real crown on your head.
2. I am going to make you king or queen of this area.
3. I am going to punch you in the head with my fist.
4. I am going to put a second checker's piece on top of your checker piece to show that it has become a king.

> **Review Video: Figures of Speech**
> Visit mometrix.com/academy and enter code: 111295

An **allusion** is a comparison of someone or something to a person or event in history or literature. Allusions that point to people or events that are a part of today's culture are called topical allusions. Those that name a specific person are known as personal allusions. For example, *His desire for power was his Achilles' heel.* This example points to Achilles: a notable hero in Greek mythology who was thought to be invincible (i.e., cannot be hurt) except for his heels. Today, the term *Achilles' heel* points to an individual's weakness.

> **Review Video: Allusions**
> Visit mometrix.com/academy and enter code: 294065

A **metaphor** is the comparison of one thing with a different thing. For example: *The bird was an arrow flying across the sky.* In this sentence, the arrow is compared to a bird. The metaphor asks you to think about the bird in another way. Let's continue with this metaphor for a bird. You are asked to view the bird's flight as the flight of an arrow. So, you may imagine the flight to be quick and purposeful.

Metaphors allow the author to describe a thing without being direct. Remember that the thing being described will not always be mentioned directly by the author. Think about a forest in winter: *Swaying skeletons reached for the sky and groaned as the wind blew through them.* In this sentence, the author uses *skeletons* as a metaphor for trees without leaves.

> **Review Video: Metaphors in Writing**
> Visit mometrix.com/academy and enter code: 133295

Hyperbole is overstatement or exaggeration. For example: *He jumped ten feet in the air when he heard the good news.* Obviously, no person can jump ten feet in the air without help. The author exaggerates because the hyperbole shares a lot of feeling. Let's say that the author shared: *He jumped when he heard the good news.* With this information, you might think that the character is not feeling very excited. Hyperbole can be dangerous if the author does not exaggerate enough. For example: *He jumped two feet in the air when he heard the good news.* You may think that the author is writing a fact. Be careful with confusing hyperboles. Some test questions may have a hyperbole and a fact listed in the answer choices.

Understatement is the opposite of hyperbole. This device discounts or downplays something. Think about someone who climbs Mount Everest. Then, they say that the journey was *a little stroll.* As with other types of figurative language, understatement has a range of uses. The device may show self-defeat or modesty as in the Mount Everest example. However, some may think of understatement as false modesty (i.e., an attempt to bring attention to you or a situation). For example, a woman is praised on her diamond engagement ring. The woman says, *Oh, this little thing?* Her understatement might be heard as stuck-up or unfeeling.

> **Review Video: Hyperbole and Understatement**
> Visit mometrix.com/academy and enter code: 308470

A **simile** is a comparison that needs the separation words *like* or *as*. Some examples: *The sun was like an orange, eager as a beaver*, and *quick as a mountain goat*. Because a simile includes *like* or *as*, the comparison uses a different tone than a simple description of something. For example: *the house was like a shoebox.* The tone is different than the author saying that the house *was* a shoebox.

> **Review Video: Similes**
> Visit mometrix.com/academy and enter code: 642949

Personification is the explanation of a nonhuman thing with human attributes. The basic purpose of personification is to describe something in a way that readers will understand. An author says that a tree *groans* in the wind. The author does not mean that the tree is giving a low, pained sound from a mouth. However, the author means that the tree is making a noise like a human groan. Of course, this personification creates a tone of sadness or suffering. A different tone would be made if the author said that the tree *sways* or *dances*.

> **Review Video: Personification**
> Visit mometrix.com/academy and enter code: 260066

Irony is a statement that hints at the opposite of what you expect. In other words, the device is used when an author or character says one thing but means another. For example, imagine a man who is covered in mud and dressed in tattered clothes. He walks in his front door to meet his wife. Then, his wife asks him, "How was your day?" He says, "Great!" The man's response to his wife is an example of irony. There is a difference between irony and sarcasm. Sarcasm is similar to irony. However, sarcasm is hurtful for the person receiving the sarcastic statement. A sarcastic statement points to the foolishness of a person to believe that a false statement is true.

> **Review Video: What is the Definition of Irony?**
> Visit mometrix.com/academy and enter code: 374204

As you read, you will see more words in the context of a sentence. This will strengthen your vocabulary. Be sure to read on a regular basis. This practice will increase the number of ways that you have seen a word in context. Based on experience, a person can remember how a word was used in the past and use that knowledge for a new context. For example, a person may have seen the word *gull* used to mean a bird that is found near the seashore. However, a *gull* can be a person who is tricked easily. If the word in context is used for a person, you will see the insult. After all, gulls are not thought to be very smart. Use your knowledge of a word to find comparisons. This knowledge can be used to learn a new use of a word.

Essay Writing

PRACTICE MAKES PREPARED WRITERS

Writing is a skill that continues to need development throughout a person's life. For some people, writing seems to be a natural gift. They rarely struggle with writer's block. When you read their papers, they have persuasive or entertaining ideas. For others, writing is an intimidating task that they endure. As you practice, you can improve your skills and be better prepared for writing a time-sensitive essay.

Remember that you are practicing for more than an exam. Two of the most valuable skills in life are the abilities to **read critically** and to **write clearly**. When you work on evaluating the arguments of a passage and explain your thoughts well, you are developing skills that you will use for a lifetime. In this overview of essay writing, you will find strategies and tools that will prepare you to write better essays.

CREATIVE WRITING

Take time to read a story or hear stories read aloud and use those opportunities to learn more about how stories are put together. This offers a frame for you to talk about a story with others and will help you to write better stories. With each new story that you read, try to predict what could happen in the story. Try to understand the setting by picturing the scenes and sounds that are described and the behaviors of characters. Then, try to summarize the events to understand more of the story.

If you need more help with understanding a story, you can try to relate narrative characters and events to your own life. For example, when reading a story, you can ask the following: Who is the main character in the story? What happened first? What happened next? What happened at the end of the story? Where does this story take place? And what is the theme or point of this story?

ESTABLISH A CONTEXT

When writing a narrative, an author must establish the context of the story. In other words, the stage needs to be set for the story to begin. Sometimes this is done by establishing the setting of the story and then introducing a narrator and characters. A character or the narrator can be introduced first. A narrator and/or characters can be introduced in many ways: through the use of dialogue, through description, or through the reactions of the narrator or characters to an event. Whatever means an that you choose, the beginning of a narrative must be compelling for your audience.

Discuss the introduction of the character in the following passage.

> Her parents named her Milagro, which means "miracle" in Spanish, but they called her Milly. She was a premature baby, very tiny, and it was a miracle that she survived. That was the beginning of her good fortune.

The author uses a dramatic way to introduce the character. Readers are told that *Milagro* means "miracle" in Spanish. Readers are told that it was a miracle that Milagro survived her birth because she was born prematurely. The way Milagro is introduced is dramatic because the author uses information to hint at what may come next. This is a form of foreshadowing. The author has established an interesting beginning with how the character is introduced, and this captures the attention of readers.

POINT OF VIEW

Point of view is the perspective from which writing occurs. There are several possibilities:

- *First person* is written so that the *I* of the story is a participant or observer. First-person narratives let narrators express inner feelings and thoughts. The narrator may be a close friend of the protagonist, or the narrator can be less involved with the main characters and plot.
- *Second person* is a device to draw the reader in more closely. It is really a variation or refinement of the first-person narrative. In some cases, a narrative combines both second-person and first-person voices, speaking of "you" and "I." When the narrator is also a character in the story, the narrative is better defined as first-person even though it also has addresses of "you."
- *Third person* may be either objective or subjective, and either omniscient or limited. Objective third-person narration does not include what the characters are thinking or feeling, while subjective third-person narration does include this information. The third-person omniscient narrator knows everything about all characters, including their thoughts and emotions; and all related places, times, and events. The third-person limited narrator may know everything about a particular character of focus, but is limited to that character. In other words, the narrator cannot speak about anything that character does not know.

SEQUENCE OF EVENTS

The sequence of events in a narrative should follow naturally out of the action and the plot. Rather than being forced, the sequence should follow the natural flow of a dialogue or plot and enhance what happens in the story. The only time that the sequence is not in the order that events naturally happen is when an author decides to use the literary device called flashback. In this case the action does not flow in sequence; instead, the action jumps back and forth in time. Events in a narrative are extremely important in helping the reader understand the intent or message of a narrative, which is why it is important to take note of the way in which the plot unfolds.

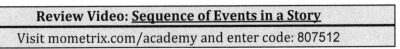

Review Video: Sequence of Events in a Story
Visit mometrix.com/academy and enter code: 807512

Remember from the Reading section that a plot shows the order of a story. The introduction is the beginning of the story. Next, the rising action, conflict, climax, and falling action are the middle. Then, the resolution or conclusion is the ending. So, stay focused on the goal of writing a story that needs those main parts: a beginning, a middle, and an ending.

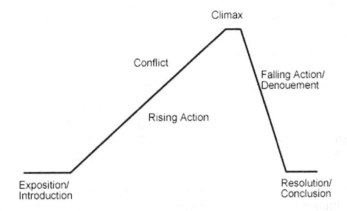

AUTHOR TECHNIQUES

You can employ many techniques to make your narrative essay come alive in a fresh and interesting way. Dialogue is an important one. Often, dialogue is the means that helps readers understand what is happening and what a character is like. Equally important are the descriptions that you can use to help readers visualize a setting and what a character looks or acts like. Remember that you have limited time to write a whole story. So, don't be concerned with providing description for everything that you put in your story.

DEVELOPMENT OF CHARACTERS

Characters are important to a story, and the problems that they face make a story interesting and complex. As you write your story, be sure to show more information about the characters through their actions. The actions of characters are important to advancing the plot because they show the different stages of the story. If your story teaches a lesson, hey also help the reader understand the theme or lesson that the story teaches.

CONFLICT

A conflict is a problem that needs to be solved. Many stories include at least one conflict, and the characters' efforts to solve conflicts move the story forward. The protagonist is the character who has the main goal of solving the conflict. Conflicts can be external or internal to any of the characters. A major type of internal conflict is some inner personal battle that is called *man against himself*. This type of conflict is when a character struggles with his or her thoughts or emotions.

Major types of external conflicts include *man against nature*, *man against man*, and *man against society*. The man against nature conflict is

    You can recognize conflicts in story plots by asking:

    Who is the protagonist?

    Who or what is the antagonist?

    Why are the protagonist and antagonist in conflict?

    What event(s) develop the conflict?

    Which event is the climax?

TRANSITIONS WORDS

Transition words can be helpful when writing a narrative so that readers can follow the events in a seamless manner. Sequence words such as *first*, *second*, and *last* assist readers in understanding the order in which events occur. Words such as *then* or *next* also show the order in which events occur. *After a while* and *before this* are other sequence expressions.

Additionally, transition words can indicate a change from one time frame or setting to another: "We were sitting on a rock near the lake when we heard a strange sound."At this point we decided to look to see where the noise was coming from by going further into the woods." In this excerpt the phrase *at this point* signals a shift in setting between what was happening and what came next.

PRECISE LANGUAGE

Your use of precise language, phrases, and sensory language (i.e., language that appeals to the five senses) helps readers imagine a place, situation, or person in the way that you intended. Details of character's actions, the setting, and the events in a narrative help create a lively and thought-provoking story. Sensory language helps convey the mood and feeling of the setting and characters and can highlight the theme of your story.

Read the excerpt and analyze the language.

At dawn, in a stuffy and smoky second-class car in which five people had already spent the night, a bulky woman in deep mourning was hoisted in—almost like a shapeless bundle. Behind her, puffing and moaning, followed her husband—a tiny man, thin and weakly, his face death-white, his eyes small and bright and looking shy and uneasy.

The language selected by the author is filled with fresh and precise words that describe and color the two passengers as well as the setting of the paragraph. The author describes the car as *stuffy and smoky*, *second-class*, and *in which five people had already spent the night*. All this conjures up a dreary train car. The author describes the woman as *a shapeless bundle*. Her husband is *tiny*, *thin*, and *weakly* with a *death-white* face. These words give a clear image of what the people look like for readers which should be a goal of your creative writing.

ROLE OF A CONCLUSION

The conclusion of a narrative is extremely important because it shapes the entire story and is the resolution of the characters' conflict(s). Some conclusions may be tragic (e.g., classic tragedies), and other endings may be lighthearted (e.g., classic comedies). Modern stories tend to have endings that are more complex than the clear-cut endings of classic literature. They often leave readers without a clear sense of how a character fares at the end. Nonetheless, this element can show how life is not always clear in its conclusions.

A student is writing a story about a boy who pushes himself to become an athlete. The student has written about how hard the boy has trained for an upcoming race. He has noted that winning has become a huge force in his life. Now, a conclusion is needed for the story. Describe what he should look for when he writes the conclusion.

The student should think about what the theme of the story is meant to be. Is it a story about someone who works hard and gets what he wants? Or is it about someone who loses an important race and how he deals with it? Then, the student should carry that theme through to the ending of the story which in this case would be whether he won or lost the race. A conclusion should bring the entire story to an appropriate ending so that readers have a sense of closure.

TRADITIONAL ESSAY OVERVIEW

A traditional way to prepare for the writing section is to read. When you read newspapers, magazines, and books, you learn about new ideas. You can read newspapers and magazines to become informed about issues that affect many people.

As you think about those issues and ideas, you can take a position and form opinions. Try to develop these ideas and your opinions by sharing them with friends. After you develop your opinions, try writing them down as if you were going to spread your ideas beyond your friends.

For your exam you need to write an essay that shows your ability to understand and respond to an assignment. When you talk with others, you give beliefs, opinions, and ideas about the world around you. As you talk, you have the opportunity to share information with spoken words, facial expressions, or hand motions. If your audience seems confused about your ideas, you can stop and explain. However, when you write, you have a different assignment. As you write, you need to share information in a clear, precise way. Your readers will not have the chance to ask questions about your ideas. So, before you write your essay, you need to understand the assignment. As you write, you should be clear and precise about your ideas.

BRAINSTORM

Spend the first three to five minutes brainstorming for ideas. Write down any ideas that you might have on the topic. The purpose is to pull any helpful information from the depths of your memory. In this stage, anything goes down on note paper regardless of how good or bad the idea may seem at first glance. You may not bring your own paper for these notes. Instead, you will be provided with paper at the time of your test.

STRENGTH THROUGH DIFFERENT VIEWPOINTS

The best papers will contain several examples and mature reasoning. As you brainstorm, you should consider different perspectives. There are more than two sides to every topic. In an argument, there are countless perspectives that can be considered. On any topic, different groups are impacted and many reach the same conclusion or position. Yet, they reach the same conclusion through different paths. Before writing your essay, try to *see* the topic through as many different *eyes* as you can.

Once you have finished with your creative flow, you need to stop and review what you brainstormed. *Which idea allowed you to come up with the most supporting information?* Be sure to pick an angle that will allow you to have a thorough coverage of the prompt.

Every garden of ideas has weeds. The ideas that you brainstormed are going to be random pieces of information of different values. Go through the pieces carefully and pick out the ones that are the best. The best ideas are strong points that will be easy to write a paragraph in response.

Now, you have your main ideas that you will focus on. So, align them in a sequence that will flow in a smooth, sensible path from point to point. With this approach, readers will go smoothly from one idea to the next in a reasonable order. Readers want an essay that has a sense of continuity (i.e., Point 1 to Point 2 to Point 3 and so on).

START YOUR ENGINES

Now, you have a logical flow of the main ideas for the start of your essay. Begin by expanding on the first point, then move to your second point. Pace yourself. Don't spend too much time on any one of the ideas that you are expanding on. You want to have time for all of them. *Make sure that you watch your time*. If you have twenty minutes left to write out your ideas and you have four ideas, then you can only use five minutes per idea. Writing so much information in so little time can be an intimidating task. Yet, when you pace yourself, you can get through all of your points. If you find that you are falling behind, then you can remove one of your weaker arguments. This will allow you to give enough support to your remaining paragraphs.

Once you finish expanding on an idea, go back to your brainstorming session where you wrote out your ideas. You can scratch through the ideas as you write about them. This will let you see what you need to write about next and what you have left to cover.

Your introductory paragraph should have several easily identifiable features.

1. First, the paragraph should have a quick description or paraphrasing of the topic. Use your own words to briefly explain what the topic is about.
2. Second, you should list your writing points. What are the main ideas that you came up with earlier? If someone was to read only your introduction, they should be able to get a good summary of the entire paper.
3. Third, you should explain your opinion of the topic and give an explanation for why you feel that way. What is your decision or conclusion on the topic?

Each of your following paragraphs should develop one of the points listed in the main paragraph. Use your personal experience and knowledge to support each of your points. Examples should back up everything.

Once you have finished expanding on each of your main points, you need to conclude your essay. Summarize what you written in a conclusion paragraph. Explain once more your argument on the prompt and review why you feel that way in a few sentences. At this stage, you have already backed up your statements. So, there is no need to do that again. You just need to refresh your readers on the main points that you made in your essay.

DON'T PANIC

Whatever you do during the essay, do not panic. When you panic, you will put fewer words on the page and your ideas will be weak. Therefore, panicking is not helpful. If your mind goes blank when you see the prompt, then you need to take a deep breath. Remember to brainstorm and put anything on scratch paper that comes to mind.

Also, don't get clock fever. You may be overwhelmed when you're looking at a page that is mostly blank. Your mind is full of random thoughts and feeling confused, and the clock is ticking down faster. You have already brainstormed for ideas. Therefore, you don't have to keep coming up with ideas. If you're running out of time and you have a lot of ideas that you haven't written down, then don't be afraid to make some cuts. Start picking the best ideas that you have left and expand on them. Don't feel like you have to write on all of your ideas.

A short paper that is well written and well organized is better than a long paper that is poorly written and poorly organized. Don't keep writing about a subject just to add sentences and avoid repeating a statement or idea that you have explained already. The goal is 1 to 2 pages of quality writing. That is your target, but you should not mess up your paper by trying to get there. You want to have a natural end to your work without having to cut something short. If your essay is a little long, then that isn't a problem as long as your ideas are clear and flow well from paragraph to paragraph. Just be sure that your writing stays inside the assigned borders of the papers. Remember to expand on the ideas that you identified in the brainstorming session.

Leave time at the end (at least three minutes) to go back and check over your work. Reread and make sure that everything you've written makes sense and flows well. Clean up any spelling or grammar mistakes. Also, go ahead and erase any brainstorming ideas that you weren't able to include. Then, clean up any extra information that you might have written that doesn't fit into your paper.

As you proofread, make sure that there aren't any fragments or run-ons. Check for sentences that are too short or too long. If the sentence is too short, then look to see if you have a specific subject and an active verb. If it is too long, then break up the long sentence into two sentences. Watch out

for any "big words" that you may have used. Be sure that you are using difficult words correctly. Don't misunderstand; you should try to increase your vocabulary and use difficult words in your essay. However, your focus should be on developing and expressing ideas in a clear and precise way.

THE SHORT OVERVIEW

Depending on your preferences and personality, the essay may be your hardest or your easiest section. You are required to go through the entire process of writing a paper in a limited amount of time which is very challenging.

Stay focused on each of the steps for brainstorming. Go through the process of creative flow first. You can start by generating ideas about the prompt. Next, organize those ideas into a smooth flow. Then, pick out the ideas that are the best from your list.

Create a recognizable essay structure in your paper. Start with an introduction that explains what you have decided to argue. Then, choose your main points. Use the body paragraphs to touch on those main points and have a conclusion that wraps up the topic.

Save a few moments to go back and review what you have written. Clean up any minor mistakes that you might have made and make those last few critical touches that can make a huge difference. Finally, be proud and confident of what you have written!

Practice Test #1

Want to take this practice test in an online interactive format?
Check out the bonus page, which includes interactive practice questions and
much more: **https://www.mometrix.com/bonus948/ssatmiddle**

Writing

Instructions: Read the following prompt, taking a few moments to plan a response. Then, write your response in essay form.

Prompt: *NSA wiretapping and spying policies have been a topic of interest lately with much discussion taking place over the need for security as it relates to the right to individual privacy.*

Do you agree or disagree with this statement? Use examples from history, literature, or your own personal experience to support your point of view.

Quantitative

1. Janice makes x phone calls. Elaina makes 23 more phone calls than Janice. June makes 14 more phone calls than Janice. In terms of x, what is the sum of their phone calls minus 25 calls?

    a. $3x + 37$
    b. $3x + 12$
    c. $x + 12$
    d. $3x - 25$
    e. $9x - 25$

2. Olga drew the regular figure shown here. She painted part of the figure a light color and part of it a darker color. She left the rest of the figure white.

Which of the following equations best models the part of the figure Olga left white?

    a. $1 - \dfrac{1}{3} - \dfrac{1}{3} = \dfrac{1}{3}$
    b. $1 - \dfrac{1}{6} - \dfrac{1}{6} = \dfrac{2}{3}$
    c. $1 - \dfrac{1}{6} - \dfrac{1}{2} = \dfrac{1}{3}$
    d. $1 - \dfrac{1}{2} - \dfrac{1}{3} = \dfrac{2}{3}$
    e. $1 - \dfrac{1}{2} - \dfrac{1}{6} = \dfrac{2}{3}$

3. On a floor plan drawn at a scale of 1:100, the area of a rectangular room is 30 cm^2. What is the actual area of the room?

    a. 30 m^2
    b. 300 cm^2
    c. 300 m^2
    d. $3{,}000 \text{ m}^2$
    e. $30{,}000 \text{ cm}^2$

4. Restaurant customers tip their server only 8 percent for poor service. If their tip was $4, how much was their bill?

    a. $40
    b. $42
    c. $46
    d. $48
    e. $50

5. The number of flights a flight attendant made per month is represented by the line graph below.

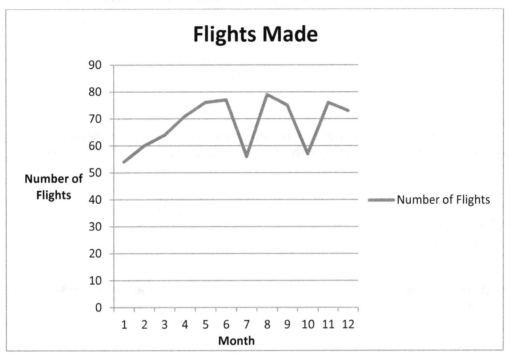

What is the range in the number of flights the flight attendant made?

    a. 20
    b. 22
    c. 25
    d. 29
    e. 32

6. In Figure 1 (pictured below), the distance from *A* to *D* is 48. The distance from *A* to *B* is equal to the distance from *B* to *C*. If the distance from *C* to *D* is twice the distance of *A* to *B*, how far apart are *B* and *D*?

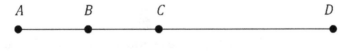

Figure 1

    a. 12
    b. 16
    c. 19
    d. 24
    e. 36

7. John buys 100 shares of stock at $100 per share. The price goes up by 10% and he sells 50 shares. Then, prices drop by 10% and he sells his remaining 50 shares. How much did he get for the last 50?

  a. $4000
  b. $4900
  c. $4950
  d. $5000
  e. $5500

8. A long distance runner does a first lap around a track in exactly 50 seconds. As she tires, each subsequent lap takes 20% longer than the previous one. How long does she take to run 3 laps?

  a. 72 seconds
  b. 160 seconds
  c. 180 seconds
  d. 182 seconds
  e. 190 seconds

9. Hannah draws two supplementary angles. One angle measures 34°. What is the measure of the other angle?

  a. 56°
  b. 66°
  c. 146°
  d. 168°
  e. 326°

10. Jeremy put a heavy chalk mark on the tire of his bicycle. His bike tire is 27 inches in diameter. When he rolled the bike, the chalk left marks on the sidewalk. Which expression can be used to best determine the distance, in inches, the bike rolled from the first mark to the fourth mark?

  a. $3(27\pi)$
  b. $4\pi(27)$
  c. $(27 \div 3)\pi$
  d. $(27 \div 4)\pi$
  e. $4\pi(27 \div 3)$

11. A data set has five values: 5, 10, 12, 13, and one unknown value. The average of the data set is 9.6. What is the unknown value?

  a. 4.6
  b. 5
  c. 6
  d. 7.2
  e. 8

12. A hat contains 6 red dice, 4 green dice, and 2 blue dice. What is the probability that Sarah pulls out a blue die, replaces it, and then pulls out a green die?

   a. $\frac{1}{18}$

   b. $\frac{1}{16}$

   c. $\frac{2}{12}$

   d. $\frac{1}{3}$

   e. $\frac{1}{2}$

13. If $a- 16 = 8b + 6$, what does $a + 3$ equal?

   a. $b + 3$
   b. $8b + 9$
   c. $8b + 22$
   d. $8b + 25$
   e. $b + 6$

14. A bag of coffee costs $9.85 and contains 16 ounces of coffee. Which of the following best represents the cost per ounce?

   a. $0.62
   b. $0.64
   c. $0.65
   d. $0.67
   e. $0.70

15. What is the slope of the line shown in the graph?

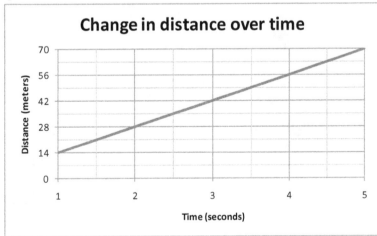

   a. 7
   b. 14
   c. 16
   d. 21
   e. 28

16. Adam builds a bridge that is 12 feet long. If 1 foot equals 0.3048 meters, which of the following best represents the length of the bridge, in meters?

   a. 1.83 meters
   b. 3.66 meters
   c. 4.96 meters
   d. 5.7 meters
   e. 39.37 meters

17. Amy saves $450 every 3 months. How much does she save after 3 years?

   a. $4,800
   b. $5,200
   c. $5,400
   d. $5,800
   e. $6,000

18. The figure below shows a square. If side $\overline{AD} = 10$ and if $\overline{AE} = \overline{EB}$ and $\overline{BF} = \overline{FC}$, what is the area of the shaded region?

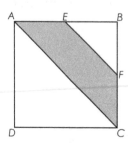

   a. 16.5
   b. 24
   c. 28
   d. 37.5
   e. 42.5

19. Simplify the following equation: $4(6-3)^2 - (-2)$

   a. 34
   b. 36
   c. 38
   d. 42
   e. 48

20. If $\sqrt{x} - 2 = 8$, determine the value of x.

   a. 64
   b. 66
   c. 100
   d. 110
   e. 144

21. Which of the following transformations has been applied to △ABC?

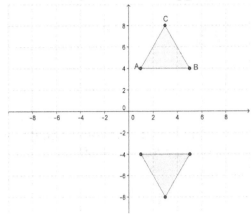

a. translation
b. rotation of 90 degrees
c. reflection
d. dilation
e. rotation of 180 degrees

22. The distance between two towns is 275 miles. A truck driver must leave one town and arrive at the other at 9:30 p.m. If the trucker drives at an average rate of 55 miles per hour, at what time should the trucker depart?

a. 4:00 p.m.
b. 4:30 p.m.
c. 5:00 p.m.
d. 4:00 a.m.
e. 4:30 a.m.

23. The chart below shows the annual number of visitors to the Augusta Planetarium. Which year shows the greatest increase in visitors over the prior year?

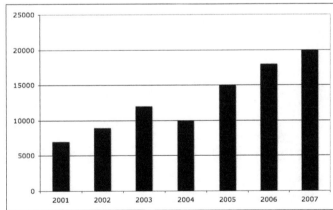

a. 2001
b. 2002
c. 2003
d. 2004
e. 2005

24. What is the simplest way to write the following expression?

$5x - 2y + 4x + y$

a. $9x - y$
b. $9x - 3y$
c. $9x + 3y$
d. $x - y$
e. $9x + y$

25. A wall clock has the numbers 1 through 12 written on it. If you spin the second hand, what is the probability of landing on an even number?

a. 10%
b. 20%
c. 30%
d. 40%
e. 50%

Reading Comprehension

Global Warming

Global warming and the depletion of natural resources are constant threats to the future of our planet. All people have a responsibility to be proactive participants in the fight to save Earth by working now to conserve resources for later. Participation begins with our everyday choices. From what you buy to what you do to how much you use, your decisions affect the planet and everyone around you. Now is the time to take action.

When choosing what to buy, look for sustainable products made from renewable or recycled resources. The packaging of the products you buy is just as important as the products themselves. Is the item minimally packaged in a recycled container? How did the product reach the store? Locally grown food and other products manufactured within your community are the best choices. The fewer miles a product traveled to reach you, the fewer resources it required.

You can continue to make a difference for the planet in how you use what you bought and the resources you have available. Remember the locally grown food you purchased? Don't pile it on your plate at dinner. Food that remains on your plate is a wasted resource, and you can always go back for seconds. You should try to be aware of your consumption of water and energy. Turn off the water when you brush your teeth, and limit your showers to five minutes. Turn off the lights, and don't leave appliances or chargers plugged in when not in use.

Together, we can use less, waste less, recycle more, and make the right choices. It may be the only chance we have.

1. What is the author's primary purpose in writing this article?
   a. The author's purpose is to scare people.
   b. The author's purpose is to warn people.
   c. The author's purpose is to inspire people.
   d. The author's purpose is to inform people.
   e. The author's purpose is to scold people.

2. How does the author make a connection between the second and third paragraphs (lines 7-19)?
   a. The author indicates he will now make suggestions for how to use what you bought.
   b. The author indicates he will continue to give more examples of what you should buy.
   c. The author indicates he will make suggestions for how to keep from buying more items.
   d. The author indicates he will make suggestions for how to tell other people what to buy.
   e. The author indicates he will continue to encourage people to be aware of their energy consumption.

3. What is the main idea of this article?
   a. People should use less water and energy.
   b. People should make responsible choices in what they purchase and how they use their available resources.
   c. People are quickly destroying the earth, and there is no way to stop the destruction.
   d. People should organize everyone they know to join the fight to save the environment.
   e. A few people need to keep the majority encouraged to save the planet's resources.

4. Which organizational pattern did the author use?
- a. Comparison and contrast
- b. Chronological order
- c. Cause and effect
- d. Problem/solution
- e. None of the above

5. What does the author say is the place to begin saving our planet?
- a. The place to begin is with getting rid of products that are not earth friendly.
- b. The place to begin is with using less water when we take a shower.
- c. The place to begin is with a commitment to fight for the improvement of Earth.
- d. The place to begin is with buying locally-grown food.
- e. The place to begin is with the choices we make every day.

6. What does the author imply will happen if people do not follow his suggestions?
- a. The author implies we will run out of resources in the next 10 years.
- b. The author implies water and energy prices will rise sharply in the near future.
- c. The author implies global warming and the depletion of natural resources will continue.
- d. The author implies local farmers will lose their farms.
- e. The author implies that we will other opportunities to save the planet.

<u>The Educational Market Town</u>

Aberystwyth is a market town on the West Coast of Wales within the United Kingdom. A market town refers to European areas that have the right to have markets, which differentiates it from a city or village. The town is located where two rivers meet, the River Ystwyth and River Rheidol and is best known as an educational center, housing an established university since 1872.

The town is situated between North Wales and South Wales, and is a large vacation destination as well as a tourist attraction. Constitution Hill is a hill on the north end of Aberystwyth, which provides excellent views of Cardigan Bay and which is supported by the Aberystwyth Electric Cliff Railway. Although Aberystwyth is known as a modern Welsh town, it is home to several historic buildings, such as the remnants of a castle.

Although there are several grocery, clothing, sporting goods, and various other miscellaneous shops, Aberystwyth is best known for its educational services. Aberystwyth University, formerly known as University College Wales, as well as the National Library of Wales, which is the legal deposit library for Wales and which houses all Welsh publications, are both located within Aberystwyth. The two main languages traditionally spoken in Aberystwyth are English and Welsh. With local live music, arts center, and educational opportunities in gorgeous scenery, Aberystwyth is a hidden luxury within the United Kingdom.

7. Where is Aberystwyth located?
- a. England
- b. Ireland
- c. Scotland
- d. Wales
- e. Isle of Man

8. What is the purpose of this essay?

    a. To explain that the university was established in 1872
    b. To explain the legal deposit library in Wales
    c. To provide a portrait of a town
    d. To explain the views in Aberystwyth
    e. To help tourists

9. What does the word *situated* mean in paragraph 2?

    a. located
    b. fighting
    c. luxurious
    d. hidden
    e. indefinite

10. Which of the following statements is an opinion?

    a. Although Aberystwyth is known as a modern Welsh town, it is home to several historic buildings, such as the remnants of a castle
    b. With local live music, arts center, and educational opportunities in gorgeous scenery, Aberystwyth is a hidden luxury within the United Kingdom
    c. The two main languages traditionally spoken in Aberystwyth are English and Welsh
    d. Aberystwyth is a market town on the West Coast of Wales within the United Kingdom
    e. Aberystwyth is best known for its educational services

11. How many languages are traditionally spoken in Aberystwyth?

    a. One
    b. Two
    c. Three
    d. Four
    e. More than four

12. What makes Aberystwyth a market town?

    a. It is a city
    b. It is a village
    c. It has the right to have a market
    d. There are markets in town every day
    e. The local live music, arts center, and educational opportunities

13. What is Constitution Hill supported by?

    a. Cardigan Bay
    b. The ocean
    c. North Wales
    d. Aberystwyth Electric Cliff Railway
    e. Tourism

14. What is Aberystwyth best known as?

    a. An educational center
    b. A market town
    c. A music center
    d. A hiking center
    e. A large vacation destination

An Excerpt from <u>The Fifty-First Dragon</u> by Heywood Broun

Of all the pupils at the knight school Gawaine le Cœur-Hardy was among the least promising. He was tall and sturdy, but his instructors soon discovered that he lacked spirit. He would hide in the woods when the jousting class was called, although his companions and members of the faculty sought to appeal to his better nature by shouting to him to come out and break his neck like a man. Even when they told him that the lances were padded, the horses no more than ponies and the field unusually soft for late autumn, Gawaine refused to grow enthusiastic. The Headmaster and the Assistant Professor of Pleasaunce were discussing the case one spring afternoon and the Assistant Professor could see no remedy but expulsion.

"No," said the Headmaster, as he looked out at the purple hills which ringed the school, "I think I'll train him to slay dragons."

"He might be killed," objected the Assistant Professor.

"So he might," replied the Headmaster brightly, but he added, more soberly, "we must consider the greater good. We are responsible for the formation of this lad's character."

"Are the dragons particularly bad this year?" interrupted the Assistant Professor. This was characteristic. He always seemed restive when the head of the school began to talk ethics and the ideals of the institution.

"I've never known them worse," replied the Headmaster. "Up in the hills to the south last week they killed a number of peasants, two cows and a prize pig. And if this dry spell holds there's no telling when they may start a forest fire simply by breathing around indiscriminately."

"Would any refund on the tuition fee be necessary in case of an accident to young Cœur-Hardy?"

"No," the principal answered, judicially, "that's all covered in the contract. But as a matter of fact he won't be killed. Before I send him up in the hills I'm going to give him a magic word."

"That's a good idea," said the Professor. "Sometimes they work wonders."

15. What is this passage about?

    a. The problems that may arise from fighting dragons
    b. How the educators would change Gawaine's course of study
    c. The way the Professor and the Headmaster taught about dragons
    d. Giving Gawaine a magic word to help him fight dragons
    e. A shy boy's troubles in a new school environment

16. **What can be inferred about Gawaine le Couer-Hardy from the first paragraph (lines 1-9)?**
    a. Gawaine does not want to be a knight
    b. Gawaine is not as strong as the other pupils at the knight school
    c. Gawaine's family history is made of unremarkable knights
    d. Gawaine enjoys playing in the forest
    e. Gawaine has no friends at the school

17. **What is the best way to describe Gawaine's character?**
    a. Fearless and excitable
    b. Careless and frigid
    c. Spiritual and careful
    d. Cowardly and apathetic
    e. Rebellious and misunderstood

18. **What is the meaning of "his better nature"?**
    a. An increased sense of honesty
    b. Gawaine's love interest
    c. A desire for ownership
    d. A man's nobler instincts
    e. His knowledge of the forests

19. **Why does the Headmaster mention some "peasants, two cows, and a prize pig"?**
    a. To help the professor understand dragon behavior
    b. To show that Gawaine would be perfect for fighting dragons
    c. To illustrate how much trouble dragons are this year
    d. To explain why Gawaine's talents were needed
    e. To remind the professor of the painful event

20. **How does the Headmaster put the professor at ease about Gawaine?**
    a. He tells him that Gawaine will only fight small dragons.
    b. He assures him that Gawaine's contract has not expired.
    c. He talks to him about the animals that have been killed by the dragons.
    d. He reminds him of their responsibility for the boy's character.
    e. He mentions that Gawaine will be given a magic word.

Charles Darwin on the Galapagos Islands

During the 1800s, Charles Darwin became known for his studies of plants and animals on the Galapagos Islands. He is often referred to as "the father of evolution," because he was first to describe a mechanism by which organisms change over time.

The Galapagos Islands are situated off the coast of South America. Much of Darwin's work on the islands focused on the birds. He noticed that island birds looked similar to finches on the South American continent and resembled a type of modified finch. The only differences in the finches Darwin saw were in their beaks and the kind of food they ate. Finches on the mainland were seed-eating birds, but the island finches ate insects, seeds, plant matter, egg yolks, and blood.

Darwin theorized that the island finches were offspring of one type of mainland finch. The population of finches was changing over time due to their environment. He believed the finches' eating habits changed because of the island's limited food supply. As the finches began to eat

105

differently, the way their beaks worked and looked changed as well. For instance, insect-eating finches needed longer beaks for digging in the ground. Seed-eating and nut-eating finches required thicker beaks to crack the seed shells.

The process by which the finches changed happened over many generations. Among the population of beetle-eating finches, those finches born with longer, sharper beaks naturally had access to more beetles than those finches with shorter beaks. As a result, the sharp-beaked, insect-eating finches thrived and produced many offspring, while the short-beaked insect-eating finches gradually died out. The sharp beak was in effect selected by nature to thrive. The same thing happened in each finch population until finches within the same population began to look similar to each other and different from finches of other populations. These observations eventually led Darwin to develop the theory of natural selection.

21. Why is Charles Darwin called "the father of evolution"?
   a. because he coined the term "evolution"
   b. because he was the first scientist to study species on the Galapagos Islands
   c. because he was the first to describe how organisms changed over time
   d. because he was the first to suggest that birds adapted to their environment
   e. because he was the first to develop the theory of natural selection

22. What is the main point of this passage?
   a. to inform
   b. to entertain
   c. to critique
   d. to persuade
   e. to shock

23. According to the passage, why did finches with sharp, long beaks thrive while other finches died off?
   a. They were able to reproduce faster than other types of finches on the island.
   b. They were more numerous and eventually outlived the other finches on the island.
   c. They were randomly selected by nature to reproduce over other types of finches on the island.
   d. They had a diet that improved their fitness for their environment.
   e. They had better access to insects than other types of finches on the island.

24. Based on Darwin's studies on the islands, what could also be inferred about how geography affects the diversity of species?
   a. Geographical barriers decrease diversity of a species.
   b. Geographical barriers increase diversity of a species.
   c. Geographical barriers have an insignificant impact on the diversity of a species.
   d. Geographical barriers left the finches open to predators.
   e. There is no relationship between geographical barriers and the diversity of a species.

25. Which of the following statements correctly compares the finches Darwin observed in the Galapagos Islands with the finches found on the mainland?

   a. The island finches were very similar with no visible differences.
   b. The island finches differed only in the shape of their beaks.
   c. The island finches differed only in size.
   d. The island finches differed in the shape of their beaks and their diet.
   e. The island finches produced fewer offspring.

<u>New Zealand Inhabitants</u>

The islands of New Zealand are among the most remote of all the Pacific islands. New Zealand is an archipelago, with two large islands and a number of smaller ones. Its climate is far cooler than the rest of Polynesia. According to Maori legends, it was colonized in the early fifteenth century by a wave of Polynesian voyagers who traveled southward in their canoes and settled on North Island. At this time, New Zealand was already known to the Polynesians, who had probably first landed there some 400 years earlier.

The Polynesian southward migration was limited by the availability of food. Traditional Polynesian tropical crops such as taro and yams will grow on North Island, but the climate of the South Island is too cold for them. Coconuts will not grow on either island. The first settlers were forced to rely on hunting and gathering, and, of course, fishing. Especially on the South Island, most settlements remained close to the sea. At the time of the Polynesian influx, enormous flocks of moa birds had their rookeries on the island shores. These flightless birds were easy prey for the settlers, and within a few centuries had been hunted to extinction. Fish, shellfish and the roots of the fern were other important sources of food, but even these began to diminish in quantity as the human population increased. The Maori had few other sources of meat: dogs, smaller birds, and rats. Archaeological evidence shows that human flesh was also eaten, and that tribal warfare increased markedly after the moa disappeared.

By far the most important farmed crop in prehistoric New Zealand was the sweet potato. This tuber is hearty enough to grow throughout the islands, and could be stored to provide food during the winter months, when other food-gathering activities were difficult. The availability of the sweet potato made possible a significant increase in the human population. Maori tribes often lived in encampments called *pa*, which were fortified with earthen embankments and usually located near the best sweet potato farmlands.

26. A definition for the word *archipelago* is

   a. A country
   b. A place in the southern hemisphere
   c. A group of islands
   d. A roosting place for birds
   e. A place with few visitors

27. This article is primarily about what?

   a. The geology of New Zealand
   b. New Zealand's early history
   c. New Zealand's prehistory
   d. Food sources used by New Zealand's first colonists
   e. The differences between the North Island and the South Island

28. Why did early settlements remain close to the sea?
   a. The people liked to swim
   b. The people didn't want to get far from the boats they had come in
   c. Taro and yams grow only close to the beaches
   d. They were dependent upon sea creatures for their food
   e. They would be able to leave the island quickly if they were attacked

29. Why do you suppose tribal warfare increased after the moa disappeared?
   a. Increased competition for food led the people to fight
   b. Some groups blamed others for the moa's extinction
   c. They had more time on their hands since they couldn't hunt the moa, so they fought
   d. One group was trying to consolidate political control over the entire country
   e. None of the above

30. How did the colder weather of New Zealand make it difficult for the Polynesians to live there?
   a. The Polynesians weren't used to making warm clothes
   b. Cold water fish are harder to catch
   c. Some of them froze
   d. Some of their traditional crops would not grow there
   e. They had to use too many resources to make their shelters

31. Why was it important that sweet potatoes could be stored?
   a. They could be eaten in winter, when other foods were scarce
   b. They could be traded for fish and other goods
   c. They could be taken along by groups of warriors going to war
   d. They tasted better after a few weeks of storage
   e. It allowed farmers to use more space for other foods

"The Road Not Taken" by Robert Frost

Two roads diverged in a yellow wood,

And sorry I could not travel both

And be one traveler, long I stood

And looked down one as far as I could

To where it bent in the undergrowth;

Then took the other, as just as fair,

And having perhaps the better claim,

Because it was grassy and wanted wear;

Though as for that the passing there

Had worn them really about the same,

And both that morning equally lay

In leaves no step had trodden black.

Oh, I kept the first for another day!

Yet knowing how way leads on to way,

I doubted if I should ever come back.

I shall be telling this with a sigh

Somewhere ages and ages hence:

Two roads diverged in a wood, and I—

I took the one less traveled by,

And that has made all the difference.

32. In the second stanza, is there a big difference between one road and the other?
   a. Yes, because one path is more dangerous than the other.
   b. Yes, because one road is much less traveled than the other.
   c. No, because one road is only a little less traveled than the other.
   d. No, because both roads lead to the same place in the end.
   e. There is not enough information given to the reader to make a decision.

33. Why does the narrator of the poem say that he will tell the story of the two roads "With a sigh/ Somewhere ages and ages hence"?
   a. The narrator is regretting the choice he has made.
   b. The narrator is sad that he had to walk alone.
   c. The narrator is looking back on a fond memory.
   d. The narrator does not remember what happened.
   e. The narrator knows that the two roads were removed many years ago.

34. Why is the path in the middle of the woods, rather than a road through the city?
   a. There are no signs to point out which road is faster.
   b. There are no distractions from the decision that the narrator has to make.
   c. There are no other people who can give the narrator advice.
   d. All of the above
   e. None of the above

35. Why does the narrator of the poem take so long to make a decision?
   a. He is not sure where the roads will lead him.
   b. He is trying to guess which road will be best for exploring.
   c. He is trying to remember if he has walked this way before.
   d. He is sure that one of the choices will be a wrong turn.
   e. He thinks the choice he makes represents who he is.

36. What does it say about the narrator that he wants to take the road less traveled?
- a. He wants to explore a place that no one has ever been to before.
- b. He wants to feel unique by making a less popular journey.
- c. He wants to take a shortcut through the woods.
- d. He wants to avoid other people.
- e. He wants to show off his bravery to other people.

The Inventions of Technology

Stories have been a part of the world since the beginning of recorded time. For centuries before the invention of the printing press, stories of the world were passed down to generations through oral tradition. With the invention of the printing press, which made written material available to wide ranges of audiences, books were mass-produced and introduced into greater society.

For the last several centuries, books have been at the forefront of education and entertainment. With the invention of the Internet, reliance on books for information quickly changed. Soon, almost everything that anyone needed to know could be accessed through the Internet. Large, printed volumes of encyclopedias became unnecessary as all of the information was easily available on the Internet.

Despite the progression of the Internet, printed media was still very popular in the forms of both fiction and non-fiction books. While waiting for an appointment, enduring a several-hour flight, or relaxing before sleep, books have been a reliable and convenient source of entertainment, and one that society has not been willing to give up.

With the progression and extreme convenience of technology, printed books are going to soon become a thing of the past. Inventions such as the iPad from Macintosh and the Kindle have made the need for any kind of printed media unnecessary. With a rechargeable battery, a large screen, and the ability to have several books saved on file, electronic options will soon take over and society will no longer see printed books.

Although some people may say that the act of reading is not complete without turning a page, sliding a finger across the screen or pressing a button to read more onto the next page is just as satisfying to the reader. The iPad and Kindle are devices that have qualities similar to a computer and can be used for so much more than just reading. These devices are therefore better than books because they have multiple uses.

In a cultural society that is part of the world and due to a longstanding tradition, stories will always be an important way to communicate ideas and provide information and entertainment. Centuries ago, stories could only be remembered and retold through speech. Printed media changed the way the world communicated and was connected, and now, as we move forward with technology, it is only a matter of time before we must say goodbye to the printed past and welcome the digital and electronic future.

37. What is the main argument of this essay?
- a. iPad and Kindles are easier to read than books
- b. The printing press was a great invention
- c. The Internet is how people receive information
- d. Technology will soon replace printed material
- e. People need frequent changes in how they receive stories

38. What is the main purpose of paragraph 1?

a. To explain oral tradition
b. To explain the importance of the printing press
c. To explain the progression of stories within society
d. To introduce the essay
e. To show why iPads and Kindles are necessary today

39. According to the essay, what was the first way that stories were communicated and passed down?

a. Oral tradition
b. Printed books
c. Technology
d. Hand writing
e. Cave drawings

40. Which of the following statements is an opinion?

a. Despite the progression of the Internet, printed media was still very popular in the forms of both fiction and non-fiction books.
b. The iPad and Kindle are devices that have qualities similar to a computer and can be used for so much more than just reading.
c. With the invention of the Internet, reliance on books for information quickly changed.
d. Stories have been a part of the world since the beginning of recorded time.
e. Although some people may say that the act of reading is not complete without turning a page, sliding a finger across the screen or pressing a button to read more onto the next page is just as satisfying to the reader.

Verbal

Synonyms

Directions: Select the one word whose meaning is closest to the word in capital letters.

1. ABROAD
  a. harsh
  b. overseas
  c. selfish
  d. truthful
  e. reception

2. RUMINATE
  a. concern
  b. decision
  c. hesitation
  d. reflect
  e. neglect

3. CONCISE
  a. brief
  b. difficult
  c. lengthy
  d. reasonable
  e. repetitive

4. MOURN
  a. cry
  b. direction
  c. approve
  d. help
  e. praise

5. RESIDENCE
  a. home
  b. area
  c. office
  d. resist
  e. warehouse

6. LEVITY
  a. attended
  b. delivered
  c. happiness
  d. prepared
  e. serious

7. RASH

- a. wise
- b. careless
- c. plan
- d. shy
- e. event

8. BANISH

- a. experiences
- b. pleasures
- c. remove
- d. solutions
- e. welcome

9. OPPORTUNITY

- a. direction
- b. chance
- c. conclusion
- d. caution
- e. sequence

10. DISABLE

- a. improve
- b. lecture
- c. rebuke
- d. replace
- e. damage

11. FRAGILE

- a. reliable
- b. firm
- c. constant
- d. delicate
- e. healthy

12. LOYAL

- a. cover
- b. proof
- c. calm
- d. faithful
- e. healthy

13. PRINCIPLE

- a. end
- b. overall
- c. punctual
- d. standard
- e. uncertain

14. ASSESS

  a. anger
  b. ignore
  c. determine
  d. loneliness
  e. guess

15. MORAL

  a. arrive
  b. fake
  c. honest
  d. portion
  e. unfair

16. SUPERIOR

  a. short
  b. similar
  c. better
  d. weak
  e. usual

17. REMARK

  a. rebuke
  b. comment
  c. lecture
  d. replace
  e. question

18. SPECIFY

  a. confuse
  b. indicate
  c. solid
  d. sturdy
  e. unsettle

19. COMMENCE

  a. begin
  b. progress
  c. finish
  d. comment
  e. exhaust

20. SWIFTLY

  a. surely
  b. quickly
  c. slowly
  d. lightly
  e. lazy

21. WILY

a. clever
b. dainty
c. open
d. trustworthy
e. direct

22. HUMANE

a. cold
b. fed
c. friendly
d. hunted
e. selfish

23. ASSERT

a. deny
b. argue
c. hesitate
d. perform
e. surrender

24. PERILOUS

a. normal
b. secure
c. emblem
d. guarded
e. hazardous

25. DONATE

a. interrupt
b. excessive
c. contribute
d. petition
e. reserve

26. FINITE

a. described
b. intended
c. limited
d. wanted
e. endless

27. DOCILE

a. disagree
b. obedient
c. relate
d. state
e. determined

28. TAINT

   a. built
   b. clean
   c. damage
   d. improve
   e. unite

29. FALTER

   a. criticism
   b. delivery
   c. statement
   d. stumble
   e. steady

30. ABRUPTLY

   a. commonly
   b. homely
   c. slowly
   d. suddenly
   e. gradually

Analogies

Directions: For each of the following questions, you will find terms and five answer choices designated a, b, c, d, and e. Select the one answer choice that best completes the analogy.

31. Historian is to perspective as

   a. explorer is to questionable
   b. victim is to autopsy
   c. native is to insight
   d. fact is to opinion
   e. director is to spirit

32. Geography is to mountains as history is to

   a. preserved
   b. events
   c. roots
   d. future
   e. behavior

33. Exhale is to inhale as

   a. annual is to yearly
   b. reckless is to brave
   c. spontaneous is to chaos
   d. invert is to reverse
   e. consent is to prohibit

34. Fiction is to myth as nonfiction is to

   a. drama
   b. poem
   c. legend
   d. biography
   e. hero

35. Astronomer is to encounter as

   a. vendor is to protect
   b. commander is to resign
   c. prophet is to inform
   d. academic is to camouflage
   e. architect is to disorient

36. Dual is to duel as

   a. docile is to fossil
   b. seam is to seem
   c. factor is to feature
   d. finite is to ample
   e. twice is to double

37. Nausea is to illness as

   a. bacteria is to infection
   b. surgery is to fracture
   c. frail is to vulnerable
   d. disease is to potent
   e. pollen is to flower

38. Evidence is to condemn

   a. generator is to restore
   b. gauge is to dignity
   c. antidote is to tension
   d. destruction is to chariot
   e. preamble is to threat

39. Liberty is to freedom as faithful is to

   a. triumph
   b. nimble
   c. sincere
   d. advantage
   e. inspect

40. Masculine is to feminine as

   a. paternal is to dad
   b. invincible is to undefeatable
   c. community is to individual
   d. defiant is to resistant
   e. concise is to summary

41. Artist is to imagination as advisor is to

    a. despair
    b. clarity
    c. oppress
    d. regal
    e. renew

42. Temple is to sacred as

    a. furnace is to basement
    b. auditorium is to musical
    c. church is to member
    d. sanctuary is to lofty
    e. cocoon is to violent

43. Gourmet is to critic as

    a. menu is to diverse
    b. meager is to portion
    c. cuisine is to exotic
    d. brick is to mason
    e. spice is to ingredient

44. Summit is to mountain as king is to

    a. battlefield
    b. powerful
    c. monarchy
    d. liberator
    e. parliament

45. Tactics is to marine

    a. data is to researcher
    b. navigate is to inspector
    c. forecast is to conductor
    d. distract is to editor
    e. incompetent is to trader

46. Chamber is to contain as

    a. throne is to cower
    b. agenda is to organize
    c. nook is to comfort
    d. chronicle is to story
    e. banjo is to instrument

47. Altar is to alter as

    a. loom is to whom
    b. shrine is to change
    c. denial is to veto
    d. rain is to reign
    e. align is to adjust

48. Nutrition is to physician as

   a. refugee is to nomad
   b. wildlife is to guide
   c. pottery is to navigator
   d. pitfall is to colonist
   e. tyranny is to tourist

49. Bravery is to cowardice as comedy is to

   a. glee
   b. grief
   c. celebrate
   d. relief
   e. inspire

50. Child is to naive as

   a. novice is to wisdom
   b. medal is to exhibit
   c. mother is to censor
   d. baptism is to custom
   e. soldier is to disciplined

51. Colonel is to kernel as

   a. agile is to fragile
   b. serial is to cereal
   c. mantle is to dismantle
   d. concept is to sonnet
   e. imply is to ally

52. Proton is to electron as

   a. productive is to efficient
   b. wept is to mourn
   c. renewable is to energy
   d. potent is to ineffective
   e. chromosome is to neutron

53. Documentary is to protestor as

   a. persist is to director
   b. banished is to renegade
   c. unpopular is to resident
   d. rotor is to mechanic
   e. fashion is to patriot

54. Tear is to tier as air is to

   a. breath
   b. ozone
   c. heir
   d. dare
   e. spare

55. Epidemic is to plague as vigor is to

a. pneumonia
b. endurance
c. incompetence
d. apathy
e. postseason

56. Eternal is to momentary as

a. frequent is to periodic
b. express is to rash
c. hinder is to interfere
d. exotic is to ordinary
e. termination is to decline

57. Meadow is to tranquility as

a. tributary is to consoling
b. suburbs is to danger
c. prairie is to campfire
d. traffic is to boring
e. exercise is to rural

58. Verses is to versus as

a. autobiography is to competition
b. lane is to cane
c. receive is to recieve
d. carat is to carrot
e. poetry is to confront

59. Aviator is to destination as sculptor is to

a. originals
b. restore
c. unrest
d. cathedral
e. strategy

60. Constellation is to star as

a. president is to campaign
b. child is to prank
c. sprout is to bloom
d. movement is to locomotive
e. orchestra is to instrument

Quantitative

1. How many one-fourths are contained in $8\frac{1}{2}$?

    a. 17
    b. 34
    c. 36
    d. 42
    e. 64

2. Given the sequence represented in the table below, where n represents the position of the term and a_n represents the value of the term, which of the following describes the relationship between the position number and the value of the term?

n	1	2	3	4	5	6
a_n	5	2	−1	−4	−7	−10

    a. Multiply n by 2 and subtract 4
    b. Multiply n by 2 and subtract 3
    c. Multiply n by −3 and add 8
    d. Multiply n by −4 and add 1
    e. Multiply n by −3 and subtract 8

3. A triangle has the following angle measures: 98°, 47°, and 35°. What type of triangle is it?

    a. equidistant
    b. right
    c. equiangular
    d. acute
    e. obtuse

4. The TV weatherman warned of a snowstorm approaching the area. If the snow is supposed to fall at a rate of 2 inches per hour, which of the following equations represents the total snowfall (t) after it has been snowing for h hours?

    a. $t = \frac{2}{h}$
    b. $t = h + 2$
    c. $t = h - 2$
    d. $t = 2h$
    e. $t = 2 - h$

5. Student scores on Mrs. Thompson's last math test are shown below. Which of the following is the best representation of class performance?

    76, 39, 87, 85, 91, 93, 86, 90, 77, 89, 74, 82, 68, 86, 79

    a. mean
    b. median
    c. mode
    d. range
    e. None of the above

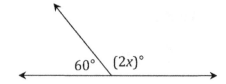

6. In the figure below, find the value of *x*:

60° (2*x*)°

   a. 30
   b. 60
   c. 80
   d. 100
   e. 120

7. If number *x* is subtracted from 27, the result is -5. What is number *x*?

   a. 19
   b. 22
   c. 23
   d. 25
   e. 32

8. Which of the following is equivalent to $4^3 + 12 \div 4 + 8^2 \times 3$?

   a. 211
   b. 249
   c. 259
   d. 278
   e. 393

9. The original price of a jacket is $36.95. The jacket is discounted by 25%. Before tax, which of the following best represents the cost of the jacket?

   a. $27.34
   b. $27.71
   c. $28.11
   d. $28.82
   e. $29.56

10. The number 123 is the 11th term in a sequence with a constant rate of change. Which of the following sequences has this number as its 11th term?

   a. 5, 17, 29, 41, …
   b. 3, 15, 27, 39, …
   c. −1, 11, 23, 35, …
   d. 1, 13, 25, 37, …
   e. 3, 17, 23, 40, …

11. What is the product of four squared and six?

   a. 22
   b. 28
   c. 55
   d. 96
   e. 104

12. A rectangular prism has a length of 14.3 cm, a width of 8.9 cm, and a height of 11.7 cm. Which of the following is the best estimate for the volume of the rectangular prism?

   a. $1{,}287 \text{ cm}^3$
   b. $1{,}386 \text{ cm}^3$
   c. $1{,}512 \text{ cm}^3$
   d. $1{,}573 \text{ cm}^3$
   e. $1{,}620 \text{ cm}^3$

13. Each month, Aisha invests twice the amount invested the previous month. If she invested $26.25 during the first month, how much did she invest during the sixth month?

   a. $157.50
   b. $420.00
   c. $768.50
   d. $840.00
   e. $900.00

14. Find the value of x in the figure below:

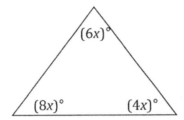

   a. 10
   b. 16
   c. 18
   d. 40
   e. 60

15. Elijah drove 45 miles to his job in an hour and ten minutes in the morning. On the way home in the evening, however, traffic was much heavier and the same trip took an hour and a half. What was his average speed in miles per hour for the round trip?

   a. 30
   b. $32\frac{1}{2}$
   c. $33\frac{3}{4}$
   d. 40
   e. 45

16. Chan receives a bonus from his job. He pays 30% in taxes, gives 30% to charity, and uses another 25% to pay off an old debt. He has $600 left. What was the total amount of Chan's bonus?

   a. $3000
   b. $3200
   c. $3600
   d. $4000
   e. $4200

17. If $3x + 5 = 11$, then $x = ?$

   a. 1
   b. 2
   c. 3
   d. 4
   e. 6

18. Which of the following fractions is halfway between 2/5 and 4/9?

   a. 2/3
   b. 2/20
   c. 17/40
   d. 19/45
   e. 7/10

19. Solve for y in the following equation if $x = -3$

$$y = x + 5$$

   a. $y = -2$
   b. $y = 2$
   c. $y = 3$
   d. $y = 6$
   e. $y = 8$

20. Which of the following is the symbol that represents the negative square root of 100?

   a. $\sqrt{-100}$
   b. $\sqrt{100}$
   c. $\sqrt{10}$
   d. $-\sqrt{10}$
   e. $-\sqrt{100}$

21. Anna wants to buy a new bicycle that costs $125, but she currently only has $40. If Anna can earn $5 each week for doing chores around the house, how many weeks will it take for Anna have enough money to buy the bicycle?

   a. 3 weeks
   b. 8 weeks
   c. 17 weeks
   d. 20 weeks
   e. 25 weeks

22. A sequence is formed from the equation, $y = 6x + 2$, where x represents the term number and y represents the value of the term. What is the value of the 18th term in the sequence?

   a. 98
   b. 104
   c. 110
   d. 116
   e. 120

23. Simplify $\frac{5}{9} \times \frac{3}{4}$.

   a. $\frac{5}{12}$

   b. $\frac{8}{13}$

   c. $\frac{20}{27}$

   d. $\frac{47}{36}$

   e. $\frac{52}{26}$

24. Rachel spent $24.15 on vegetables. She bought 2 pounds of onions, 3 pounds of carrots, and $1\frac{1}{2}$ pounds of mushrooms. If the onions cost $3.69 per pound, and the carrots cost $4.29 per pound, what is the price per pound of mushrooms?

   a. $2.25
   b. $2.35
   c. $2.60
   d. $2.80
   e. $3.10

25. At a picnic, cans of soda are put into a cooler. In the cooler, there are 12 colas, 6 diet colas, 9 lemon-limes, 2 root beers, 4 ginger ales, and 3 orange sodas. What would be the probability of reaching into the cooler without looking and pulling out a ginger ale?

   a. $\frac{1}{9}$

   b. $\frac{1}{8}$

   c. $\frac{1}{6}$

   d. $\frac{1}{5}$

   e. $\frac{1}{3}$

Answer Key and Explanations for Test #1

Quantitative

1. B: Translate this word problem into a mathematical equation. Let the number of Janice's phone calls $= x$. Let the number of Elaina's phone calls $= x + 23$. Let the number June's calls $= x + 14$. Add their calls together and subtract 25 calls:

$$= x + x + 23 + x + 14 - 25$$
$$= 3x + 37 - 25$$
$$= 3x + 12$$

2. C: To answer this question, notice that this figure is a regular hexagon, having 6 equal sides and angles. The part painted darker can be represented by $\frac{1}{6}$. The part painted lighter is clearly $\frac{1}{2}$, which is equivalent to $\frac{3}{6}$. The whole figure is represented by the number 1. So, 1 minus $\frac{1}{6}$ minus $\frac{3}{6}$ equals $\frac{2}{6}$ which is equivalent to $\frac{1}{3}$. Therefore, the equation, $1 - \frac{1}{6} - \frac{1}{2} = \frac{1}{3}$ best models the part of the figure Olga left white.

3. A: Since there are 100 cm in a meter, on a 1:100 scale drawing, each centimeter represents one meter. Therefore, an area of one square centimeter on the drawing represents one square meter in actuality. Since the area of the room in the scale drawing is 30 cm^2, the room's actual area is 30 m^2.

Another way to determine the area of the room is to write and solve an equation, such as this one: $\frac{l}{100} \times \frac{w}{100} = 30$ cm^2 , where l and w are the dimensions of the actual room

$$\frac{lw}{10,000} = 30 \text{ cm}^2$$

$$\text{Area} = 300,000 \text{ cm}^2$$

Since this is not one of the answer choices, convert cm^2 to m^2:

$$300,000 \text{ cm}^2 \times \frac{1 \text{ m}}{100 \text{ cm}} \times \frac{1 \text{ m}}{100 \text{ cm}} = 30 \text{ m}^2.$$

4. E: The total amount of the bill is: $\frac{4}{x} = \frac{8}{100}$; $400 = 8x$; $x = \$50$.

5. C: The line graph shows the largest number of flights made during a month as 79 with the smallest number of flights made during a month as 54. The range is equal to the difference between the largest number of flights and smallest number of flights, i.e., $79 - 54 = 25$. Therefore, the range is equal to 25.

6. E: Segment $\overline{AD} = 48$. Because the length of $\overline{CD}$ is 2 times the length of $\overline{AB}$, let $\overline{AB} = x$ and let $\overline{CD} = 2x$. Since $\overline{AB} = \overline{BC}$, let $\overline{BC} = x$ also. Thus:

$$\overline{AD} = \overline{AB} + \overline{BC} + \overline{CD}$$
$$= x + x + 2x$$
$$= 4x$$

Since $\overline{AD} = 48$, $x = 12$ and therefore $\overline{BC} + \overline{CD} = x + 2x = 3x = 3 \times 12 = 36$.

7. C: The stock first increased by 10%, that is, by \$10 (10% of \$100) to \$110 per share. Then, the price decreased by \$11 (10% of \$110) so that the sale price was \$110 − \$11 = \$99 per share, and the sale price for 50 shares was 99 × \$50 = \$4950.

8. D: We know that the first lap takes 50 seconds, and the second one takes 20% more time to complete. This can be written as an equation: $T_2 = 1.2 \times T_1$. In the equation, T_1 is the time required for the first lap, and T_2 is the time required for the second lap. So, you can put in the known information and have: $1.2 \times 50 = 60$ seconds. For the third lap, you would start with the equation: $T_3 = 1.2 \times T_2$. When you put in the numbers, you have: $1.2 \times 60 = 72$ seconds. Now, you can add the times for the three laps: $50 + 60 + 72 = 182$.

9. C: Supplementary angles add to 180 degrees. Therefore, the other angle is equal to the difference between 180 degrees and 34 degrees: $180 − 34 = 146$. Thus, the other angle measures 146°.

10. A: The distance given from the top to the bottom of the tire through the center is the diameter. Finding the distance the bike traveled in one complete roll of the tire is the same as finding the circumference. Using the formula, $C = \pi d$, we multiply 27 by π. From the first mark to the fourth, the tire rolls three times. Then, you would multiply by 3, and the equation would be $3(27\pi)$.

11. E: First: Add the known values together: $5 + 10 + 12 + 13 = 40$. Now, set up an equation with the sum of the known values in the divisor. Then, put the number of values in the dividend.

For this question, you have 5 values. So, you would write the equation as $\frac{40+?}{5} = 9.6$. Now, multiply both sides by 5: $5 \times \frac{40+?}{5} = 9.6 \times 5$. You are left with $40+? = 48$. Now, subtract 40 from both sides: $40 − 40+? = 48 − 40$. Now, you know that the missing value is 8.

12. A: The events are independent since Sarah replaces the first die. The probability of two independent events can be found using the formula $P(A \text{ and } B) = P(A) \times P(B)$. The probability of pulling out a blue die is $\frac{2}{12}$. The probability of pulling out a green die is $\frac{4}{12}$. The probability of pulling out a blue die and a green die is $\frac{2}{12} \times \frac{4}{12}$, which simplifies to $\frac{1}{18}$.

13. D: Isolate a: $a = 8b + 6 + 16$. Thus, $a = 8b + 22$.

Next, add 3 to both side of the equation: $a + 3 = 8b + 22 + 3 = 8b + 25$

14. A: The cost per ounce can be calculated by dividing the cost of the bag by the number of ounces the bag contains. Thus, the cost per ounce can be calculated by writing $9.85 ÷ 16, which equals approximately \$0.62 per ounce.

15. B: The slope of a line describes the change in the dependent variable divided by the change in the independent variable, i.e. the change in y over the change in x. To calculate the slope, consider any two points on the line. Let the first point be (1, 14), and let the second point be (2, 28).

$$\frac{y_2 - y_1}{x_2 - x_1} = \frac{28 - 14}{2 - 1} = \frac{14}{1} = 14$$

16. B: Since 1 foot equals 0.3048 meters, The proportion can be written as: $\frac{1}{0.3048} = \frac{12}{x}$. Solving for x gives $x = 3.6576$, which rounds to 3.66. Thus, the length of the bridge is approximately 3.66 meters.

17. C: There are 36 months in 3 years. The following proportion may be written: $\frac{450}{3} = \frac{x}{36}$. The equation $3x = 16,200$, may be solved for x. Dividing both sides of the equation by 3 gives $x = 5,400$.

18. D: The area of the shaded region must be equal to the area of the square minus the areas of the two triangular areas $\triangle ACD$ and $\triangle BEF$. The area of a triangle is given by $A = \frac{1}{2}bh$, where b is the base and h is the height. Since $\triangle ACD$ and $\triangle BEF$ are both right triangles, one of the orthogonal sides is the base and the other is the height. Further, since $\overline{AE} = \overline{EB}$ and $\overline{BF} = \overline{FC}$, it follows that $\overline{EB} = \overline{BF} = 5$, this being one half the side $\overline{AB}$. Thus, $A_{ADC} = \frac{1}{2}(10 \times 10) = 50$, and $A_{BEF} = \frac{1}{2}(5 \times 5) = 12.5$. The area of the square is the product of its two sides, or $10 \times 10 = 100$. Therefore, for the shaded region, $A = 100 - 50 - 12.5 = 37.5$.

19. C: Remember to use the order of operations when simplifying this equation. The acronym *PEMDAS* will help you remember the correct order: Parenthesis, Exponentiation, Multiplication/Division, Addition/Subtraction.

$$4(6 - 3)^2 - (-2) = 4 \times 3^2 - (-2)$$
$$= 4 \times 9 - (-2)$$
$$= 36 - (-2)$$
$$= 36 - (-2)$$
$$= 38$$

20. C: Isolate the variable on one side of the equal sign by adding 2 to both sides of the equation. This yields $\sqrt{x} = 8 + 2 = 10$. Now, solve the equation by squaring both sides: $x = 10^2 = 100$.

21. C: The original triangle was reflected across the x-axis. When reflecting across the x-axis, the x-values of each point remain the same, but the y-values of the points will be opposites.

$$(1, 4) \rightarrow (1, -4), (5, 4) \rightarrow (5, -4), (3, 8) \rightarrow (3, -8)$$

22. B: To solve this problem, you need to find the time needed to drive 275 miles at a speed of 55 miles per hour. If $rate \times time = distance$, then $time = distance \div rate$:

$$275 \text{ miles} \div 55 \frac{\text{miles}}{\text{hour}} = 5 \text{ hours}$$

The truck driver needs to arrive at 9:30 p.m., so subtract 5 hours from 9:30. The truck driver needs to leave at 4:30 p.m. to arrive on time.

23. E: Attendance in 2004 decreased from about 12,000 to 10,000 visitors. In 2005 it rebounded to 15,000 visitors, an increase of 5,000. This is the greatest year-to-year increase shown on the chart.

24. A: Add the coefficients of the 'x-terms' together as follows: $5x + 4x = 9x$
Add the coefficients of the 'y-terms' as follows: $-2y + y = -y$
Put the x- and y-terms back into the same equation: $9x - y$.

25. E: Out of the twelve numbers, half are even. That means there is a 50% chance that the spinner will land on an even number.

Reading Comprehension

1. D: Various parts of the article are intended to scare (choice A), warn (choice B), and inspire (choice C) people, but the primary purpose of the article is to offer practical advice about what products people should buy and how to use their available resources to make responsible decisions for the future of our planet.

2. A: The author begins the third paragraph with, "You can continue to make a difference for the planet in how you use what you bought and the resources you have available." This sentence makes the connection between the second paragraph which deals with what people should buy and the third paragraph which makes suggestions for how to use what they have.

3. B: The author does suggest that people should use less water and energy (choice A), but these are only two suggestions among many and not the main idea of the article. The article does not say that people are destroying the earth (choice C) or make a suggestion that people organize their acquaintances (choice D).

4. D: The author presents the problems of global warming and the rapid depletion of the planet's natural resources and offers several practical suggestions for how to stop global warming and use remaining resources judiciously.

5. E: The author makes suggestions to use less water (choice B) and buy locally grown food (choice D), but they are not suggested as the place to begin saving the planet. The author does not suggest getting rid of products that are not earth friendly (choice A). The author states: "Participation begins with our everyday choices."

6. C: The author does not mention running out of resources in a specific time period (choice A), the cost of water and energy (choice B), or the possibility of hardship for local farmers (choice D).

7. D: Paragraph 1 states that Aberystwyth is located on the West Coast of Wales.

8. C: The essay provides information on various aspects of the town of Aberystwyth, providing a portrait of the town as a whole.

9. A: Situated means to be located in a certain place.

10. B: In an essay that is factual, proclaiming that the scenery is "gorgeous" or that a town is a "hidden luxury" is an opinion.

11. B: Paragraph 3 states that two main languages are traditionally spoken in Aberystwyth.

12. C: Paragraph 1 states, "A market town refers to European areas that have the right to have markets, which differentiates it from a city or village."

13. D: Paragraph 2 states, "Constitution Hill is a hill on the north end of Aberystwyth, which provides excellent views of Cardigan Bay and which is supported by the Aberystwyth Electric Cliff Railway."

14. A: Paragraph 1 explains that Aberystwyth is best known as an education center, and this is repeated in paragraph 3, which states that Aberystwyth is best known for its educational services.

15. B: While some of the other choices are mentioned in the selection, they do not adequately explain what the entire selection is about.

16. A: From the first paragraph, you can determine that Gawaine has little or no interest in becoming a knight.

17. D: Gawaine is said to be tall and sturdy, but he would run away and hide at the smallest sign of trouble.

18. D: "His better nature" is one way of talking about a person's deeper character.

19. C: This forms part of the answer to the professor's question, "Are the dragons particularly bad this year?"

20. D: Choice A is not mentioned in the text, and the other choices do not directly answer the question.

21. C: The passage states that he was given this title since he was the first to explain how organisms change over time.

22. A: The tone and purpose of this passage is to inform the reader.

23. E: The passage explains that finches with longer, sharper beaks were able to reach insects more easily than finches with shorter beaks, giving them an advantage over the other finches on the island.

24. B: The island finches were different from the mainland finches, so geographical separation over time increased the diversity of finches.

25. D: The passage states that the island finches differed from the mainland finches by the shape of their beaks and in their diet.

26. C: An archipelago is a large group or chain of islands.

27. D: The article deals primarily with the ways the colonists fed themselves: their crops and the foods they hunted. While the history and agriculture discussed are part of the Māori culture, that is not the focus of the passage.

28. D: The passage states that the first settlers were forced to rely on fishing for their food.

29. A: When an increased population had driven a major food source to extinction, they began to fight for control over the remaining food supply.

30. D: The article tells us that coconuts did not grow in New Zealand, and that some of the other crops would grow only on North Island.

31. A: The sweet potato provided a winter food source through storage, allowing the population to increase.

32. C: Both roads in the woods are more or less equally covered in leaves. One is only a little more traveled than the other, but this is enough for the narrator to choose the less-traveled path.

33. C: Looking back on the memory, the narrator is proud that he "chose the [road] less traveled by," and he will make sure that other people know that, too.

34. D: The poem is based on the narrator having to decide upon a path based only on his own personality and how well traveled the road is. It is a decision that he must make alone.

35. E: The narrator thinks that whatever road he chooses will say something about his character. He waits a long time because he wants to be sure of his choice.

36. B: The narrator wants to be as unique as he can, and so takes the road less traveled. However, he cannot be truly unique, as he is not the first person to have walked that road.

37. D: The main argument is stated in paragraph 4: "With the progression and extreme convenience of technology, printed books are going to soon become a thing of the past."

38. C: Paragraph 1 explains how stories have progressed, beginning with oral tradition and past the invention of the printing press. In context with the rest of the essay, this paragraph is important in explaining how stories progress and are provided within society.

39. A: In paragraph 1, it is stated that oral tradition was the main medium for storytelling before the invention of the printing press.

40. E: It is not a fact that "sliding a finger across the screen or pressing a button to move onto the next page is just as satisfying to the reader." Satisfaction is not something universal that can be proven for every reader. This statement is an opinion.

Verbal

1. B: When someone is abroad, it usually means that they are away, overseas, or in a foreign country.

2. D: When someone ruminates, it means that they are reflecting, thinking, or brainstorming about something or someone.

3. A: When something is described as concise, it usually means that it is brief or compact.

4. A: When someone mourns, it means that they are crying or filled with regret.

5. A: Residence is a place where a person lives. So, a home is the best answer choice.

6. C: Levity means happiness or silliness.

7. B: When something is described as rash, it usually means that it is careless or bold.

8. C: When it is said that someone has been banished, it means that they have been removed or dismissed from a place.

9. B: When you are extended an opportunity, you are being offered a chance to try something.

10. E: To disable means that something is damaged or harmed.

11. D: An object that is fragile is something that can be broken very easily. So, one could say that the object is delicate.

12. D: A loyal person is someone who is committed and faithful.

13. D: The principle is something that is the standard or source. This should be confused with principal who may the head of a school or an organization.

14. C: To assess something is to evaluate or determine something.

15. C: If somebody is moral, it means that they are honest or good and correct in their behavior.

16. C: Something that is superior is understood to be preferable or better.

17. B: A remark is a statement or comment.

18. B: Specify is when you indicate or name something to give a clear understanding to others. For example, there are several trees in a yard, and you are talking about one tree. So, you would need to be clear or specify which tree that you meant.

19. A: To commence something is to begin or start something.

20. B: Something that is moving swiftly is something that is moving at a high speed or quickly.

21. A: Someone that is wily is clever or mischievous. For example, a child who avoids something that he or she doesn't want to do will be creative with excuses or deceptive about their plans.

22. C: Humane is another word for friendly. Saying someone is humane is the same as saying that they are very helpful and generous.

23. B: When someone is asserting something, they are insisting or arguing that something is the case.

24. E: A situation that is perilous is one that is risky or hazardous.

25. C: To donate means to offer a service or gift something as a contribution.

26. C: When something is finite, we mean that it is limited or fixed. Saying that there is a finite amount of gold in the world has the same meaning as saying that there is a limited amount of gold in the world.

27. B: When somebody is docile, it means that they are obedient or easily led. A student who respects and obeys their teachers will be a docile student.

28. C: To taint has a similar meaning to harm or damage. If you say that a shirt is tainted, for example, you are saying that the shirt is ruined or damaged.

29. D: When a person falters, we mean that they stumbled or hesitated. For example, a good character in a story has to make a difficult decision, and he or she struggles to make the decision in time. So, we could say that the character faltered to make a decision.

30. D: Something that is done suddenly means that it is done unexpectedly or without warning. For example, saying that the car stopped suddenly and saying it stopped unexpectedly convey the same meaning.

31. C: The analogy focuses on a characteristic of historians who need to consider an event with the surrounding context of time before and after an event. The best choice is the comparison to a native who has insight about his or her village or country and provide context to events of their area.

32. B: This analogy is about the use of geography and how one thing that it studies is mountains. Among the choices, one use of history is the study of events and how they have made an important influence.

33. E: This comparison is about the antonyms exhale and inhale. The other answer choices are synonyms, and choice E has the antonyms of consent and prohibit.

34. D: This comparison is about the synonyms of fiction and myth. The other answer choices are antonyms or something that is incompatible with nonfiction. So, the correct choice that remains is biography.

35. C: A simple sentence for this analogy could be "An astronomer's task is to encounter new things." The other users in the answer choices do not match with this sentence, and their "tasks" are not typical jobs for them. Answer choice C could be written as "A prophet's task is to inform about new things."

36. B: This analogy is about the homonyms *dual* and *duel* which sound similar but have different meanings. The only answer choice that makes sense is choice B which has the homonyms of *seam* and *seem*.

37. A: This analogy of degree focuses on a symptom that is part of an illness. The best answer is choice A which starts with a bacteria that develops into an infection.

38. A: Evidence that is used in a court of law can be condemning for someone by bringing a punishment on him or her. The best comparison for this question is choice A where the use of a generator is to restore energy or electricity to something.

39. C: *Liberty* and *freedom* are close synonyms, and *sincere* is a close synonym of *faithful*.

40. C: This comparison is about the antonyms *masculine* and *feminine*. The other answer choices are synonyms. So, the best answer is choice C which has the antonyms *community* and *individual*.

41. B: An artist brings imagination to complete their tasks and help others. In a similar way, an advisor uses clarity to complete their tasks and help others.

42. D: This comparison shows that one characteristic of a temple is that it is sacred. The best answer choice is the comparison of a sanctuary to its loftiness or grandness and beauty.

43. E: A gourmet is a person who is very familiar with food, and this person would fall under the category of a critic. With the topic of food in mind, a spice is an item that provides flavor to meals and can come under the category of ingredient.

44. C: As a part to whole analogy, a summit is the highest point of a mountain. Now, you need to judge how a king is a part of a whole. The best answer is choice C as a member of a monarchy government.

45. A: The analogy highlights a product to producer relationship. The tactics of a mission are made and developed by marines. In a similar way, data is developed by a researcher.

46. B: A chamber is needed to contain or hold items. Choice A is nearly a product to producer as some rulers on thrones can be intimidating to the point that people bow or cower before the throne. Choice C is a characteristic analogy. Answer choice D is a synonym. Answer choice E is a category analogy. So, the best choice is B as an agenda is used to organize the use of time.

47. D: This analogy is about the homonyms *altar* and *alter*. The correct answer choice D has the homonyms *rain* and *reign*.

48. B: To help more patients, a physician would study the nutritional value of certain items and harm from other items. So, this analogy focuses on a user. The other answer choices do not focus on the relationship of an item or field of study and a user, or they make incorrect connections. Thus, the best answer choice is choice B because wildlife would be studied by a guide for future tours.

49. B: The terms *bravery* and *cowardice* are antonyms in this analogy. So, the best answer choice is the one that is an antonym for *comedy*, and the best choice is choice B for *grief.*

50. E: When we say that a child is *naïve*, we are naming one of their characteristics. The correct answer choice is choice E which has *disciplined* as a characteristic of a *soldier*.

51. B: This analogy focuses on the homonyms of *colonel* and *kernel*. So, the correct answer choice is the homonyms *serial* and *cereal.*

52. D: You may recall from science classes that protons and electrons are parts of an atom. A proton has a positive charge, and an electron has a negative charge. So, the comparison focuses on these as opposites or antonyms. Therefore, the best answer choice is choice D which compares *potent* and *ineffective* as antonyms.

53. D: A documentary can be used by a protestor to bring more attention to his or her cause. So, this analogy highlights the comparison of someone who uses something. The best answer choice is choice D which has a *rotor* being used by a *mechanic*.

54. C: Again, we have a homonym analogy with the terms *tear* and *tier*. You are provided with the term *air*, and the best choice available is choice C which has *heir*.

55. B: An *epidemic* is a disease that is far reaching. The same definition applies to *plague*. So, you know that we are working with a comparison of synonyms. You are supplied with the term *vigor* which means high energy and strength. So, the best available synonym is *endurance*.

56. D: You may recognize that *eternal* means that something continues without an end. *Momentary* means that something is brief or short-lived. So, the best answer choice is choice D which has the antonyms of *exotic* (i.e., unusual or mysterious) and *ordinary* (i.e., plain or familiar).

57. A: Often, an open field of a meadow is described as a peaceful and restful place to rest. So, one could say that a meadow has the characteristic of being tranquil. The best match for this analogy would be choice A as a *tributary* (i.e., river or stream) can be a *consoling* or restful place to visit.

58. D: This analogy highlights another homonym relationship. The other answer choices are terms that rhyme or have no understandable relationship. So, the best answer choice is choice D of *carat* and *carrot*.

59. A: An *aviator* is a person who flies an aircraft. So, this relationship can be understood as an *aviator* is responsible for flying an aircraft to a certain *destination*. In a similar way, choice A can be understood as a *sculptor* or artist is responsible for creating *original* works of art.

60. E: A *constellation* is a group of stars that form an outline of a person, animal, or object. So, this analogy can be understood as a whole moving to a part. The *constellation* is the whole, and a *star* is a part of the whole. Now, the best answer choice would be choice E as an *orchestra* is a group of musicians playing music with their respective *instruments*. Thus, an *instrument* would a part of the whole *orchestra*.

Quantitative

1. B: The number of one-fourths contained in $8\frac{1}{2}$ can be determined by dividing $8\frac{1}{2}$ by $\frac{1}{4}$. In order to find the quotient, $8\frac{1}{2}$ can be multiplied by the reciprocal of $\frac{1}{4}$, or 4. Thus, the quotient can be found by writing $\frac{17}{2} \times 4$, which equals 34.

2. C: The equation that represents the relationship between the position number, n, and the value of the term, a_n, is $a_n = -3n + 8$. Notice each n is multiplied by –3, with 8 added to that value. Substituting position number 1 for n gives $a_n = -3(1) + 8$, which equals 5. Substitution of the remaining position numbers does not provide a counterexample to this procedure.

3. E: A triangle with an obtuse angle (an angle greater than 90°) is called an obtuse triangle.

4. D: Since the snow will fall at a constant rate, the snowfall follows a directly proportional relationship. Then, Total Snowfall = (Snowfall rate) × (Number of hours of snowfall), $t = 2h$. In Answer A, the values were set up as an inversely proportional relationship. In Answer B, the snowfall rate was incorrectly added to the number of hours of snowfall. In Answer C, the snowfall rate was incorrectly subtracted from the number of hours of snowfall.

5. B: Whenever the data includes an extreme outlier, such as 39, the median is the best representation of the data. The mean would include that score and heavily skew the data.

6. B: Angles that form a straight line add up to 180 degrees. Such angles are sometimes referred to as being "supplementary."

$$60 + 2x = 180$$
$$2x = 120$$
$$x = 60$$

7. E: In this problem, if you do not know how to solve, try filling in the answer choices to see which one checks out. Many math problems may be solved by a guess and check method when you have a selection of answer choices.

$$27 - x = -5$$
$$x = 32$$

8. C: The order of operations states that numbers with exponents must be evaluated first. Thus, the expression can be rewritten as $64 + 12 \div 4 + 64 \times 3$. Next, multiplication and division must be computed as they appear from left to right in the expression. Thus, the expression can be further simplified as $64 + 3 + 192$, which equals 259.

9. B: The discounted price is 25% less than the original price. Therefore, the discounted price can be written as 36.95 − ((0.25)(36.95)), which equals approximately 27.71. Thus, the discounted price of the jacket is $27.71.

10. B: All given sequences have a constant difference of 12. Subtraction of 12 from the starting term, given for Choice B, gives a y-intercept of −9. The equation $123 = 12x − 9$ can thus be written. Solving for x gives $x = 11$; therefore, 123 is indeed the 11th term of this sequence. Manual computation of the 11th term by adding the constant difference of 12 also reveals 123 as the value of the 11th term of this sequence.

11. D: Turn the word problem into an equation. Remember that product means multiplication:

$$4^2 \times 6 = 96$$

12. C: The dimensions of the rectangular prism can be rounded to 14 cm, 9 cm, and 12 cm. The volume of a rectangular prism can be determined by finding the product of the length, width, and height. Therefore, the volume is approximately equal to $14 \times 9 \times 12$, or 1,512 cm^3.

13. D: The amount Aisha invests doubles each month. Thus, the invested amounts for months $1 − 6$ are as follows: $26.25, $52.50, $105, $210, $420, and $840. She invests $840 during the sixth month.

14. A: The sum of the measures of the angels in a triangle equals 180°. Use the numbers given in the figure to make the following equation:

$$6x + 8x + 4x = 180$$
$$18x = 180$$
$$x = 10$$

15. C: To determine this, first determine the total distance of the round trip. This is twice the 45 miles of the one-way trip to work in the morning, or 90 miles. Then, to determine the total amount of time Elijah spent on the round trip, first convert his travel times into minutes. One hour and ten minutes equals 70 minutes, and an hour and a half equals 90 minutes. So, Elijah's total travel time was $70 + 90 = 160$ minutes. Elijah's average speed can now be determined in miles per minute:

$$\text{Speed} = \frac{90 \text{ miles}}{160 \text{ min}} = 0.5625 \text{ miles per minute}$$

Finally, to convert this average speed to miles per hour, multiply by 60, since there are 60 minutes in an hour:

$$\text{Average speed (mph)} = 60 \times 0.5625 = 33.75 \text{ miles per hour}$$

16. D: Besides the $600 he has remaining; Chan has paid out a total of 85% (30% + 30% + 25%) of his bonus for the expenses described in the question. Therefore, the $600 represents the remaining 15%. Remember that 15% can be written as 15/100. To determine his total bonus, solve

$$\frac{15}{100}x = \$600$$
$$x = \frac{100}{15} \times \$600$$
$$x = \$4,000$$

17. B: Since $11 - 5 = 6$, then $3x = 6$, and $x = \frac{6}{3} = 2$.

18. D: Find the common denominator for the two fractions so that you can compare them. You can use the common denominator of 45, as follows:

$$\frac{2}{5} = \frac{18}{45}$$
$$\frac{4}{9} = \frac{20}{45}$$

Look at the numerators: 18 and 20. The number halfway between them is 19, so the answer is $\frac{19}{45}$

19. B: $y = x + 5$, and you were told that $x = -3$. Fill in the missing information for x, then solve.

$$y = (-3) + 5$$
$$y = 2$$

20. E: You would write the negative square root of 100 as follows: $-\sqrt{100}$

21. C: The equation to determine how Anna can earn the $125 is set up as:

$$Weekly\ Pay \times Number\ of\ Weeks + Money\ Anna\ Already\ Has = \$125$$

If w = number of weeks, substitute for the remaining values to get the equation: $\$5w + \$40 = \$125$. To solve that equation, start by subtracting $40 from both sides: $\$5w = \$85$. Then, divide both sides by 5 to get $h = 17$. In Answer A, the equation was incorrectly set up as $(\$5 + \$40)w = \$125$. In Answer B, the equation was incorrectly set up as $\$5w = \$40$. In Answer D, the equation was incorrectly set up as $\$5w = \$125$.

22. C: The value of the 18th term can be found by substituting 18 for the variable, x, in the equation, $y = 6x + 2$. Doing so gives: $y = 6(18) + 2$, or $y = 110$. Therefore, the value of the 18th term is 110.

23. A: When multiplying fractions, multiply the terms straight across the fraction: $\frac{5}{9} \times \frac{3}{4} = \frac{15}{36}$. Then, simplify the fraction. Since 15 and 36 are both multiples of 3, divide each term by 3 to reach the final result: $\frac{5}{12}$.

24. C: You know the price for each pound of onions and carrots. So, start by finding the total cost of the onions and carrots: $(2 \times \$3.69) + (3 \times \$4.29) = \$20.25$. Next, this sum is subtracted from the total cost of the vegetables. This is done to find the cost of the mushrooms: $\$24.15 - \$20.25 = \$3.90$. Finally, the cost of the mushrooms is divided by the quantity (lbs) to find the cost per pound:

$$Cost\ per\ pound = \frac{\$3.90}{1.5\ lb} = \frac{\$2.60}{lb}$$

25. A: There are 36 total cans in the cooler. Four of the cans are Ginger Ale. Therefore, there is a $\frac{4}{36} = \frac{1}{9}$ probability of pulling a Ginger Ale out of the cooler.

Practice Test #2

Writing

25 Minutes

Instructions: Read the following prompt, taking a few moments to plan a response. Then, write your response in essay form.

<u>Prompt</u>: *Fast food restaurants should be held legally responsible for the current rise in obesity in children.*

Do you agree or disagree with this statement? Use examples from history, literature, or your own personal experience to support your point of view.

Mometrix

Quantitative

Read each question, perform the appropriate calculations, and determine the correct answer.

1. Harold learned that 6 out of 10 students at his school live within two miles of the school. If 240 students attend Grade 6 at his school, about how many of these students should Harold expect to live within two miles of the school?

    a. 24
    b. 40
    c. 144
    d. 180

2. Given the counters shown below, where ⬤ represents negative 1 and ⬤ represents positive 1, what is the sum?

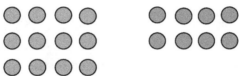

    a. −20
    b. 4
    c. 20
    d. −4

3. Akita is thinking of a number. The number is the opposite of 7. What must be true about Akita's number?

    I.   The number is 7
    II.   The number is −7
    III.   The number has an absolute value of 7
    IV.   The number has an absolute value of −7

    a. II and III
    b. I and III
    c. II and IV
    d. I and IV

4. Given the sequence represented in the table below, where n represents the position of the term and a_n represents the value of the term, which of the following describes the relationship between the position number and the value of the term?

n	1	2	3	4	5	6
a_n	5	2	−1	−4	−7	−10

    a. Multiply n by 2 and subtract 4
    b. Multiply n by 2 and subtract 3
    c. Multiply n by −3 and add 8
    d. Multiply n by −4 and add 1

139

5. A trash company charges a fee of $80 to haul off a load of trash. There is also a charge of $0.05 per mile the load must be hauled. Which equation can be used to find c, the cost for hauling a load of trash m miles?

    a. $80(m + 0.05)$
    b. $0.05(m + 80)$
    c. $80m + 0.05$
    d. $0.05m + 80$

6. A clothing company is reviewing their quarterly report. Last quarter, 36% of their customers purchased sweatshirts. Which fraction is equivalent to the percentage of customers who purchased sweatshirts last quarter?

    a. $\frac{36}{50}$
    b. $\frac{9}{25}$
    c. $\frac{1}{36}$
    d. $\frac{13}{50}$

7. Which of the following scenarios can be represented by the equation $14 + x = 52$?

    a. Stella has $14 in her wallet. How much money does she have if she adds the $52 she earned babysitting last night?
    b. Marcus earns $52 mowing yards. How much money does he save if he buys his brother a birthday present that costs $14 and saves the rest?
    c. Troy earns $52 working for a neighbor. How much money does he have if he earns an additional $14 working for his aunt?
    d. Izzy has $14 of money in her piggy bank. How much money does she have if she adds the $52 she receives for her birthday?

8. Which situation best represents the inequality $12.5x \geq 375$?

    a. Dustin can ride his bike 12.5 miles per hour and rides 375 miles in x hours.
    b. Darla needs to drive at least 375 minutes to get her driver's permit and has driven 12.5 minutes so far and has x number of minutes remaining.
    c. Desiree makes $12.5 per hour and made more than $375 over x hours.
    d. Desmond has a goal of making at least 375 bracelets and makes 12.5 bracelets each day for x days.

9. A tree casts a shadow that is 4 feet long. At the same time, a 5-foot girl standing next to the tree casts a shadow that is 2.5 feet long. Which of the following proportions can be used to determine the height of the tree?

    a. $\frac{x}{4} = \frac{5}{2.5}$
    b. $\frac{x}{4} = \frac{2.5}{5}$
    c. $\frac{x}{2.5} = \frac{4}{2.5}$
    d. $\frac{x}{4} = \frac{2.5}{5}$

10. According to the order of operations, which of the following steps should be completed immediately following the evaluation of the squared number when evaluating the expression

$$9 - 18^2 \times 2 + 12 \div 4$$

a. Subtract 18^2 from 9
b. Multiply the squared value by 2
c. Divide 12 by 4
d. Add 2 and 12

11. Tomas needs $100 to buy a telescope he wants. He received $40 as a gift and spent $10 on a book about telescopes. He earned $35 doing small jobs for his family. The steps Tomas can use to find the amount he still needs to save to buy the telescope are shown here in incorrect order.

Step R: Subtract 65 from 100.
Step S: Subtract 10 from 40.
Step T: Add 35 to 30.

Which sequence shows the steps in the correct order?

a. T, S, R
b. T, R, S
c. S, T, R
d. R, S, T

12. Caroline put 3 drops of blue food coloring in 2 cups of water. Devon put 5 drops of blue food coloring in 4 cups of water. If more blue food coloring makes a darker shade of blue, what is true about Caroline 's and Devon's water?

a. Caroline's water is a darker blue than Devon's because 3 : 2 is greater than 5 : 4.
b. Devon's water is a darker blue than Caroline's because 5 drops is greater than 3 drops.
c. The water is the same shade of blue because 3 : 2 is equivalent to 5 : 4.
d. Devon's water is a darker blue than Caroline's because 5 : 4 is greater than 3 : 2.

13. A figure is depicted below. Use the ruler to measure the figure to the nearest $\frac{1}{2}$ inch.

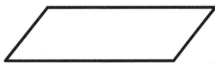

What is the area of the parallelogram in square inches?

a. 32 in^2
b. $43\frac{3}{4} \text{ in}^2$
c. $36\frac{1}{4} \text{ in}^2$
d. 50 in^2

14. Which of the following statements is NOT true about this figure?

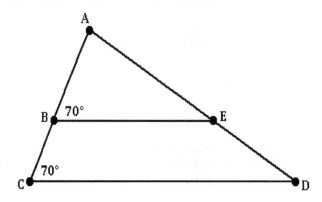

a. $\triangle ABE$ is similar to $\triangle ACD$
b. $BE = CD$
c. $\angle B \cong \angle C$
d. $\dfrac{AB}{AC} = \dfrac{AE}{AD}$

15. Which situation best represents the inequality $\dfrac{n}{4} > 36$?

a. Theresa packaged more than 36 packages when she packaged n cupcakes into packages of 4.
b. Tyler has more than 36 pages to read and reads 4 pages each day for n days.
c. Tamar practiced for n hours on the piano. She practiced the piano for more than 36 hours each day for 4 days.
d. Tamika ran n miles over 4 days, which is less than 36 miles.

16. Xi wrote an expression that is equivalent to $9z + (z - 3)$. Which expression could be the one Xi wrote?

a. $9z \cdot z - 27z$
b. $(z - 3) + 9z$
c. $10z + 3$
d. $(z - 3) - 9z$

17. Ana has completed approximately $\dfrac{2}{7}$ of her research paper. Which of the following best represents the percentage of the paper she has completed?

a. 24%
b. 26%
c. 27%
d. 29%

18. A display at the bottom of the laptop computer Erica was using showed that the battery had a 70% charge. Which decimal is equivalent to 70%?

a. 0.07
b. 70.0
c. 7.0
d. 0.7

19. Which number line represents the solution to $17 - x \geq 9$?

a.

b.

c.

d.

20. Nova is redecorating her bedroom and spent $\frac{7}{25}$ of her time painting. What percentage of her time did Nova spend painting?
a. 28%
b. 7%
c. 25%
d. 48%

21. Which statement is true about the product of 5 and $\frac{1}{2}$?
a. The product is less than 5.
b. The product is greater than 5.
c. The product is less than 1.
d. The product is less than $\frac{1}{2}$.

22. Which expression is equivalent to $81 \div 9 + 36$?
a. $3^2 + 6^2$
b. $3 \cdot 3 + 3 \cdot 3 \cdot 3$
c. $\frac{9^2}{3^3} + (12 \cdot 3)$
d. $(9 \cdot 9) \div (3 \cdot 3 \cdot 5)$

23. Which of the following correctly represents the solution to the following inequality on a number line?

$$-2x + 5 > 13$$

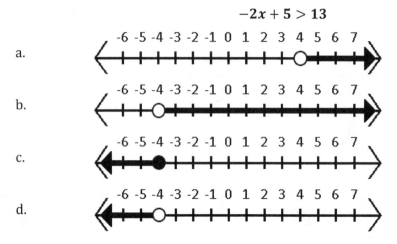

a.

b.

c.

d.

24. The volume of a cylinder is equal to the product of the area of one base and the height. Which of the following represents the area of one of the bases?

    a. πr
    b. πd
    c. πd^2
    d. πr^2

25. The total number of views on a new video increased by a scale factor of 13 each day. What does that mean about the number of views on the video?

    a. The number of views increased by adding 13 to the total each day.
    b. Each day the number of views increased by 13,000.
    c. Each day the number of views increased by multiplying the number of days by 13.
    d. The number of views increased by multiplying the previous day's total by 13.

Reading Comprehension

Read each passage closely and answer the associated questions. Be sure to choose the answer that BEST answers the question being asked.

Questions 1-4 refer to the following passage:

It is most likely that you have never had diphtheria. You probably don't even know anyone who has suffered from this disease. In fact, you may not even know what diphtheria is. Similarly, diseases like whooping cough, measles, mumps, and rubella may all be unfamiliar to you. In the nineteenth and early twentieth centuries, these illnesses struck hundreds of thousands of people in the United States each year, mostly children, and tens of thousands of people died. The names of these diseases were frightening household words. Today, they are all but forgotten. That change happened largely because of vaccines.

You probably have been vaccinated against diphtheria. You may even have been exposed to the bacterium that causes it, but the vaccine prepared your body to fight off the disease so quickly that you were unaware of the infection. Vaccines take advantage of your body's natural ability to learn how to combat many disease-causing germs, or microbes. What's more, your body remembers how to protect itself from the microbes it has encountered before. Collectively, the parts of your body that remember and repel microbes are called the immune system. Without the proper functioning of the immune system, the simplest illness—even the common cold—could quickly turn deadly.

On average, your immune system needs more than a week to learn how to fight off an unfamiliar microbe. Sometimes, that isn't enough time. Strong microbes can spread through your body faster than the immune system can fend them off. Your body often gains the upper hand after a few weeks, but in the meantime you are sick. Certain microbes are so virulent that they can overwhelm or escape your natural defenses. In those situations, vaccines can make all the difference.

Traditional vaccines contain either parts of microbes or whole microbes that have been altered so that they don't cause disease. When your immune system confronts these harmless versions of the germs, it quickly clears them from your body. In other words, vaccines trick your immune system in order to teach your body important lessons about how to defeat its opponents.

1. What is the main idea of the passage?
   a. The nineteenth and early twentieth centuries were a dark period for medicine.
   b. You have probably never had diphtheria.
   c. Traditional vaccines contain altered microbes.
   d. Vaccines help the immune system function properly.

2. Which statement is not a detail from the passage?

a. Vaccines contain microbe parts or altered microbes.
b. The immune system typically needs a week to learn how to fight a new disease.
c. The symptoms of disease do not emerge until the body has learned how to fight the microbe.
d. A hundred years ago, children were at the greatest risk of dying from now-treatable diseases.

3. What is the meaning of the word virulent as it is used in the third paragraph?

a. tiny
b. malicious
c. contagious
d. annoying

4. What is the author's primary purpose in writing the essay?

a. to entertain
b. to persuade
c. to inform
d. to analyze

Questions 5-8 refer to the following passage:

Foodborne illnesses are contracted by eating food or drinking beverages contaminated with bacteria, parasites, or viruses. Harmful chemicals can also cause foodborne illnesses if they have contaminated food during harvesting or processing. Foodborne illnesses can cause symptoms ranging from upset stomach to diarrhea, fever, vomiting, abdominal cramps, and dehydration. Most foodborne infections are undiagnosed and unreported, though the Centers for Disease Control and Prevention estimates that every year about 76 million people in the United States become ill from pathogens in food. About 5,000 of these people die.

Harmful bacteria are the most common cause of foodborne illness. Some bacteria may be present at the point of purchase. Raw foods are the most common source of foodborne illnesses because they are not sterile; examples include raw meat and poultry contaminated during slaughter. Seafood may become contaminated during harvest or processing. One in 10,000 eggs may be contaminated with Salmonella inside the shell. Produce, such as spinach, lettuce, tomatoes, sprouts, and melons, can become contaminated with Salmonella, Shigella, or Escherichia coli (E. coli). Contamination can occur during growing, harvesting, processing, storing, shipping, or final preparation. Sources of produce contamination vary, as these foods are grown in soil and can become contaminated during growth, processing, or distribution. Contamination may also occur during food preparation in a restaurant or a home kitchen. The most common form of contamination from handled foods is the calicivirus, also called the Norwalk-like virus.

When food is cooked and left out for more than two hours at room temperature, bacteria can multiply quickly. Most bacteria don't produce an odor or change in color or texture, so they can be impossible to detect. Freezing food slows or stops bacteria's growth but does not destroy the bacteria. The microbes can become

146

reactivated when the food is thawed. Refrigeration also can slow the growth of some bacteria. Thorough cooking is required to destroy the bacteria.

5. What is the subject of the passage?
   a. foodborne illnesses
   b. the dangers of uncooked food
   c. bacteria
   d. proper food preparation

6. Which statement is not a detail from the passage?
   a. Every year, more than 70 million Americans contract some form of foodborne illness.
   b. Once food is cooked, it cannot cause illness.
   c. Refrigeration can slow the growth of some bacteria.
   d. The most common form of contamination in handled foods is calicivirus.

7. What is the meaning of the word pathogens as it is used in the first paragraph?
   a. diseases
   b. vaccines
   c. disease-causing substances
   d. foods

8. What is the meaning of the word sterile as it is used in the second paragraph?
   a. free of bacteria
   b. healthy
   c. delicious
   d. impotent

Questions 9-12 refer to the following passage:

There are a number of health problems related to bleeding in the esophagus and stomach. Stomach acid can cause inflammation and bleeding at the lower end of the esophagus. This condition, usually associated with the symptom of heartburn, is called esophagitis, or inflammation of the esophagus. Sometimes a muscle between the esophagus and stomach fails to close properly and allows the return of food and stomach juices into the esophagus, which can lead to esophagitis. In another unrelated condition, enlarged veins (varices) at the lower end of the esophagus rupture and bleed massively. Cirrhosis of the liver is the most common cause of esophageal varices. Esophageal bleeding can be caused by a tear in the lining of the esophagus (Mallory-Weiss syndrome). Mallory-Weiss syndrome usually results from vomiting but may also be caused by increased pressure in the abdomen from coughing, hiatal hernia, or childbirth. Esophageal cancer can cause bleeding.

The stomach is a frequent site of bleeding. Infections with Helicobacter pylori (H. pylori), alcohol, aspirin, aspirin-containing medicines, and various other medicines (such as nonsteroidal anti-inflammatory drugs [NSAIDs]—particularly those used for arthritis) can cause stomach ulcers or inflammation (gastritis). The stomach is often the site of ulcer disease. Acute or chronic ulcers may enlarge and erode through a blood vessel, causing bleeding. Also, patients suffering from burns, shock, head injuries, cancer, or those who have undergone extensive surgery may develop

147

stress ulcers. Bleeding can also occur from benign tumors or cancer of the stomach, although these disorders usually do not cause massive bleeding.

9. What is the main idea of the passage?
- a. The digestive system is complex.
- b. Of all the digestive organs, the stomach is the most prone to bleeding.
- c. Both the esophagus and the stomach are subject to bleeding problems.
- d. Esophagitis afflicts the young and old alike.

10. Which statement is not a detail from the passage?
- a. Alcohol can cause stomach bleeding.
- b. Ulcer disease rarely occurs in the stomach.
- c. Benign tumors rarely result in massive bleeding.
- d. Childbirth is one cause of Mallory-Weiss syndrome.

11. What is the meaning of the word rupture as it is used in the first paragraph?
- a. tear
- b. collapse
- c. implode
- d. detach

12. What is the meaning of the word erode as it is used in the second paragraph?
- a. avoid
- b. divorce
- c. contain
- d. wear away

Questions 13-16 refer to the following passage:

We met Kathy Blake while she was taking a stroll in the park . . . by herself. What's so striking about this is that Kathy is completely blind, and she has been for more than 30 years.

The diagnosis from her doctor was retinitis pigmentosa, or RP. It's an incurable genetic disease that leads to progressive visual loss. Photoreceptive cells in the retina slowly start to die, leaving the patient visually impaired.

"Life was great the year before I was diagnosed," Kathy said. "I had just started a new job; I just bought my first new car. I had just started dating my now-husband. Life was good. The doctor had told me that there was some good news and some bad news. 'The bad news is you are going to lose your vision; the good news is we don't think you are going to go totally blind.' Unfortunately, I did lose all my vision within about 15 years."

Two years ago, Kathy got a glimmer of hope. She heard about an artificial retina being developed in Los Angeles. It was experimental, but Kathy was the perfect candidate.

Dr. Mark Humayun is a retinal surgeon and biomedical engineer. "A good candidate for the artificial retina device is a person who is blind because of retinal blindness," he said. "They've lost the rods and cones, the light-sensing cells of the eye, but the

148

rest of the circuitry is relatively intact. In the simplest rendition, this device basically takes a blind person and hooks them up to a camera."

It may sound like the stuff of science fiction . . . and just a few years ago it was. A camera is built into a pair of glasses, sending radio signals to a tiny chip in the back of the retina. The chip, small enough to fit on a fingertip, is implanted surgically and stimulates the nerves that lead to the vision center of the brain. Kathy is one of twenty patients who have undergone surgery and use the device.

It has been about two years since the surgery, and Kathy still comes in for weekly testing at the University of Southern California's medical campus. She scans back and forth with specially made, camera-equipped glasses until she senses objects on a screen and then touches the objects. The low-resolution image from the camera is still enough to make out the black stripes on the screen. Impulses are sent from the camera to the 60 receptors that are on the chip in her retina. So, what is Kathy seeing?

"I see flashes of light that indicate a contrast from light to dark—very similar to a camera flash, probably not quite as bright because it's not hurting my eye at all," she replied.

Humayun underscored what a breakthrough this is and how a patient adjusts. "If you've been blind for 30 or 50 years, (and) all of a sudden you get this device, there is a period of learning," he said. "Your brain needs to learn. And it's literally like seeing a baby crawl—to a child walk—to an adult run."

While hardly perfect, the device works best in bright light or where there is a lot of contrast. Kathy takes the device home. The software that runs the device can be upgraded. So, as the software is upgraded, her vision improves. Recently, she was outside with her husband on a moonlit night and saw something she hadn't seen for a long time.

"I scanned up in the sky (and) I got a big flash, right where the moon was, and pointed it out. I can't even remember how many years ago it's been that I would have ever been able to do that."

This technology has a bright future. The current chip has a resolution of 60 pixels. Humayun says that number could be increased to more than a thousand in the next version.

"I think it will be extremely exciting if they can recognize their loved ones' faces and be able to see what their wife or husband or their grandchildren look like, which they haven't seen," said Humayun.

Kathy dreams of a day when blindness like hers will be a distant memory. "My eye disease is hereditary," she said. "My three daughters happen to be fine, but I want to know that if my grandchildren ever have a problem, they will have something to give them some vision."

13. What is the primary subject of the passage?

a. a new artificial retina
b. Kathy Blake
c. hereditary disease
d. Dr. Mark Humayun

14. What is the meaning of the word progressive as it is used in the second paragraph?

a. selective
b. gradually increasing
c. diminishing
d. disabling

15. Which statement is not a detail from the passage?

a. The use of an artificial retina requires a special pair of glasses.
b. Retinal blindness is the inability to perceive light.
c. Retinitis pigmentosa is curable.
d. The artificial retina performs best in bright light.

16. What is the author's intention in writing the essay?

a. to persuade
b. to entertain
c. to analyze
d. to inform

Questions 17-21 refer to the following passage:

Usher syndrome is the most common condition that affects both hearing and vision. The major signs of Usher syndrome are hearing loss and an eye disorder called retinitis pigmentosa, or RP. Retinitis pigmentosa causes night blindness and a loss of peripheral vision (side vision) through the progressive degeneration of the retina. The retina, which is crucial for vision, is a light-sensitive tissue at the back of the eye. As RP progresses, the field of vision narrows, until only central vision (the ability to see straight ahead) remains. Many people with Usher syndrome also have severe balance problems.

There are three clinical types of Usher syndrome. In the United States, types 1 and 2 are the most common. Together, they account for approximately 90 to 95 percent of all cases of juvenile Usher syndrome. Approximately three to six percent of all deaf and hearing-disabled children have Usher syndrome. In developed countries, such as the United States, about four in every 100,000 newborns have Usher syndrome.

Usher syndrome is inherited as an autosomal recessive trait. The term autosomal means that the mutated gene is not located on either of the chromosomes that determine sex; in other words, both males and females can have the disorder and can pass it along to a child. The word recessive means that in order to have Usher syndrome, an individual must receive a mutated form of the Usher syndrome gene from each parent. If a child has a mutation in one Usher syndrome gene but the other gene is normal, he or she should have normal vision and hearing. Individuals with a mutation in a gene that can cause an autosomal recessive disorder are called carriers, because they carry the mutated gene but show no symptoms of the disorder. If both parents are carriers of a mutated gene for Usher syndrome, they will have a one-in-four chance of producing a child with Usher syndrome.

Usually, parents who have normal hearing and vision do not know if they are carriers of an Usher syndrome gene mutation. Currently, it is not possible to determine whether an individual without a family history of Usher syndrome is a carrier. Scientists at the National Institute on Deafness and Other Communication Disorders (NIDCD) are hoping to change this, however, as they learn more about the genes responsible for Usher syndrome.

17. What is the main idea of the passage?
   a. Usher syndrome is an inherited condition that affects hearing and vision.
   b. Some people are carriers of Usher syndrome.
   c. Usher syndrome typically skips a generation.
   d. Scientists hope to develop a test for detecting the carriers of Usher syndrome.

18. What is the meaning of the word *signs* as it is used in the first paragraph?
   a. qualifications
   b. conditions/diseases
   c. subjective markers
   d. measurable indicators

19. Which statement is not a detail from the passage?
   a. Types 1 and 2 Usher syndrome are the most common in the United States.
   b. Usher syndrome affects both hearing and smell.
   c. Right now, there is no way to identify a carrier of Usher syndrome.
   d. Central vision is the ability to see straight ahead.

20. What is the meaning of the word juvenile as it is used in the second paragraph?
   a. bratty
   b. serious
   c. occurring in children
   d. improper

21. What is the meaning of the word mutated as it is used in the third paragraph?
   a. selected
   b. altered
   c. composed
   d. destroyed

Questions 22-27 refer to the following passage:

The immune system is a network of cells, tissues, and organs that defends the body against attacks by foreign invaders. These invaders are primarily microbes—tiny organisms such as bacteria, parasites, and fungi—that can cause infections. Viruses also cause infections but are too primitive to be classified as living organisms. The human body provides an ideal environment for many microbes. It is the immune system's job to keep the microbes out or destroy them.

The immune system is amazingly complex. It can recognize and remember millions of different enemies, and it can secrete fluids and cells to wipe out nearly all of them.

The secret to its success is an elaborate and dynamic communications network. Millions of cells, organized into sets and subsets, gather and transfer information in response to an infection. Once immune cells receive the alarm, they produce powerful chemicals that help to regulate their own growth and behavior, enlist other immune cells, and direct the new recruits to trouble spots.

Although scientists have learned much about the immune system, they continue to puzzle over how the body destroys invading microbes, infected cells, and tumors without harming healthy tissues. New technologies for identifying individual immune cells are now allowing scientists to determine quickly which targets are triggering an immune response. Improvements in microscopy are permitting the first-ever observations of living B cells, T cells, and other cells as they interact within lymph nodes and other body tissues.

In addition, scientists are rapidly unraveling the genetic blueprints that direct the human immune response, as well as those that dictate the biology of bacteria, viruses, and parasites. The combination of new technology with expanded genetic information will no doubt reveal even more about how the body protects itself from disease.

22. What is the main idea of the passage?

    a. Scientists fully understand the immune system.
    b. The immune system triggers the production of fluids.
    c. The body is under constant invasion by malicious microbes.
    d. The immune system protects the body from infection.

23. Which statement is not a detail from the passage?

    a. Most invaders of the body are microbes.
    b. The immune system relies on excellent communication.
    c. Viruses are extremely sophisticated.
    d. The cells of the immune system are organized.

24. What is the meaning of the word ideal as it is used in the first paragraph?

    a. thoughtful
    b. confined
    c. hostile
    d. perfect

25. Which statement is not a detail from the passage?

    a. Scientists can now see T cells.
    b. The immune system ignores tumors.
    c. The ability of the immune system to fight disease without harming the body remains mysterious.
    d. The immune system remembers millions of different invaders.

26. What is the meaning of the word enlist as it is used in the second paragraph?

    a. call into service
    b. write down
    c. send away
    d. put across

27. What is the author's primary purpose in writing the essay?

    a. to persuade

    b. to analyze

    c. to inform

    d. to entertain

Questions 28-31 refer to the following passage:

> The federal government regulates dietary supplements through the United States Food and Drug Administration (FDA). The regulations for dietary supplements are not the same as those for prescription or over-the-counter drugs. In general, the regulations for dietary supplements are less strict.
>
> To begin with, a manufacturer does not have to prove the safety and effectiveness of a dietary supplement before it is marketed. A manufacturer is permitted to say that a dietary supplement addresses a nutrient deficiency, supports health, or is linked to a particular body function (such as immunity), if there is research to support the claim. Such a claim must be followed by the words "This statement has not been evaluated by the Food and Drug Administration. This product is not intended to diagnose, treat, cure, or prevent any disease."
>
> Also, manufacturers are expected to follow certain good manufacturing practices (GMPs) to ensure that dietary supplements are processed consistently and meet quality standards. Requirements for GMPs went into effect in 2008 for large manufacturers and are being phased in for small manufacturers through 2010.
>
> Once a dietary supplement is on the market, the FDA monitors safety and product information, such as label claims and package inserts. If it finds a product to be unsafe, it can take action against the manufacturer and/or distributor and may issue a warning or require that the product be removed from the marketplace. The Federal Trade Commission (FTC) is responsible for regulating product advertising; it requires that all information be truthful and not misleading.
>
> The federal government has taken legal action against a number of dietary supplement promoters or Web sites that promote or sell dietary supplements because they have made false or deceptive statements about their products or because marketed products have proven to be unsafe.

28. What is the main idea of the passage?

    a. Manufacturers of dietary supplements have to follow good manufacturing practices.

    b. The FDA has a special program for regulating dietary supplements.

    c. The federal government prosecutes those who mislead the general public.

    d. The FDA is part of the federal government.

29. Which statement is not a detail from the passage?

    a. Promoters of dietary supplements can make any claims that are supported by research.

    b. GMP requirements for large manufacturers went into effect in 2008.

    c. Product advertising is regulated by the FTC.

    d. The FDA does not monitor products after they enter the market.

30. **What is the meaning of the phrase *phased in* as it is used in the third paragraph?**
    a. stunned into silence
    b. confused
    c. implemented in stages
    d. legalized

31. **What is the meaning of the word deceptive as it is used in the fifth paragraph?**
    a. misleading
    b. malicious
    c. illegal
    d. irritating

Questions 32-35 refer to the following passage:

Anemia is a condition in which there is an abnormally low number of red blood cells (RBCs). This condition also can occur if the RBCs don't contain enough hemoglobin, the iron-rich protein that makes the blood red. Hemoglobin helps RBCs carry oxygen from the lungs to the rest of the body.

Anemia can be accompanied by low numbers of RBCs, white blood cells (WBCs), and platelets. Red blood cells are disc-shaped and look like doughnuts without holes in the center. They carry oxygen and remove carbon dioxide (a waste product) from your body. These cells are made in the bone marrow and live for about 120 days in the bloodstream. Platelets and WBCs also are made in the bone marrow. White blood cells help fight infection. Platelets stick together to seal small cuts or breaks on the blood vessel walls and to stop bleeding.

If you are anemic, your body doesn't get enough oxygenated blood. As a result, you may feel tired or have other symptoms. Severe or long-lasting anemia can damage the heart, brain, and other organs of the body. Very severe anemia may even cause death.

Anemia has three main causes: blood loss, lack of RBC production, or high rates of RBC destruction. Many types of anemia are mild, brief, and easily treated. Some types can be prevented with a healthy diet or treated with dietary supplements. However, certain types of anemia may be severe, long lasting, and life threatening if not diagnosed and treated.

If you have the signs or symptoms of anemia, you should see your doctor to find out whether you have the condition. Treatment will depend on the cause and severity of the anemia.

32. **What is the main idea of the passage?**
    a. Anemia presents in a number of forms.
    b. Anemia is a potentially dangerous condition characterized by low numbers of RBCs.
    c. Anemia is a deficiency of WBCs and platelets.
    d. Anemia is a treatable condition.

33. Which statement is not a detail from the passage?

a. There are different methods for treating anemia.
b. Red blood cells remove carbon dioxide from the body.
c. Platelets are made in the bone marrow.
d. Anemia is rarely caused by blood loss.

34. What is the meaning of the word oxygenated as it is used in the third paragraph?

a. containing low amounts of oxygen
b. containing no oxygen
c. consisting entirely of oxygen
d. containing high amounts of oxygen

35. What is the meaning of the word severity as it is used in the fifth paragraph?

a. seriousness
b. disconnectedness
c. truth
d. swiftness

Questions 36-39 refer to the following passage:

Contrary to previous reports, drinking four or more cups of coffee a day does not put women at risk of rheumatoid arthritis (RA), according to a new study partially funded by the National Institute of Arthritis and Musculoskeletal and Skin Diseases (NIAMS). The study concluded that there is little evidence to support a connection between consuming coffee or tea and the risk of RA among women.

Rheumatoid arthritis is an inflammatory autoimmune disease that affects the joints. It results in pain, stiffness, swelling, joint damage, and loss of function. Inflammation most often affects the hands and feet and tends to be symmetrical. About one percent of the U.S. population has rheumatoid arthritis.

Elizabeth W. Karlson, M.D., and her colleagues at Harvard Medical School and Brigham and Women's Hospital in Boston, Massachusetts, used the Nurses' Health Study, a long-term investigation of nurses' diseases, lifestyles, and health practices, to examine possible links between caffeinated beverages and RA risk. The researchers were able to follow up more than 90 percent of the original pool of 83,124 participants who answered a 1980 food frequency questionnaire, and no links were found. They also considered changes in diet and habits over a prolonged period of time, and when the results were adjusted for other factors, such as cigarette smoking, alcohol consumption, and oral contraceptive use, the outcome still showed no relationship between caffeine consumption and risk of RA.

Previous research had suggested an association between consuming coffee or tea and RA risk. According to Dr. Karlson, the data supporting that conclusion were inconsistent. Because the information in the older studies was collected at only one time, she says, consideration was not given to the other factors associated with RA, such as cigarette smoking and changes in diet and lifestyle over a follow-up period. The new study presents a more accurate picture of caffeine and RA risk.

36. **What is the main idea of the passage?**
    a. In the past, doctors have cautioned older women to avoid caffeinated beverages.
    b. Rheumatoid arthritis affects the joints of older women.
    c. A recent study found no link between caffeine consumption and RA among women.
    d. Cigarette smoking increases the incidence of RA.

37. **Which statement is not a detail from the passage?**
    a. Alcohol consumption is linked with RA.
    b. The original data for the study came from a 1980 questionnaire.
    c. Rheumatoid arthritis most often affects the hands and feet.
    d. This study included tens of thousands of participants.

38. **What is the meaning of the word symmetrical as it is used in the second paragraph?**
    a. affecting both sides of the body in corresponding fashion
    b. impossible to treat
    c. sensitive to the touch
    d. asymptomatic

39. **What is the author's primary purpose in writing the essay?**
    a. to entertain
    b. to inform
    c. to analyze
    d. to persuade

40. **This passage describes Toni Morrison's writing as all of the following EXCEPT:**

    Toni Morrison, who name was originally Chloe Anthony Wofford, is a writer of great distinction who has won many awards, one of which was the Pulitzer Prize in 1988. From her very first novel, *The Bluest Eye*, the writer has portrayed the struggles of black people, and especially black women, in America. Her writing is multifaceted and profound with the distinctive African-American culture as the backbone. Morrison's novels are literary epics with strong, descriptive dialogue and black characters with powerful depth.

    a. multifaceted
    b. award-winning
    c. profound
    d. struggling

Verbal

30 minutes, 60 questions

For questions 1-30: Select the synonym. Each question has a word in all capital letters followed by five answer choices in all lower-case letters. Select the answer choice with a definition closest to the capitalized word.

1. OBSCURE:
- a. opinionated
- b. unclear
- c. offensive
- d. benign

2. REMISS:
- a. timely
- b. diligent
- c. negligent
- d. meticulous

3. GRIEVOUS:
- a. casual
- b. frightening
- c. delighted
- d. serious

4. EXHILARATION:
- a. exhalation
- b. aimlessness
- c. curiosity
- d. elation

5. SIEGE:
- a. slip
- b. blockade
- c. severity
- d. odor

6. COURTEOUS:
- a. conscientious
- b. polite
- c. interested
- d. aware

7. RECEDE:
- a. excel
- b. increase
- c. abut
- d. wane

157

8. BRANDISHED:

    a. threw
    b. waved menacingly
    c. smacked
    d. peered

9. BESOTTED:

    a. infatuated
    b. infuriated
    c. perplexed
    d. engrossed

10. VICINITY:

    a. neighborhood
    b. parish
    c. mindset
    d. idea

11. PROGNOSIS:

    a. forecast
    b. description
    c. outline
    d. schedule

12. ABSTAIN:

    a. offend
    b. retrain
    c. to refrain from
    d. defenestrate

13. OMINOUS:

    a. threatening
    b. emboldening
    c. destructive
    d. insightful

14. INCIDENCE:

    a. random events
    b. sterility
    c. autonomy
    d. rate of occurrence

15. OCCLUDED:

    a. closed
    b. deformed
    c. enlarged
    d. engorged

16. POTENT:

    a. frantic

    b. determined

    c. feverish

    d. powerful

17. PRECIPITOUS:

    a. detached

    b. sordid

    c. encompassed

    d. steep

18. INSIDIOUS:

    a. stealthy

    b. deadly

    c. collapsed

    d. new

19. PROSCRIBE:

    a. anticipate

    b. prevent

    c. defeat

    d. forbid

20. DISTENDED:

    a. concave

    b. sore

    c. swollen

    d. empty

21. OVERT:

    a. concealed

    b. apparent

    c. expert

    d. delectable

22. CARNIVORE:

    a. hungry

    b. meat-eating

    c. infected

    d. demented

23. BELLIGERENT:

    a. retired

    b. sardonic

    c. pugnacious

    d. acclimated

24. FLACCID:
a. defended
b. limp
c. slender
d. outdated

25. TERRESTRIAL:
a. alien
b. earthly
c. foreign
d. domestic

26. ENDOGENOUS:
a. contagious
b. painful to the touch
c. continuous
d. growing from within

27. DISCRETE:
a. calm
b. subtle
c. hidden
d. separate

28. EXACERBATE:
a. implicate
b. aggravate
c. heal
d. decondition

29. HOLISTIC:
a. insensitive
b. ignorant
c. specialized
d. concerned with the whole rather than the parts

30. REPUGNANT:
a. destructive
b. selective
c. collective
d. offensive

For questions 31-60: These questions ask you to identify and compare relationships between pairs of words. Select the answer that best completes the comparison.

31. shovel is to dig as spoon is to
a. stir
b. knife
c. silverware
d. eat

32. shoot is to gun as drive is to

a. road
b. way
c. automobile
d. golf

33. simmer is to boil as tremor is to

a. earth
b. earthquake
c. shake
d. nervous

34. intelligent is to stupid as enthusiastic is to

a. happy
b. passionate
c. action
d. indifferent

35. bouquet is to flowers as recipe is to

a. success
b. cookbook
c. ingredients
d. chef

36. cool is to freezing as warm is to

a. boiling
b. summer
c. heat
d. cozy

37. France is to Europe as China is to

a. Japan
b. Asia
c. country
d. continent

38. fable is to story as sandal is to

a. strap
b. summer
c. foot
d. shoe

39. shell is to beach as rock is to

a. roll
b. stone
c. mountain
d. dune

40. kitchen is to cook as library is to

    a. peace
    b. read
    c. play
    d. pray

41. rug is to floor as sheet is to

    a. pillowcase
    b. bedspread
    c. sail
    d. bed

42. smokestack is to factory as steeple is to

    a. church
    b. chase
    c. dome
    d. high

43. rain is to wet as fire is to

    a. ash
    b. ember
    c. hot
    d. spark

44. sentence is to paragraph as brick is to

    a. mortar
    b. cement
    c. slate
    d. wall

45. try is to attempt as dare is to

    a. challenge
    b. devil
    c. fear
    d. defy

46. laugh is to joy as sneer is to

    a. snicker
    b. snob
    c. contempt
    d. face

47. hospital is to surgeon as store is to

    a. clerk
    b. inventory
    c. warehouse
    d. customer

48. weave is to basket as knit is to

   a. brow
   b. scarf
   c. sew
   d. needle

49. hungry is to eat as tired is to

   a. bed
   b. awake
   c. sick
   d. sleep

50. desert is to dune as ocean is to

   a. deep
   b. continent
   c. sea
   d. wave

51. oil is to squeak as salve is to

   a. burn
   b. medicine
   c. soothe
   d. ointment

52. nudge is to shove as nibble is to

   a. morsel
   b. devour
   c. tiny
   d. swallow

53. cavity is to tooth as wart is to

   a. hog
   b. blemish
   c. skin
   d. virus

54. had is to have as saw is to

   a. tool
   b. sawed
   c. see
   d. wood

55. racket is to tennis as paddle is to

   a. hit
   b. punishment
   c. wheel
   d. ping pong

56. etch is to glass as paint is to

    a. canvas
    b. draw
    c. color
    d. brush

57. debt is to pay as law is to

    a. obey
    b. break
    c. order
    d. legal

58. president is to government as principal is to

    a. belief
    b. teacher
    c. school
    d. student

59. pearl is to oyster as seed is to

    a. plant
    b. grape
    c. sow
    d. grow

60. rake is to hoe as hammer is to

    a. head
    b. build
    c. pound
    d. screwdriver

Quantitative

Read each question, perform the appropriate calculations, and determine the correct answer.

1. Jason chooses a number that is the square root of four less than two times Amy's number. If Amy's number is 20, what is Jason's number?

   a. 6
   b. 7
   c. 8
   d. 9

2. Fred designs a candy box in the shape of a triangular prism. The base of each triangular face measures 4 inches, while the height of the prism is 7 inches. Given that the length of the prism is 11 inches, what is the volume of the candy box?

   a. 102 in^3
   b. 128 in^3
   c. 154 in^3
   d. 308 in^3

3. Which of the following is equivalent to $4^3 + 12 \div 4 + 8^2 \times 3$?

   a. 249
   b. 393
   c. 211
   d. 259

4. A car holds 12 gallons of gasoline. How many quarts of gasoline does the car hold?

   a. 3 quarts
   b. 48 quarts
   c. $\frac{1}{3}$ quarts
   d. 4 quarts

5. The bar graph shows the number of views a viral video has on four different platforms.

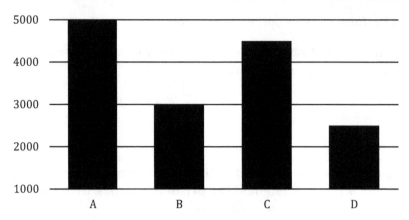

Which statement is supported by the data?

a. The number of views on platform B is twice the number of views on platform C.
b. The number of views on platform A is greater than the number of views on platform B and D combined.
c. The number of views on platform D is half the number of views on platform C
d. The number of views on platform A is double the number of views on platform D

6. Points W, X, Y, and Z are placed on the number line.

NUMBER LINE

Which point best represents the placement of $-\frac{4}{3}$ on the number line?

a. W
b. X
c. Y
d. Z

7. Four points are graphed on a coordinate grid.

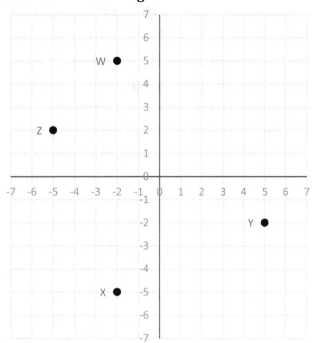

Which point is located at $(-2, 5)$?

    a. Point W
    b. Point X
    c. Point Y
    d. Point Z

8. Which expression is equivalent to $5^3 + 4 \cdot 7 + 6$?

    a. $(125 + 4) \cdot 13$
    b. $(25 \cdot 5) + (4 \cdot 13)$
    c. $(5 \cdot 5 \cdot 5) + (4 \cdot 7 \cdot 6)$
    d. $25 \cdot 5 + 34$

9. Which expression is equivalent to $3 - (x + 4)$?

    a. $3 + 4x$
    b. $-3 + 4x$
    c. $-x + 4 + 3$
    d. $3 - x - 4$

10. What is the solution for the equation $\frac{x}{24} = -6$?

    a. 4
    b. -4
    c. 144
    d. -144

11. Antonio wants to buy a roll of border to finish an art project. At four different shops, he found four different borders he liked. He wants to use the widest of the borders. The list shows the width, in inches, of the borders he found.

$$1\frac{7}{10}, 1.72, 1\frac{3}{4}, 1.695$$

Which roll of border should Antonio buy if he wants to buy the widest border?

a. $1\frac{7}{10}$

b. 1.72

c. $1\frac{3}{4}$

d. 1.695

12. Which list includes values that are all equivalent?

a. $20\%, \frac{1}{20}, 0.2$

b. $1.5, 15\%, \frac{15}{100}$

c. $\frac{7}{20}, 35\%, 0.35$

d. $10\%, \frac{1}{10}, 0.01$

13. Which of the following values of x makes this equation a true statement?

$$-2 - 3x = -14$$

a. -4

b. 4

c. 3

d. -5

14. Which of the following is the solution to the equation $320 - 12d = 80$?

a. -20

b. 12

c. 20

d. -12

15. Which equation is true when $x = -4$?

a. $25 = 5x$

b. $x - 36 = 32$

c. $\frac{68}{x} = -17$

d. $17 - x = 13$

16. A mathematics test has a 4:2 ratio of data analysis problems to algebra problems. If the test has 18 algebra problems, how many data analysis problems are on the test?

a. 24

b. 36

c. 38

d. 28

17. A scientist tracked the population of cicadas in an area over 5 years. The table shows the population of cicadas each year in millions.

Year 1	Year 2	Year 3	Year 4	Year 5
4	12	36	108	324

By what scale factor did the population of cicadas increase each year?

    a. 4
    b. 8
    c. 3
    d. 6

18. What expression is NOT equal to 5?

    a. the absolute value of −5
    b. the reciprocal of −5
    c. the absolute value of 5
    d. the opposite of −5

19. The histogram below represents the overall GRE scores for a sample of college students. Which of the following is a true statement?

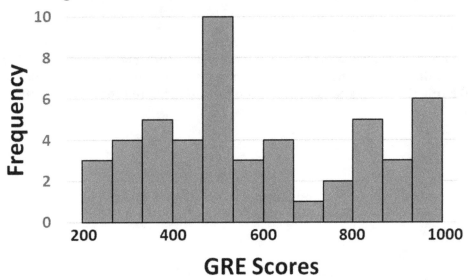

    a. The range of GRE scores is approximately 600.
    b. The average GRE score is 750.
    c. The median GRE score is approximately 500.
    d. The fewest number of college students had an approximate score of 800.

20. A publishing company has been given 29 manuscripts to review. If the company divides the work equally amongst 8 editors, which of the following represents the number of manuscript each editor will review?

    a. $3\frac{3}{5}$
    b. $3\frac{5}{8}$
    c. $3\frac{7}{9}$
    d. $3\frac{2}{3}$

21. Which of the following is equivalent to $-8^2 + (17 - 9) \times 4 + 7$?

   a. -217
   b. 24
   c. -64
   d. -25

22. If 1 mile = 5,280 feet, which of the following proportions can be used to determine the number of miles equal to 26,400 feet?

   a. $\dfrac{5{,}280}{1} = \dfrac{26{,}400}{x}$
   b. $\dfrac{5{,}280}{1} = \dfrac{x}{26{,}400}$
   c. $\dfrac{5{,}280}{x} = \dfrac{26{,}400}{1}$
   d. $\dfrac{5{,}280}{26{,}400} = \dfrac{x}{1}$

23. Allison is making lemonade. She uses 3 cups of sugar for every 2 gallons of water. Which ratio of sugar to water would make a lemonade with the same sweetness?

   a. $10:6$
   b. $2:3$
   c. $12:8$
   d. $27:16$

24. Large boxes of canned beans hold 24 cans of beans and small boxes hold 12 cans. One afternoon, Gerald brought 4 large boxes of canned beans and 6 small boxes of canned beans to the food bank. How many cans of beans did Gerald bring to the food bank that afternoon?

   a. 168
   b. 192
   c. 288
   d. 360

25. Castor collects only baseball and football cards. He has 40 baseball cards and 10 football cards. Which decimal best shows the part of his entire card collection represented by his baseball cards?

   a. 0.8
   b. 0.75
   c. 0.4
   d. 0.25

Answer Key and Explanations for Test #2

Quantitative

1. C: One way to find this answer is to set up a proportion: $\frac{6}{10} = \frac{G}{240}$, in which G represents the number of Grade 6 students living within two miles of the school. To solve the proportion, we should cross-multiply. So, 10 times G = 6 times 240. This gives the equation:

$10G = 1,440$. To solve the equation we divide both sides of the equation by 10, which gives $G = 144$.

2. D: The counters represent the expression $-12 + 8$, which equals -4. Using the additive inverse property, the eight negative 1 integers and eight positive 1 integers cancel one another, leaving four negative 1 integers, written as -4.

3. A: The number Akita is thinking of is the opposite of 7. The opposite of a number is the value that is the same distance from zero on the other side of a number line. Akita must be thinking of the number -7. The absolute value of a number is its distance from zero. When looking at a number line, -7 is 7 away from zero, so the absolute value of -7 is 7. The true statements about Akita's number are II: the number is -7, and III: the number has an absolute value of 7.

4. C: The equation that represents the relationship between the position number, n, and the value of the term, a_n, is $a_n = -3n + 8$. Notice each n is multiplied by -3, with 8 added to that value. Substituting position number 1 for n gives $a_n = -3(1) + 8$, which equals 5. Substitution of the remaining position numbers does not provide a counterexample to this procedure.

5. D: The amount charged for miles hauled will require us to multiply the number of miles by \$0.05. The charge for each load of \$80 is not changed by the number of miles hauled. That will be added to the amount charged for miles hauled. So, the equation needs to show 0.05 times miles plus 80, or $c = 0.05m + 80$.

6. B: This problem focuses on equivalent percentages and fractions. There are a few ways to approach this problem. One way would be to convert each fraction to a percentage. Another way would be to convert the percentage to a fraction and simplify. To convert 36% to a fraction, the 36 would be written out of 100 and this fraction can be simplified. $36\% = \frac{36}{100}$, which can be simplified to $\frac{18}{50}$ and $\frac{9}{25}$.

7. B: Let x represent the amount of money saved, \$52 the amount earned mowing yards, and \$14 the amount spent on a birthday present. Then \$52 – \$14 = x. This can be rearranged as $14 + x = 52$. Therefore, choice B is correct. 2.7.10

8. D: The inequality $12.5x \geq 375$ means that 375 is less than or equal to 12.5 times a value x, or a value x times 12.5 is greater than or equal to 375. Option A describes an equation where $12.5x = 375$. Option B describes the inequality $12.5 + x \geq 375$. Option C describes the inequality $12.5x > 375$. Option D describes the inequality $375 \leq 12.5x$ because Desmond makes 12.5 bracelets each day for x days, $12.5x$, and has a goal of making at least 375 bracelets, which means that $12.5x$ must be greater than or equal to 375.

9. A: When setting up a proportion, like quantities need to be placed in the numerators and like quantities need to be placed in the denominators. For this problem, the proportion has the form of $\frac{\text{object}}{\text{shadow}} = \frac{\text{object}}{\text{shadow}}$. The proportion in the correct format is $\frac{x}{4} = \frac{5}{2.5}$. Therefore, choice A is correct.

10. B: The order of operations states that multiplication and division, as they appear from left to right in the expression, should be completed following the evaluation of exponents. Therefore, after evaluating the squared number, that value should be multiplied by 2.

11. C: The first step would be to subtract the $10 he spent on the book from the gift, $40. This gives us $30. This is how much Tomas still has. We add the $35 he earned to the $30 remaining from the gift, which gives $65, the amount Tomas has in total. Then we subtract $65 from the $100 cost of the telescope to find the amount Tomas still needs to save.

12. A: This problem focuses on comparing ratios. There are many ways to compare 3 : 2 and 5 : 4. One way would be by finding the unit ratio of coloring to cups using division. Caroline uses a ratio of 3 : 2 drops to cups, which is equivalent to 1.5 drops to 1 cup because $3 \div 2 = 1.5$. Devon uses a ratio of 5 : 4 drops to cups, which is equivalent to 1.25 drops to 1 cup because $5 \div 4 = 1.25$. If Caroline uses more drops per cup of water, her water is darker because 3 : 2 is greater than 5 : 4.

13. B: This problem focuses on using the area formula of a parallelogram. The reference sheet can be used to find the area formula of a parallelogram: $A = bh$. The height of a parallelogram is the length of a line that connects and is perpendicular to the bases. Based on the diagram, the base of the figure is $12\frac{1}{2}$ inches and the height of the figure is $3\frac{1}{2}$ inches. The equation to find the area is $A = 12\frac{1}{2}$ in $\cdot\ 3\frac{1}{2}$ in $= 43\frac{3}{4}$ in^2.

14. B: Since $\triangle ABE$ and $\triangle ACD$ have two congruent angles (notice that both triangles have $\angle A$ in common, and $\angle B \cong \angle C$ since both angles measure 70°), their third angles must also be congruent. Thus, $\triangle ABE$ is similar to $\triangle ACD$. Since the corresponding sides of similar triangles are proportional, $\frac{AB}{AC} = \frac{AE}{AD}$. However, the lengths BE and CD are not equal. Therefore, choice B is correct.

15. A: This problem focuses on writing situations that represent inequalities. In this example, 36 is less than n divided by 4. This means that a number n is being divided by 4, and this value is greater than 36. The only situation that describes a total, n divided by 4, being greater than 36 is Theresa packaging n number of cupcakes into packages of 4, which makes more than 36 packages.

16. B: There are many ways to approach this problem. One way to solve this would be to review each option and compare them to the given expression. When the expression $9z \cdot z - 27z$ is compared to $9z + (z - 3)$, it is evident that they are not equivalent because $9z \cdot z = 9z^2$ and no term in $9z + (z - 3)$ contains or can be simplified to contain a factor of z^2. When the expression $9z + (z - 3)$ is compared to $(z - 3) + 9z$, it can be observed that these expressions are equivalent because of the commutative property, so the expressions $9z$ and $z - 3$ can be added in any order. When $10z + 3$ is compared to $9z + (z - 3)$, it is evident that these expressions are not equivalent because, while $9z + z = 10z$, the 3 should be subtracted, not added. Lastly, when $(z - 3) - 9z$ is compared to $9z + (z - 3)$, it is evident that these expressions are not equivalent because the sum of $9z$ and $(z - 3)$ is not equivalent to the difference between $(z - 3)$ and $9z$.

17. D: In order to convert the given fraction to a percentage, divide 2 by 7. Doing so gives a decimal of approximately 0.29. The decimal can be converted to a percentage by multiplying by 100, which moves the decimal point two places to the right and gives 29%.

18. D: To correctly write a percent as a decimal, the percent sign is dropped and the number is rewritten with the decimal point two places to the left. This is because a percent is always a value out of 100 and the second place after the decimal point is the hundredths place. So, 70% = 0.70 and the zero at the end after the decimal can be dropped.

19. A: This problem focuses on graphing solutions to inequalities on a number line. Given the inequality $17 - x \geq 9$, this can be solved by isolating x by simplifying the inequality. $17 - x \geq 9$ is simplified by first adding x to each side to get $17 \geq 9 + x$, and this can be further simplified by subtracting 9 from each side to get $8 \geq x$. This solution can be graphed on a number line using a closed circle over the 8, because x could be equal to 8, and an arrow to the left because if x is not equal to 8, it is less than 8.

20. A: This problem focuses on converting a fraction $\frac{7}{25}$ to a percentage. Converting fractions to percentages can be performed by converting the fraction to a value out of 100, or converting the fraction to a decimal. $\frac{7}{25}$ can be converted to a fraction out of 100 by multiplying the numerator and denominator by 4: $\frac{7}{25} = \frac{28}{100}$, which is equivalent to 28%

21. A: The product of 5 and $\frac{1}{2}$ is the same as the value of $5 \cdot \frac{1}{2}$. The product of a whole number multiplied by a fraction is less than the whole number. 5 times $\frac{1}{2}$ must be less than 5. The product cannot be greater than 5, and the product must be greater than 1 and $\frac{1}{2}$ because $5 \cdot \frac{1}{2} = \frac{5}{2}$ which is greater than 1 and $\frac{1}{2}$.

22. A: This problem focuses on equivalent expressions using exponents and order of operations. There are many ways to approach this problem. One strategy is to simplify each expression and compare. The given expression $81 \div 9 + 36$ is equivalent to 45 because $81 \div 9 = 9$ and $9 + 36 = 45$. The expression in option A, $3^2 + 6^2$, is also equivalent to 45 because $3^2 = 9, 6^2 = 36$, and $9 + 36 = 45$. The expression in option B, $3 \cdot 3 + 3 \cdot 3 \cdot 3$, is equivalent to 36 because $3 \cdot 3 = 9, 3 \cdot 3 \cdot 3 = 27$, and $9 + 27 = 36$. The expression in option C, $\frac{9^2}{3^3} + (12 \cdot 3)$, is equivalent to 39 because $9^2 = 81$, $3^3 = 27$, and $\frac{81}{27} = 3$. Then, $12 \cdot 3 = 36$, and finally, $3 + 36 = 39$. The expression in option D, $(9 \cdot 9) \div (3 \cdot 3 \cdot 5)$, is equivalent to 1.8 because $9 \cdot 9 = 81, 3 \cdot 3 \cdot 5 = 45$, and $81 \div 45 = 1.8$. The only expression that is equivalent to the given expression is the expression $3^2 + 6^2$.

23. D: First, subtract 5 from both sides of the inequality, which yields $-2x > 8$. Then, divide both sides by -2. Remember to reverse the symbol since the inequality is being divided by a negative number. This yields $x < -4$, which is graphed on a number line with an open circle at -4 and shading to the left. Therefore, choice D is correct.

24. D: The volume of a cylinder can be determined by using the following formula: $V = Bh$, where B represents the area of the base and h represents the height. The area of one of the bases refers to the area of one of the circular bases. The area of a circle is determined by πr^2; thus, the area of one of the cylindrical bases is represented by πr^2.

25. D: This problem focuses on the definition of scale factors. If the views on a video increase by a scale factor of 13 each day, this means that the change in views from each day increased by a multiplicative factor of 13. For example, if there are 5 views on day 1, there will be $5 \cdot 13 = 65$ views on day 2 and $65 \cdot 13 = 845$ views on day 3. The number of views increases by multiplying the previous day's total by 13.

Reading Comprehension

1. D: The main idea of this passage is that vaccines help the immune system function properly. Identifying main ideas is one of the key skills tested by the exam. One of the common traps that many test-takers fall into is assuming that the first sentence of the passage will express the main idea. Although this will be true for some passages, often the author will use the first sentence to attract interest or to make an introductory, but not central, point. On this question, if you assume that the first sentence contains the main idea, you will incorrectly choose answer B. Finding the main idea of a passage requires patience and thoroughness; you cannot expect to know the main idea until you have read the entire passage. In this case, a diligent reading will show you that answer choices A, B, and C express details from the passage, but only answer choice D is a comprehensive summary of the author's message.

2. C: This passage does not state that the symptoms of disease will not emerge until the body has learned to fight the disease. The reading comprehension section of the exam will include several questions that require you to identify details from a passage. The typical structure of these questions is to ask you to identify the answer choice that contains a detail not included in the passage. This question structure makes your work a little more difficult, because it requires you to confirm that the other three details are in the passage. In this question, the details expressed in answer choices A, B, and D are all explicit in the passage. The passage never states, however, that the symptoms of disease do not emerge until the body has learned how to fight the disease-causing microbe. On the contrary, the passage implies that a person may become quite sick and even die before the body learns to effectively fight the disease.

3. B: In the third paragraph, the word *virulent* means "malicious." The reading comprehension section of the exam will include several questions that require you to define a word as it is used in the passage. Sometimes the word will be one of those used in the vocabulary section of the exam; other times, the word in question will be a slightly difficult word used regularly in academic and professional circles. In some cases, you may already know the basic definition of the word. Nevertheless, you should always go back and look at the way the word is used in the passage. The exam will often include answer choices that are legitimate definitions for the given word, but which do not express how the word is used in the passage. For instance, the word *virulent* could in some circumstances mean contagious. However, since the passage is not talking about transfer of the disease, but the effects of the disease once a person has caught it, malicious is the more appropriate answer.

4. C: The author's primary purpose in writing this essay is to inform. The reading comprehension section of the exam will include a few questions that ask you to determine the purpose of the author. The answer choices are always the same: The author's purpose is to entertain, to persuade, to inform, or to analyze. When an author is *writing to entertain*, he or she is not including a great deal of factual information; instead, the focus is on vivid language and interesting stories. *Writing to persuade* means "trying to convince the reader of something." When a writer is just trying to provide the reader with information, without any particular bias, he or she is *writing to inform*. Finally, *writing to analyze* means to consider a subject already well known to the reader. For instance, if the above passage took an objective look at the pros and cons of various approaches to fighting disease, we would say that the passage was a piece of analysis. Because the purpose of this passage is to present new information to the reader in an objective manner, it is clear that the author's intention is to inform.

5. A: The subject of this passage is foodborne illnesses. Identifying the subject of a passage is similar to identifying the main idea. Do not assume that the first sentence of the passage will declare the subject. Oftentimes, an author will approach his or her subject by first describing some related, familiar subject. In this passage, the author does introduce the subject of the passage in the first sentence. However, it is only by reading the rest of the passage that you can determine the subject. One way to figure out the subject of a passage is to identify the main idea of each paragraph, and then identify the common thread in each.

6. B: This passage never states that cooked food cannot cause illness. Indeed, the first sentence of the third paragraph states that harmful bacteria can be present on cooked food that is left out for two or more hours. This is a direct contradiction of answer choice B. If you can identify an answer choice that is clearly contradicted by the text, you can be sure that it is not one of the ideas advanced by the passage. Sometimes the correct answer to this type of question will be something that is contradicted in the text; on other occasions, the correct answer will be a detail that is not included in the passage at all.

7. C: In the first paragraph, the word *pathogens* means "disease-causing substances." The vocabulary you are asked to identify in the reading comprehension section of the exam will tend to be health related. The exam administrators are especially interested in your knowledge of the terminology used by doctors and nurses. Some of these words, however, are rarely used in normal conversation, so they may be unfamiliar to you. The best way to determine the meaning of an unfamiliar word is to examine how it is used in context. In the last sentence of the first paragraph, it is clear that pathogens are some substances that cause disease. Note that the pathogens are not diseases themselves; we would not say that an uncooked piece of meat "has a disease," but rather that consuming it "can cause a disease." For this reason, answer choice C is better than answer choice A.

8. A: In the second paragraph, the word *sterile* means "free of bacteria." This question provides a good example of why you should always refer to the word as it is used in the text. The word *sterile* is often used to describe "a person who cannot reproduce." If this definition immediately came to mind when you read the question, you might have mistakenly chosen answer D. However, in this passage the author describes raw foods as *not sterile*, meaning that they contain bacteria. For this reason, answer choice A is the correct response.

9. C: The main idea of the passage is that both the esophagus and the stomach are subject to bleeding problems. The structure of this passage is simple: The first paragraph discusses bleeding disorders of the esophagus, and the second paragraph discusses bleeding disorders of the stomach. Remember that statements can be true, and can even be explicitly stated in the passage, and can yet not be the main idea of the passage. The main idea given in answer choice A is perhaps true but is too general to be classified as the main idea of the passage.

10. B: The passage never states that ulcer disease rarely occurs in the stomach. On the contrary, in the second paragraph the author states that ulcer disease *can* affect the blood vessels in the stomach. The three other answer choices can be found within the passage. The surest way to answer a question like this is to comb through the passage, looking for each detail in turn. This is a time-consuming process, however, so you may want to follow any initial intuition you have. In other words, if you are suspicious of one of the answer choices, see if you can find it in the passage. Often you will find that the detail is expressly contradicted by the author, in which case you can be sure that this is the right answer.

11. A: In the first paragraph, the word *rupture* means "tear." All of the answer choices are action verbs that suggest destruction. In order to determine the precise meaning of rupture, then, you must examine its usage in the passage. The author is describing a condition in which damage to a vein causes internal bleeding. Therefore, it does not make sense to say that the vein has *collapsed* or *imploded*, as neither of these verbs suggests a ripping or opening in the side of the vein. Similarly, the word *detach* suggests an action that seems inappropriate for a vein. It seems quite possible, however, for a vein to *tear*: Answer choice A is correct.

12. D: In the second paragraph, the word *erode* means "wear away." Your approach to this question should be the same as for question 11. Take a look at how the word is used in the passage. The author is describing a condition in which ulcers degrade a vein to the point of bleeding. Obviously, it is not appropriate to say that the ulcer has *avoided*, *divorced*, or *contained* the vein. It *is* sensible, however, to say that the ulcer has *worn away* the vein.

13. A: The primary subject of the passage is a new artificial retina. This question is a little tricky, because the author spends so much time talking about the experience of Kathy Blake. As a reader, however, you have to ask yourself whether Mrs. Blake or the new artificial retina is more essential to the story. Would the author still be interested in the story if a different person had the artificial retina? Probably. Would the author have written about Mrs. Blake if she hadn't gotten the artificial retina? Almost certainly not. Really, the story of Kathy Blake is just a way for the author to make the artificial retina more interesting to the reader. Therefore, the artificial retina is the primary subject of the passage.

14. B: In the second paragraph, the word *progressive* means "gradually increasing." The root of the word is *progress*, which you may know means "advancement toward a goal." With this in mind, you may be reasonably certain that answer choice B is correct. It is never a bad idea to examine the context, however. The author is describing *progressive visual loss*, so you might be tempted to select answer choice C or D, since they both suggest loss or diminution. Remember, however, that the adjective *progressive* is modifying the noun *loss*. Since the *loss* is increasing, the correct answer is B.

15. C: The passage never states that retinitis pigmentosa (RP) is curable. This question may be somewhat confusing, since the passage discusses a new treatment for RP. However, the passage never declares that researchers have come up with a cure for the condition; rather, they have developed a new technology that allows people who suffer from RP to regain some of their vision. This is not the same thing as curing RP. Kathy Blake and others like her still have RP, though they have been assisted by this exciting new technology.

16. D: The author's intention in writing this essay is to inform. You may be tempted to answer that the author's intention is to entertain. Indeed, the author expresses his message through the story of Kathy Blake. This story, however, is not important by itself. It is clearly included as a way of explaining the new camera glasses. If the only thing the reader learned from the passage was the story of Kathy Blake, the author would probably be disappointed. At the same time, the author is not really trying to persuade the reader of anything. There is nothing controversial about these new glasses: Everyone is in favor of them. The mission of the author, then, is simply to inform the reader.

17. A: The main idea of the passage is that Usher syndrome is an inherited condition that affects hearing and vision. Always be aware that some answers may be included in the passage but not the main idea. In this question, answer choices B and D are both true details from the passage, but neither of them would be a good summary of the article. One way to approach this kind of question is to consider what you would be likely to say if someone asked you to describe the article in a single sentence. Often, the sentence you come up with will closely mimic one of the answer choices. If so, you can be sure that answer choice is correct.

18. D: In the first paragraph, the word signs means "measurable indicators." The word sign is used frequently in medical contexts, though many people do not entirely understand its meaning. Signs are those objective (measurable) indicators of illness that can be observed by someone besides the person with the illness. A stomachache, for instance, is not technically considered a sign, since it cannot be observed by anyone other than the person who has it, and therefore must be expressed by the individual experiencing it. This would be known as a symptom. Change in vital signs, a failed hearing test, or a low Snellen (vision) chart score, however, would all be considered signs because practitioners can measure or observe them. The best definition for signs, then, is "measurable indicators," that is, objective markers of a disease or condition.

19. B: The passage does not state that Usher syndrome affects both hearing and smell. On the contrary, the passage only states that Usher syndrome affects hearing and vision. You should not be content merely to note that sentence in the passage and select answer choice B. In order to be sure, you need to quickly scan the passage to determine whether there is any mention of problems with the sense of smell. This is because the mention of impaired hearing and vision does not make it impossible for smell to be damaged as well. It is a good idea to practice scanning short articles for specific words. In this case, you would want to scan the article looking for words like *smell* and *nose*.

20. C: In the second paragraph, the word *juvenile* means "occurring in children." Examine the context in which the word is used. Remember that the context extends beyond just the immediate sentence in which the word is found. It can also include adjacent sentences and paragraphs. In this case, the word juvenile is immediately followed by a further explanation of Usher syndrome as it appears in children. You can be reasonably certain, then, that juvenile Usher syndrome is the condition as it presents in children. Although the word *juvenile* is occasionally used in English to describe immature or annoying behavior, it is clear that the author is not here referring to a *bratty* form of Usher syndrome.

21. B: In the third paragraph, the word *mutated* means "altered." This word comes from the same root as mutant; a *mutant* is an organism in which the chromosomes have been changed somehow. The context in which the word is used makes it clear that the author is referring to a scenario in which one of the parent's chromosomes has been altered. One way to approach this kind of problem is to substitute the answer choice into the passage to see if it still makes sense. Clearly, it would not make sense for a chromosome to be *selected*, since chromosomes are passed on and inherited without conscious choice. Neither does it make sense for a chromosome to be destroyed, because a basic fact of biology is that all living organisms have chromosomes.

22. D: The main idea of the passage is that the immune system protects the body from infection. The author repeatedly alludes to the complexity and mystery of the immune system, so it cannot be true that scientists fully understand this part of the body. It is true that the immune system triggers the production of fluids, but this description misses the point. Similarly, it is true that the body is under constant invasion by malicious microbes; however, the author is much more interested in the body's response to these microbes. For this reason, the best answer choice is D.

23. C: The passage never states that viruses are extremely sophisticated. In fact, the passage explicitly states the opposite. However, in order to know this, you need to understand the word *primitive*. The passage says that viruses are too primitive, or early in their development, to be classified as living organisms. A primitive organism is simple and undeveloped—exactly the opposite of sophisticated. If you do not know the word *primitive*, you can still answer the question by finding all three of the answer choices in the passage.

Mometrix

24. D: In the first paragraph, the word *ideal* means "perfect." Do not be confused by the similarity of the word *ideal* to *idea* and mistakenly select answer choice A. Take a look at the context in which the word is used. The author is describing how many millions of microbes can live inside the human body. It would not make sense, then, for the author to be describing the body as a *hostile* environment for microbes. Moreover, whether or not the body is a confined environment would not seem to have much bearing on whether it is good for microbes. Rather, the paragraph suggests that the human body is a perfect environment for microbes.

25. B: The passage never states that the immune system ignores tumors. Indeed, at the beginning of the third paragraph, the author states that scientists remain puzzled by the body's ability to fight tumors. This question is a little tricky, because it is common knowledge that many tumors prove fatal to the human body. However, you should not take this to mean that the body does not at least try to fight tumors. In general, it is best to seek out direct evidence in the text rather than to rely on what you already know. You will have enough time on the exam to fully examine and research each question.

26. A: In the second paragraph, the word *enlist* means "call into service." The use of this word is an example of figurative language, the use of a known image or idea to elucidate an idea that is perhaps unfamiliar to the reader. In this case, the author is describing the efforts of the immune system as if they were a military campaign. The immune system *enlists* other cells, and then directs these *recruits* to areas where they are needed. You are probably familiar with *enlistment* and *recruitment* as they relate to describe military service. The author is trying to draw a parallel between the enlistment of young men and women and the enlistment of immune cells. For this reason, "call into service" is the best definition for *enlist*.

27. C: The author's primary purpose in writing this essay is to inform. As you may have noticed, the essays included in the reading comprehension section of the exam were most often written to inform. This should not be too surprising; after all, the most common intention of any writing on general medical subjects is to provide information rather than to persuade, entertain, or analyze. This does not mean that you can automatically assume that "to inform" will be the answer for every question of this type. However, if you are in doubt, it is probably best to select this answer. In this case, the passage is written in a clear, declarative style with no obvious prejudice on the part of the author. The primary intention of the passage seems to be providing information about the immune system to a general audience.

28. B: The main idea of the passage is that the Food and Drug Administration (FDA) has a special program for regulating dietary supplements. This passage has a straightforward structure: The author introduces his subject in the first paragraph and uses the four succeeding paragraphs to elaborate. All of the other possible answers are true statements from the passage but cannot be considered the main idea. One way to approach questions about the main idea is to take sentences at random from the passage and see which answer choice they could potentially support. The main idea should be strengthened or supported by most of the details from the passage.

29. D: The passage never states that the Food and Drug Administration (FDA) ignores products after they enter the market. In fact, the entire fourth paragraph describes the steps taken by the FDA to regulate products once they are available for purchase. In some cases, questions of this type will contain answer choices that are directly contradictory. Here, for instance, answer choices A and B cannot be true if answer choice D is true. If there are at least two answer choices that contradict another answer choice, it is a safe bet that the contradicted answer choice cannot be correct. If you are at all uncertain about your logic, however, you should refer to the passage.

Copyright © Mometrix Media. You have been licensed one copy of this document for personal use only. Any other reproduction or redistribution is strictly prohibited. All rights reserved. This content is provided for test preparation purposes only and does not imply an endorsement by Mometrix of any particular political, scientific, or religious point of view.

30. C: In the third paragraph, the phrase *phased in* means "implemented in stages." Do not be tempted by the similarity of this phrase to the word *fazed*, which can mean "confused or stunned." The author is referring to manufacturing standards that have already been implemented for large manufacturers and are in the process of being implemented for small manufacturers. It would make sense, then, for these standards to be implemented in *phases*: that is, to be *phased in*.

31. A: In the fifth paragraph, the word *deceptive* means "misleading." The root of the word *deceptive* is the same as for the words *deceive* and *deception*. Take a look at the context in which the word is used. The author states that the FDA prevents certain kinds of advertising. It would be somewhat redundant for the author to mean that the FDA prevents *illegal* advertising; this goes without saying. At the same time, it is unlikely that the FDA spends its time trying to prevent merely *irritating* advertising; the persistent presence of such advertising makes this answer choice inappropriate. Left with a choice between *malicious* and *misleading* advertising, it makes better sense to choose the latter, since being mean and nasty would be a bad technique for selling a product. It is common, however, for an advertiser to deliberately mislead the consumer.

32. B: The main idea of the passage is that anemia is a potentially dangerous condition characterized by low numbers of RBCs (red blood cells). All of the other answer choices are true (although answer C leaves out RBCs), but only answer choice C expresses an idea that is supported by the others. When you are considering a question of this type, try to imagine the answer choices as they would appear on an outline. If the passage above were placed into outline form, which answer choice would be the most appropriate title? Which answer choices would be more appropriate as supporting details? Try to get in the habit of imagining a loose outline as you are reading the passages on the exam.

33. D: The passage never states that anemia is rarely caused by blood loss. On the contrary, in the first sentence of the fourth paragraph the author lists three causes of anemia, and blood loss is listed first. Sometimes, answer choices for this type of question will refer to details not explicitly mentioned in the passage. For instance, answer choice A is true without ever being stated in precisely those terms. Since the passage mentions several different treatments for anemia, however, you should consider the detail in answer choice A to be in the passage. In other words, it is not enough to scan the passage looking for an exact version of the detail. Sometimes, you will have to use your best judgment.

34. D: In the third paragraph, the word *oxygenated* means "containing high amounts of oxygen." This word is not in common usage, so it is absolutely essential for you to refer to its context in the passage. The author states in the second paragraph that anemia is in part a deficiency of the red blood cells that carry oxygen throughout the body. Then in the first sentence of the third paragraph, the author states that anemic individuals do not get enough oxygenated blood. Given this information, it is clear that *oxygenated* must mean carrying high amounts of oxygen, because it has already been stated that anemia consists of a lack of oxygen-rich blood.

35. A: In the fifth paragraph, the word *severity* means "seriousness." This word shares a root with the word *severe*, but not with the word *sever*. As always, take a look at the word as it is used in the passage. In the final sentence of the passage, the author states that the treatment for anemia will depend on the *cause and severity* of the condition. In the previous paragraph, the author outlined a treatment for anemia and indicated that the proper response to the condition varies. The author even refers to the worst cases of anemia as being *severe*. With this in mind, it makes the most sense to define *severity* as seriousness.

36. C: The main idea of the passage is that a recent study found no link between caffeine consumption and rheumatoid arthritis (RA) among women. As is often the case, the first sentence of the passage contains the main idea. However, do not assume that this will always be the case. Furthermore, do not assume that the first sentence of the passage will only contain the main idea. In this passage, for instance, the author makes an immediate reference to the previous belief in the correlation between caffeine and RA. It would be incorrect, however, to think that this means answer choice A is correct. Regardless of whether or not the main idea is contained in the first sentence of the passage, you will need to read the entire text before you can be sure.

37. A: The passage never states that alcohol consumption is linked with RA. The passage does state that the new study took into account alcohol consumption when evaluating the long-term data. This is a good example of a question that requires you to spend a little bit of time rereading the passage. A quick glance might lead you to believe that the new study had found a link between alcohol and RA. Tricky questions like this make it even more crucial for you to go back and verify each answer choice in the text. Working through this question by using the process of elimination is the best way to ensure the correct response.

38. A: In the second paragraph, the word *symmetrical* means "affecting both sides of the body in corresponding fashion." This is an example of a question that is hard to answer even after reviewing its context in the passage. If you have no idea what *symmetrical* means, it will be hard for you to select an answer: All of them sound plausible. In such a case, the best thing you can do is make an educated guess. One clue is that the author has been describing a condition that affects the hands and the feet. Since people have both right and left hands and feet, it makes sense that inflammation would be described as *symmetrical* if it affects both the right and left hand or foot.

39. B: The author's primary purpose in writing this essay is to inform. You may be tempted to select answer choice D on the grounds that the author is presenting a particular point of view. However, there is no indication that the author is trying to persuade the reader of anything. One clear sign that an essay is written to persuade is a reference to what the reader already thinks. A persuasive essay assumes a particular viewpoint held by the reader and then argues against that viewpoint. In this passage, the author has no allegiance to any idea; he or she is only reporting the results of the newest research.

40. D: Although the passage does use the word "struggles" in the second sentence, the word does not describe the writing. The struggles are ones that Morrison's characters are dealing with rather than a description of Morrison's writing.

Verbal

1. B: The word "obscure" means "unclear" and "difficult to understand."

2. C: The word "remiss" means "negligent or forgetful."

3. D: Serious most closely means the same thing as grievous.

4. D: Elation most closely means the same thing as exhilaration.

5. B: Blockade most closely means the same thing as siege.

6. B: Polite most closely means the same things as courteous.

7. D: Wane most closely means the same thing as recede.

8. B: Brandish means to wave menacingly.

9. A: Besotted means infatuated.

10. A: Vicinity means neighborhood.

11. A: The best definition for the word *prognosis* is "forecast."

12. C: The best definition for the word *abstain* is "to refrain from."

13. A: The best synonym for *ominous* is "threatening."

14. D: The word *incidence* means "rate of occurrence."

15. A: The closest meaning for the word *occluded* is "closed."

16. D: The best definition for the word *potent* is "powerful."

17. D: The word *precipitous* means "steep."

18. A: The best definition of the word *insidious* is "stealthy."

19. D: The word *proscribe* means "forbid."

20. C: The word *distended* means "swollen."

21. B: The word *overt* means "apparent."

22. B: The word *carnivore* means "meat-eating."

23. C: The word *belligerent* means "pugnacious." *Pugnacious* means "ready to fight."

24. B: The best description for the word *flaccid* is "limp.

25. B: The word *terrestrial* means "earthly."

26. D: The word *endogenous* means "growing from within."

27. D: The best description for the word *discrete* is "separate."

28. B: The word *exacerbate* means "aggravate."

29. D: The word *holistic* means "concerned with the whole rather than the parts."

30. D: The word *repugnant* means "offensive, especially to the senses or the morals."

31. A: A shovel is used to dig and a spoon is used to stir. While a spoon can also be used to eat, it isn't the direct instrument of eating in the way that a shovel is the direct instrument of digging.

32. C: Shoot is an action done with a gun and drive is an action done with an automobile.

33. B: Simmer is a milder form of boil and tremor is a milder form of earthquake.

34. D: Intelligent is the opposite of stupid and enthusiastic is the opposite of indifferent.

35. C: A bouquet is made up of flowers and a recipe is made up of ingredients.

36. A: Cool is a mild temperature and freezing is extreme; warm is a mild temperature and boiling is extreme.

37. B: France is a country on the continent of Europe and China is a country on the continent of Asia.

38. D: A fable is a type of story and a sandal is a type of shoe.

39. C: A shell can be found on the beach and a rock can be found on a mountain.

40. B: You cook in a kitchen and you read in a library.

41. D: A rug covers the floor and a sheet covers a bed.

42. A: A smokestack extends from the roof of a factory and a steeple extends from the roof of a church.

43. C: Rain feels wet and fire feels hot.

44. D: Sentences make up a paragraph and bricks make up a wall.

45. A: Try is another word for attempt and challenge is another word for dare.

46. C: To laugh is to show joy and to sneer is to show contempt.

47. A: A surgeon works in a hospital and a clerk works in a store.

48. B: A basket can be made by weaving and a scarf can be made by knitting.

49. D: To eat is a solution to being hungry and to sleep is a solution to being tired.

50. D: A dune is a feature of the desert and a wave is a feature of the ocean.

51. A: Oil is applied to relieve a squeak and salve is applied to relieve a burn.

52. B: A nudge is less extreme as compared to a shove and nibble is less extreme as compared to devour.

53. C: A cavity is a flaw in a tooth and a wart is a flaw on the skin.

54. C: Had is the past tense of have and saw is the past tense of see.

55. D: A racket is used to play tennis and a paddle is used to play ping pong.

56. A: To etch is to embellish glass and to paint is to embellish a canvas.

57. A: A debt must be paid and a law must be obeyed.

58. C: A president heads the government and a principal heads the school.

59. B: A pearl can be found inside an oyster and a seed can be found inside a grape.

60. D: A rake and a hoe are both tools for gardening and a hammer and a screwdriver are both tools for building.

Mometrix

Quantitative

1. A: Jason's number can be determined by writing the following expression: $\sqrt{2x - 4}$, where x represents Amy's number. Substitution of 20 for x gives $\sqrt{2(20) - 4}$, which simplifies to $\sqrt{36}$, or 6. Thus, Jason's number is 6. Jason's number can also be determined by working backwards. If Jason's number is the square root of 4 less than 2 times Amy's number, Amy's number should first be multiplied by 2 with 4 subtracted from that product and the square root taken of the resulting difference.

2. C: The volume of a triangular prism can be determined using the formula $V = \frac{1}{2}bhl$, where b represents the length of the base of each triangular face, h represents the height of each triangular face, and l represents the length of the prism. Substitution of the given values into the formula gives $V = \frac{1}{2} \cdot 4 \cdot 7 \cdot 11$, which equals 154. Thus, the volume of the candy box is 154 cubic inches.

3. D: The order of operations states that numbers with exponents must be evaluated first. Thus, the expression can be rewritten as $64 + 12 \div 4 + 64 \times 3$. Next, multiplication and division must be computed as they appear from left to right in the expression. Thus, the expression can be further simplified as $64 + 3 + 192$, which equals 259.

4. B: This problem focuses on converting measurements. The conversion sheet can be used to find that 1 gallon is equivalent to 4 quarts. This means that $\frac{4 \text{ quarts}}{1 \text{ gallon}} = \frac{x}{12 \text{ gallons}}$, which is equivalent to $x = 4 \cdot 12$ quarts $= 48$ quarts.

5. D: This problem focuses on interpreting data from a bar graph. Based on the bar graph, the number of views on platform A is 5,000, platform B is 3,000, platform C is 4,500, and platform D is 2,500. These values should be compared to the statements to find the statement that is supported by the data. 3,000 is not twice the value of 4,500. 5,000 is not greater than $3,000 + 2,500 = 5,500$. 2,500 is not half of 4,500. 5,000 is double 2,500.

6. D: There are many ways to identify $-\frac{4}{3}$ on the number line. One place to start is to identify the first and last value on the number line. In this case, the number line ranges from –2 to 2. $-\frac{4}{3}$ is a negative number, so the value will be to the left of 0. Additionally, $-\frac{4}{3}$ is an improper fraction, which means that it is less than 1 ($\frac{4}{3}$ is greater than 1, so $-\frac{4}{3}$ is less than 1). So far, it has been determined that $-\frac{4}{3}$ lies between –2 and –1. The space between –1 and –2 can be divided into sections of 3 because the fraction is in thirds, and it can be determined that $-\frac{4}{3}$ is located at point Z.

7. A: This problem focuses on identifying parts and coordinate points on a graph. The given coordinates are $(-2,5)$, which describe a point that is 2 units to the left of the origin, and 5 units above the x-axis. The point that fits this description and is located at $(-2,5)$ is point W.

8. D: This problem focuses on equivalent expressions using order of operations and exponents. There are many strategies that can be used to solve this problem. One way to solve this problem is to gradually simplify the expression and compare to the options. The first step to simplify the given expression is to simplify the exponents. The expression 5^3 is equivalent to many expressions, including $5 \cdot 5 \cdot 5$, $25 \cdot 5$, and 125. Each option includes an equivalent expression to 5^3. The next step to simplifying the expression is to multiply 4 and 7, which is 28. Option A shows the expression $(125 + 4) \cdot 13$, where addition is performed before multiplication when $7 + 6$ is solved before

184

multiplying 4 and 7. Option B shows the expression $(25 \cdot 5) + (4 \cdot 13)$ where, again, addition is performed before multiplication when $7 + 6$ is solved before multiplying 4 and 7. Option C shows the expression $(5 \cdot 5 \cdot 5) + (4 \cdot 7 \cdot 6)$ where the addition operation $7 + 6$ is changed to multiplication. Option D shows the expression $25 \cdot 5 + 34$ where each operation is performed in the correct order when the multiplication of 4 and 7 is performed and then 6 is added to the product.

9. D: This problem focuses on equivalent expressions using the associative and distributive properties. There are many ways to approach this problem. One place to start would be to use the distributive property and distribute the negative sign, or -1. This can be done because $3 - (x + 4)$ can also be written as $3 - 1(x + 4)$ and because we can distribute the -1 in this problem. This means that $3 - (x + 4)$ is equivalent to $3 - x - 4$ because $-1 \cdot x = -x$ and $-1 \cdot 4 = -4$.

10. D: This problem focuses on solving equations with one variable. To solve the equation $\frac{x}{24} = -6$, the goal is to isolate x, or have x alone on one side of the equal sign. To isolate x, each side of the equal sign should be multiplied by 24. $\frac{x}{24} = -6$ can be simplified to $24 \cdot \frac{x}{24} = -6 \cdot 24$, which is further simplified to $x = -144$.

11. C: To answer this question correctly, convert all numbers to decimal form to make them easy to compare. Since two of the numbers are already in decimal form, we only need to convert $1\frac{7}{10}$ and $1\frac{3}{4}$ to decimal form.

$$7 \div 10 = 0.7, \text{ so } 1\frac{7}{10} = 1.7$$
$$\text{and } 3 \div 4 = 0.75, \text{ so } 1\frac{3}{4} = 1.75$$

Therefore, by comparing place values from left to right of 1.7, 1.72, 1.75 and 1.695, we see that 1.695 is least, 1.7 is next greatest, 1.72 is next, and 1.75 is greatest. So, Antonio should buy the border that is $1\frac{3}{4}$ inches wide.

12. C: This problem involves finding equivalent fractions, decimals, and percentages. To solve this problem, each value in the list should be compared to identify if they are equivalent. 20% is equivalent to 0.2, but is not equivalent to $\frac{1}{20}$, which is equivalent to 5%. 15% is equivalent to $\frac{15}{100}$, but is not equivalent to 1.5, which is equivalent to 150%. $\frac{7}{20}$ is equivalent to $\frac{35}{100}$ which is equivalent to 35% and 0.35. 10% is equivalent to $\frac{1}{10}$ and 0.1, but it is not equivalent to 0.01.

13. B: The first step in solving $-2 - 3x = -14$ is to add 2 to both sides. This results in $-3x = -12$. Dividing both sides by -3 yields $x = 4$. Therefore, choice B is correct.

14. C: Subtracting 320 from both sides yields $-12m = -240$. Dividing both sides by -12 yields $m = 20$. Therefore, choice C is correct.

15. C: This problem focuses on testing equations with a known value in order to identify a variable. In this case, $x = -4$, so -4 will replace each x value to see if -4 is a solution. First, $25 \neq 5 \cdot -4$ because $5 \cdot -4 = -20$. Next, $-4 - 36 \neq 32$ because $-4 - 36 = -40$. Next, $\frac{68}{-4} = -17$ because $68 \div -4 = -17$. Last, $17 - (-4) \neq 13$ because $17 - (-4) = 17 + 4 = 21$.

185

16. B: The proportion can be written as $\frac{4}{2} = \frac{x}{18}$. Solving for x gives $x = 36$. Thus, there are 36 data analysis problems on the test.

17. C: This problem focuses on scale factors. According to the table, the population of cicadas increased each year. From year 1 to year 2, the population increased from 4 to 12 million. The population increased by a factor of 3 because $4 \cdot 3 = 12$. From year 2 to year 3, the population increased from 12 to 36 million; $12 \cdot 3 = 36$. From year 3 to year 4, $36 \cdot 3 = 108$. From year 4 to year 5, $108 \cdot 3 = 324$. Each year the population increases by a scale factor of 3.

18. B: The absolute value of -5 is 5 because the absolute value represents a number's distance from zero on a number line. The reciprocal of -5 is $-\frac{1}{5}$. The absolute value of 5 is 5. The opposite of -5 is also 5.

19. C: The score that has approximately 50% above and 50% below is approximately 500 (517 to be exact). The scores can be manually written by choosing either the lower or upper end of each interval and using the frequency to determine the number of times to record each score, i.e., using the lower end of each interval shows an approximate value of 465 for the median; using the upper end of each interval shows an approximate value of 530 for the median. A score of 500 (and the exact median of 517) is found between 465 and 530.

20. B: In order to determine the number of manuscripts each editor will review, the total number of manuscripts should be divided by the number of editors; $29 \div 8$ can be written as $\frac{29}{8}$, which simplifies to the mixed fraction $3\frac{5}{8}$. Notice that the quotient is 3 with a remainder of 5.

21. D: The order of operations requires evaluation of the expression inside the parentheses as a first step. Thus, the expression can be re-written as $-8^2 + 8 \times 4 + 7$. Next, the integer with the exponent must be evaluated. Doing so gives $-64 + 8 \times 4 + 7$. The order of operations next requires all multiplications and divisions to be computed as they appear from left to right. Thus, the expression can be written as $-64 + 32 + 7$. Finally, the addition may be computed as it appears from left to right. The expression simplifies to $-32 + 7$, or -25.

22. A: When setting up a proportion, it's important to remember that like quantities must be placed in the numerators, and like quantities must be placed in the denominators. The general idea for a problem like this is $\frac{\text{feet}}{\text{miles}} = \frac{\text{feet}}{\text{miles}}$. The correct proportion is $\frac{5,280}{1} = \frac{26,400}{x}$. Therefore, choice A is correct.

23. C: In the story, Allison is making lemonade and uses a ratio of 3 cups of sugar to every 2 gallons of water, or 3 : 2. A lemonade with the same sweetness would have a ratio that is equivalent to 3 : 2. One way to solve this problem is to find equivalent ratios using multiplication. 3 : 2 is equivalent to 6 : 4, 9 : 6, 12 : 8, 15 : 10, 18 : 12, 21 : 14, 24 : 16, and so on. 12 : 8 is equivalent to 3 : 2.

24. A: Multiply 24 by 4 to get 96 and multiply 12 by 6 to get 72. Then, add 96 and 72 to get the correct answer, 168.

25. A: In order to answer this question, we add the number of baseball and football cards to realize that there are 50 total cards in Castor's collection, 40 of which are baseball cards. To convert this to a decimal, we need to divide 40 by 50. This gives the correct answer, 0.8.

Practice Test #3

Writing

25 Minutes

Instructions: Read the following prompt, taking a few moments to plan a response. Then, write your response in essay form.

<u>Prompt</u>: *A professional athlete should be held to a higher standard in his or her personal life than the average citizen.*

Do you agree or disagree with this statement? Use examples from history, literature, or your own personal experience to support your point of view.

Quantitative

Read each question, perform the appropriate calculations, and determine the correct answer.

1. 148% is equivalent to what fraction?

a. $\dfrac{148}{1}$

b. $\dfrac{37}{25}$

c. $\dfrac{50}{74}$

d. $\dfrac{1}{148}$

2. The cost of tickets to a community event is shown in the table below. Which of the following is the unit rate?

Number of tickets	5	10	20	30
Cost ($)	30	60	120	180

a. $\dfrac{6}{1}$

b. $\dfrac{1}{6}$

c. $\dfrac{5}{1}$

d. $\dfrac{1}{5}$

3. Enrique used a formula to find the total cost, in dollars, for repairs he and his helper, Jenny, made to a furnace. The expression below shows the formula he used, with 4 being the number of hours he worked on the furnace and 2 being the number of hours Jenny worked on the furnace.

$$20 + 35(4 + 2) + 47$$

What is the total cost for repairing the furnace?

a. $189

b. $269

c. $277

d. $377

4. Triangle A has side lengths of 12 cm, 8 cm, and 16 cm. Triangle B is related to Triangle A by a scale factor of $\dfrac{1}{4}$. Which of the following represents the dimensions of Triangle B?

a. 4 cm, 2 cm, 8 cm

b. 2 cm, 3 cm, 8 cm

c. 3 cm, 2 cm, 4 cm

d. 6 cm, 4 cm, 8 cm

5. Sha is packaging cupcakes in packs of 12. Which expression does NOT express the relationship between packages, p, and cupcakes, c?

a. $12c = p$

b. $p = \dfrac{c}{12}$

c. $c = 12p$

d. $\dfrac{c}{p} = 12$

6. Elaine represents an equation using the algebra tiles shown below

Given that ▭ represents x, ▢ represents positive 1, and ▢ represents negative 1, which of the following represents the solution to the equation?

   a. $x = -6$
   b. $x = 4$
   c. $x = 12$
   d. $x = -4$

7. Petra installed 10 light fixtures at a new warehouse that was being built. Each of the fixtures required 3 light bulbs. The bulbs come in packages of 5 and cost $8 per package. What was the total cost for the bulbs required for all of the fixtures Petra installed at the warehouse?

   a. $16
   b. $48
   c. $120
   d. $240

8. A unit of liquid measure in the English System of Measure is the gill. The table, shown here, gives conversions from gills to fluid ounces.

Conversion Table

Gills	Fluid Ounces
2	8
4	16
5	20
6	24
10	40

Which equation best describes the relationship between gills, g, and fluid ounces, f?

   a. $f = 8g - 8$
   b. $f = 2g + 4$
   c. $f = 4g$
   d. $4f = g$

9. Two rectangles are similar. The length and the width of the first rectangle is 3 meters by 6 meters. The second rectangle is similar by a scale factor of $\frac{1}{2}$. What are length and width of the second rectangle?

   a. 1.5 meters by 3 meters
   b. 3.5 meters by 6.5 meters
   c. 6 meters by 12 meters
   d. 1 meter by 2.5 meters

189

10. Which of the following is the correct representation for the solution of $x + 2 = 5$?

a.

b.

c.

d.

11. Tommy is 4 years older than Gianna. Which equation represents the relationship between Tommy's age, t, and Gianna's age, g?

    a. $4 + t = g$
    b. $t = 4 + g$
    c. $4 - t = g$
    d. $g - t = 4$

12. Charlie wrote a story to match the graph below.

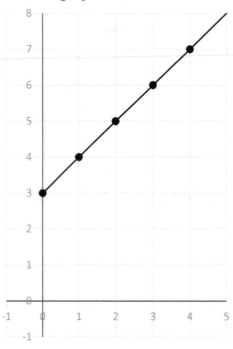

Which story below could be the story that Charlie wrote?

    a. Damien is 3 years older than Jackson.
    b. Damien sold 3 times as many candy bars as Jackson.
    c. Damien didn't make any money for 3 weeks and then made 1 dollar each week.
    d. Damien read 3 pages each day for 4 days.

13. In ΔRST, shown here, $m\angle S$ is 20° less than $m\angle R$.

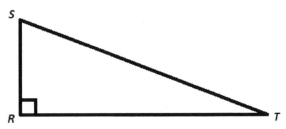

What is the measure of $\angle T$?
   a. 110°
   b. 70°
   c. 50°
   d. 20°

14. The dot plot shows the number of sandwiches sold each day by a sandwich shop.

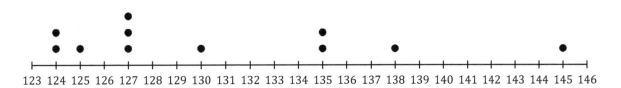

Which statement is best supported by the data?
   a. The sandwich shop sold 135 sandwiches more often than they sold 124 sandwiches.
   b. The sandwich shop sold more than 129 sandwiches on 5 days.
   c. The sandwich shop sold sandwiches for only 10 days.
   d. The sandwich shop sold fewer than 130 sandwiches exactly half of the time.

15. Kimi is saving to buy a pair of earbuds that cost $195. She makes money mowing lawns and earns $10 for each lawn she mows. Which inequality illustrates how many lawns, x, Kimi needs to mow to make at least $195?
   a. $195 < 10x$
   b. $195 > 10x$
   c. $195 \leq 10x$
   d. $195 \geq 10x$

16. A grocery store received a delivery of 250 apples. 14 apples from the delivery were rotten and could not be sold. Which equation could NOT be used to find the number of apples, a, that could be sold?
   a. $a - 14 = 250$
   b. $14 = 250 - a$
   c. $a = 250 - 14$
   d. $a + 14 = 250$

17. Four points are graphed on a coordinate plane.

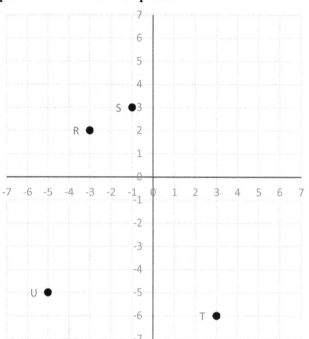

What ordered pair best represents point T?

    a. $(-3,6)$
    b. $(6,-3)$
    c. $(-6,3)$
    d. $(3,-6)$

18. A social media company creates 75 posts per hour. Which graph represents the relationship between the number of posts, y, and hours worked, x?

a.

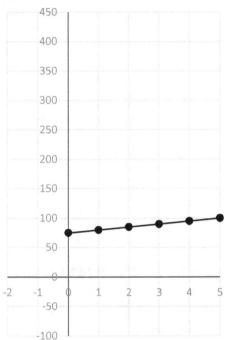

c.

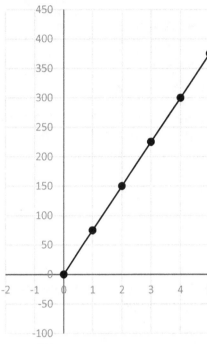

b.

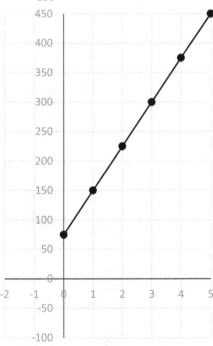

d.

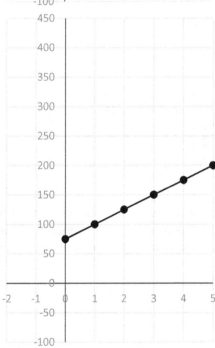

19. Which of the following options makes this inequality a true statement?

$$30b < 372$$

a. $b = 30$
b. $b = 22$
c. $b = 14$
d. $b = 12$

20. A round trip airline ticket costs $406. The airline Aidan is using charges $35 per checked bag. Which of the following equations represents the total cost for the ticket and checked bag(s)?

   a. $y = 35 + 406x$
   b. $y = 441x$
   c. $y = \frac{406}{35}x$
   d. $y = 406 + 35x$

21. Amanda has finished 80% of a grant proposal. Which of the following fractions represents the amount she has finished?

   a. $\frac{3}{4}$
   b. $\frac{7}{9}$
   c. $\frac{4}{5}$
   d. $\frac{6}{7}$

22. If 1 mile = 5,280 feet, which of the following proportions can be used to determine the number of miles equal to 26,400 feet?

   a. $\frac{5,280}{1} = \frac{26,400}{x}$
   b. $\frac{5,280}{1} = \frac{x}{26,400}$
   c. $\frac{5,280}{x} = \frac{26,400}{1}$
   d. $\frac{5,280}{26,400} = \frac{x}{1}$

23. Robert secures three new clients every eight months. After how many months has he secured 24 new clients?

   a. 64
   b. 58
   c. 52
   d. 66

24. Tanya is painting the kitchen wall and has chosen a paint mixture that has a ratio of 3 ounces of green paint to 8 ounces of white paint. To complete Tanya's paint order, how many ounces of green paint are in a container that has 192 ounces of white paint?

   a. 52
   b. 64
   c. 24
   d. 72

25. Which of the following statements is true regarding the circumference (C) and the diameter (d) of a circle?

   a. $\pi = C + d$
   b. $\pi = Cd$
   c. $\pi = \frac{C}{d}$
   d. $\pi = \frac{d}{C}$

Reading Comprehension

Read each passage closely and answer the associated questions. Be sure to choose the answer that BEST answers the question being asked.

Questions 1-4 refer to the following passage:

Protozoa are microscopic, one-celled organisms that can be free-living or parasitic in nature. They are able to multiply in humans, a factor which contributes to their survival and also permits serious infections to develop from just a single organism. Transmission of protozoa that live in the human intestine to another human typically occurs by a fecal-oral route (for example, contaminated food or water, or person-to-person contact). Protozoa that thrive in the blood or tissue of humans are transmitted to their human hosts by an arthropod vector (for example, through the bite of a mosquito or sand fly).

Helminths are large, multicellular organisms that are generally visible to the naked eye in their adult stages. Like protozoa, helminths can be either free-living or parasitic in nature. In their adult form, helminths cannot multiply in humans. There are three main groups of helminths (derived from the Greek word for worms) that are human parasites:

4. Flatworms (platyhelminths) – these include the trematodes (flukes) and cestodes (tapeworms).
5. Thorny-headed worms (acanthocephalins) – the adult forms of these worms reside in the gastrointestinal tract. The acanthocephala are thought to be intermediate between the cestodes and nematodes.
6. Roundworms (nematodes) – the adult forms of these worms can reside in the gastrointestinal tract, blood, lymphatic system or subcutaneous tissues. Alternatively, the immature (larval) states can cause disease through their infection of various body tissues.

1. As used in this passage, the word "parasite" means
   a. a person who lives in Paris
   b. an organism that live on or in another organism
   c. microscopic insects
   d. a person who takes advantage of the generosity of others

2. According to the passage, adult Roundworms can live in
   a. the arthropod vector
   b. fecal matter
   c. the subcutaneous tissue of humans
   d. contaminated water

3. You can infer from this passage that
   a. larval stages of parasites are more dangerous than the adult forms
   b. mosquitoes do not transmit parasites
   c. worms cannot infect humans
   d. clean sanitary conditions will keep you free of protozoa

4. According to the passage, which of the following is true?

> I. Protozoa live in the blood or tissue of humans.
> II. Adult helminthes cannot reproduce in humans.
> III. Adult thorny-headed worms live in the intestinal tract.

a. I only
b. II only
c. I and II only
d. I, II, and III

Questions 5-9 refer to the following passage:

What do you think is the biggest American holiday? The most significant and uniquely American holiday would have to be the Fourth of July, the day when the United States celebrates its independence from Britain. You might think that the Fourth of July became a holiday immediately after the signing of the Declaration of Independence on July 4, 1776, but actually it didn't become a tradition until after the War of 1812.

By the 1870s, the Fourth of July was the most important nonreligious holiday on the calendar. All across the country, on that day, towns and cities held celebrations with parades, barbecues, and fireworks displays.

Back in the 1870s, the Fourth of July was "the big event of the year," according to Nettie Spencer, a pioneer from Portland, Oregon. The holiday included a parade with floats, a band, and a speaker. "First, the speaker would challenge England to a fight and berate the King and say that he was a skunk. In the afternoon, we had what we called the 'plug uglies'--funny floats and clowns who took off on the political subjects of the day," said Spencer. At that time, the Fourth of July made people think about what it meant to be independent from Britain.

More than 200 years have passed since the signing of the Declaration of Independence, and our independence from Britain is sometimes taken for granted.

Today, the Fourth of July holiday is still a popular day for celebrations with family and friends. The holiday's importance has inspired the creation of everything from the lyrics to "Yankee Doodle Dandy" ("I'm a Yankee Doodle Dandy ...born on the Fourth of July...") to movies like *Independence Day*. America's independence has always been an important concept of our country, and Americans will protect it from I any and all challenges facing it.

5. The author wrote this passage to

a. tell about the Declaration of Independence
b. encourage the reader to watch movies about America's independence
c. give the reader the history of an American holiday
d. explain why America's independence from Britain is taken for granted

6. This passage is primarily about

a. the most important nonreligious holiday in America
b. how the Fourth of July did not become a tradition until after the War of 1812
c. how Americans will always protect their independence
d. how the Fourth of July no longer makes people think about independence from Britain

7. According to the passage, when did Americans first begin celebrating the Fourth of July?

   a. Immediately after signing the Declaration of Independence

   b. After the War of 1812

   c. In the 1870s

   d. Two hundred years after the Declaration of Independence was signed

8. The word "berate" in the third passage can best be replaced with

   a. compliment

   b. praise

   c. inform

   d. scold

9. The tone of this passage can best be described as

   a. confused

   b. neutral

   c. admiring

   d. condescending

Questions 10-13 refer to the following passage:

Nutria (Myocastor coypu) are large rodents that look like beavers with long, thin tails. Nutria may weigh up to 20 lbs. but on average weigh between 12-15 lbs. with males slightly larger than females. They have dense, grayish under-fur overlaid by long, glossy guard hairs that vary in color from dark brown to yellowish brown. Their large front teeth are yellow-orange to orange-red on the outer surface. The forepaws have four well-developed clawed toes and one non-functional toe. The hind feet have five clawed toes: four webbed and one that hangs free. Nutria have several other adaptations to help them in the water. Their eyes, ears and nostrils are set high on their heads. The nostrils and mouth have valves that seal out water while swimming, diving or feeding underwater. The female's teats are located high on her sides to allow the young to suckle while in the water. Nutria are primarily nocturnal (active at night), with peak activity occurring near midnight. When food is abundant, nutria rest and groom during the day and feed at night. When food is limited, daytime feeding increases, especially in wetlands free from disturbance.

Nutria inhabit fresh and brackish marshes, rivers, bayous, farm ponds, freshwater impoundments, drainage canals, swamps and various other types of wetlands. Although found in sixteen U.S. states, nutria are native to South America. Their original range includes Argentina, Chile, Bolivia, Uruguay, Paraguay and southern Brazil. After escaping from captivity in the U.S. and elsewhere, they now inhabit a much greater area. Nutria were first imported into the United States between 1899 and 1930 in an attempt to establish a fur farm industry. Many of the fur farms failed in the late 1940s because fur prices fell and nutria did not reproduce well in captivity. Many nutria were released into the wild. Nutria are now reported in every Maryland Eastern Shore county and are found from Bombay Hook National Wildlife Refuge in Delaware through the Delmarva Peninsula to Virginia's Eastern Shore. They have also been reported on the western shore of Maryland in the Potomac and Patuxent Rivers and in Virginia as far south as the Northern Neck near the Rappahanock River.

Nutria are highly prolific and breed all year. Reproductive peaks occur in late winter, early summer, and mid-autumn. Reproduction and survival may be influenced by extreme weather conditions. Nutria reach sexual maturity at four to six months. Sexually mature male nutria can breed throughout the year. Females are pregnant from 128 to 130 days and are ready to breed within forty-eight hours after giving birth. Litters average four to five young; however, nutria can have up to thirteen young per litter and may have three litters per year. Young are born fully furred and active, weighing 8 oz. at birth. They can swim and eat vegetation shortly thereafter, still feeding on mother's milk for up to eight weeks. Within five days of life, nutria can survive away from the mother.

10. Where would you most likely find this passage?

a. In a tourist guidebook
b. In a history textbook
c. In an online encyclopedia
d. In a comic book

11. It can be inferred from the passage that nutrias' eyes, ears, and nostrils are set high on their heads

a. so they can see their young while they are in the water
b. to prevent water from getting in them while they are swimming
c. so that they can eat at night
d. so that they are balanced with the rest of their body

12. According to the passage, how long does it take for nutria to reach sexual maturity?

a. 4 to 6 months
b. 128 to 130 days
c. 48 hours
d. 8 weeks

13. The author states that fur farms failed in the 1940s because

a. nutria were released into the wild
b. of limited amounts of food for the nutria
c. nutria are highly prolific
d. nutria did not reproduce well in captivity

Questions 14-18 refer to the following passage:

Born Ehrich Weiss, Harry Houdini was a master of illusion. Houdini earned an international reputation as an escape artist who dramatically freed himself from ropes, shackles, and handcuffs. He was married to Wilhelmina Rahner, who, as Beatrice Houdini, was his stage assistant. He performed on vaudeville and was also in many motion pictures.

In 1899, when Houdini decided to stop doing traditional magic and instead concentrate on escapes, his career took off. He created several dramatic escape tricks. In 1908, in St. Louis, Houdini introduced his escape from a giant milk can filled with water. It became a very popular trick and he took it on tour throughout the U.S., England, and Germany. What kind of escape could top this?

For his next escape, Houdini had to come up with something even more dramatic than the Giant Milk Can Escape, and he did. His new trick, which he began to perform in 1913, was known as the Upside Down Water Torture Cell. In this trick, Houdini's ankles were secured in a brace and he was put under water, upside down, and locked in place in full view of the audience. From this position, he freed himself and escaped from the water cell. Another escape was called the underwater burial. Houdini called this "the greatest feat I have ever attempted."

Some magicians might make a rabbit jump out of a hat or a bird disappear into thin air, but that was too easy for Houdini. He had to work with an elephant! In 1918, in the middle of the brightly lit stage of the Hippodrome Theater in New York City, Houdini made a 10,000-pound elephant named Jennie disappear. The act was called "The Vanishing Elephant," and when Houdini fired a pistol, Jennie vanished from view. Houdini had created a sensation. This incredible trick helped make Houdini a world-famous master of illusion.

14. The best title for this passage is

a. Hippodrome Theater
b. The Giant Milk Can Escape
c. The Master of Illusion
d. Rabbit in the Hat

15. The author wrote this passage to

a. inform the reader
b. entertain the reader
c. persuade the reader
d. humor the reader

16. Who was Beatrice Houdini?

a. A 10,000 pound elephant
b. Houdini's mother
c. The owner of Houdini's vaudeville show
d. Wilhelmina Rahner, Houdini's wife

17. According to the passage, what was Houdini's most sensational act?

a. The Giant Milk Can Escape
b. The Upside Down Water Torture Cell
c. The Vanishing Elephant
d. Escape from Handcuffs

18. Which word best replaces the word "feat" in the fourth paragraph without changing the meaning?

a. exploit
b. failure
c. discovery
d. surrender

Questions 19-22 refer to the following passage:

Volcanoes destroy and volcanoes create. The catastrophic eruption of Mount St. Helens on May 18, 1980, made clear the awesome destructive power of a volcano. Yet, over a time span longer than human memory and record, volcanoes have played a key role in forming and modifying the planet upon which we live. More than 80 percent of the earth's surface--above and below sea level--is of volcanic origin. Gaseous emissions from volcanic vents, scoring and shaping the earth over hundreds of millions of years, formed the earth's earliest oceans and atmosphere, and supplied the ingredients vital to generate and sustain life. Over geologic eons, countless volcanic eruptions have produced mountains, plateaus, and plains, which subsequent erosion and weathering have sculpted into majestic landscapes and fertile soils.

Ironically, these volcanic soils and inviting terrains have attracted people, and continue to attract people, to an existence on the flanks of volcanoes. Thus, as population density increases in regions of active or potentially active volcanoes, mankind must become increasingly aware of the hazards and learn not to "crowd" the volcanoes. People living in the shadow of volcanoes must live in harmony with them, expecting and planning for periodic violent unleashings of their pent-up energy.

19. According to the passage, how were the earth's early oceans and atmosphere formed?
   a. By gaseous emissions from volcanic vents
   b. Through erosion and weathering
   c. By volcanic eruptions
   d. By hurricanes

20. According to the context of the passage, "crowd" means
   a. a group of people gathered in one spot
   b. to press or throng into a space
   c. a group of people with something in common
   d. the common people

21. This passage would most likely be found in
   a. an almanac
   b. a science textbook
   c. a social studies textbook
   d. a novel

22. How does erosion and weathering affect the earth's surface?
   a. They create mountains and plateaus
   b. They create volcanic emissions
   c. They destroy the landscape
   d. They help to form fertile soils

Questions 23-27 refer to the following passage:

Jazz singer Billie Holiday, later nicknamed "Lady Day," was born on April 7, 1915, in Baltimore, Maryland. In her autobiography, "Lady Sings the Blues," Holiday says, "Mom and Pop were just a couple of kids when they got married; he was 18, she was

16, and I was three." Despite a challenging childhood and no formal musical training, Billie Holiday made her professional singing debut in Harlem nightclubs in 1931. By 1933, she had made her first recordings. Do you think her parents really named her "Billie?"

Born Eleanora Fagan, she gave herself the stage name Billie after Billie Dove, an early movie star. While becoming a star, Holiday faced racism. Laws at that time created separate facilities, public spaces, and seats on public buses for black people and, in the private sector, there were restaurants that would serve only white people. As a result, Holiday sometimes found herself singing in clubs that refused service to black people. Her 1939 version of "Strange Fruit," a song about lynching, was described in the album's liner notes as the most haunting and sad "expression of protest against man's inhumanity to man that has ever been made in the form of vocal jazz."

Billie Holiday worked with many jazz greats including Count Basie and Benny Goodman. She sang in small clubs, large concert halls, and in the film *New Orleans*. She even arranged and composed her own songs such as "I Love My Man" and "God Bless the Child." Many people mourned the loss of "Lady Day" when she died in New York at the age of 44.

23. The best title for this passage is
a. Mom and Pop
b. Harlem
c. Lady Day Sings the Blues
d. Jazz in the 1930s

24. According to the passage, which of the following is true?
I. Billie Holiday had no formal musical training.
II. Billie Holiday's parents were very young when they got married.
III. Billie Holiday sang in clubs that refused service to white people.

a. I only
b. II only
c. I and II only
d. I, II, and III

25. It can be inferred from the passage that Holiday
a. felt strongly about racism
b. despised her given name, Eleanora Fagan
c. preferred singing in large concert halls
d. died of a heart attack

26. The author wrote this passage to
a. tell a story
b. make the reader laugh
c. describe the life of a famous singer
d. convince the reader to buy a Billie Holiday CD

27. When did Billie Holiday make her professional singing debut in Harlem?

 a. 1915
 b. 1931
 c. 1933
 d. 1939

Questions 28-31 refer to the following passage:

When you think of a web, you probably don't think of earthworms, do you? What comes to mind? A spider web? The World Wide Web? How about a duck's webbed feet? Well, there's another kind of web you might not know about. It's the soil food web.

The soil food web is the set of organisms that work underground to help plants grow. There are billions of organisms that make up the soil food web. These include bacteria, fungi, protozoa, nematodes, arthropods and earthworms. Each type of organism plays an important role in keeping the soil healthy for all living things.

Earthworms eat just about every other organism in the soil. They're miniature topsoil factories—all the soil you have ever seen has passed through the stomachs of lots of earthworms. When they eat, they leave behind "castings," which are high in organic matter and plant nutrients and are a valuable fertilizer.

Earthworms move through the soil creating tunnels—areas that can be filled by air and water. Fields that are "tilled" by earthworm tunneling can absorb water at a rate 4 to 10 times that of fields without worm tunnels. This reduces water runoff, restores groundwater, and helps store more water for dry spells.

This burrowing also helps nutrients enter the subsoil at a faster rate and opens up pathways for roots to grow into. During droughts, the tunnels allow plant roots to penetrate more deeply, enabling them to reach the water they need to thrive.

Earthworms help keep soil healthy by moving organic matter from the surface into the soil. Normally, a tree leaf may take three to five years to decompose and be incorporated into the soil. In forests infested with night crawlers, this process can take as little as four weeks! By speeding up the breakdown of plant material, earthworms also speed up the rate at which nutrients are recycled back to the plants.

Earthworms and other soil organisms are a necessary part of the soil food web. Without them, all the organic matter would build up on the soil surface and never get down into the soil. To grow healthy, productive plants, you need healthy, productive soil. Organisms in the soil provide the food for plants—when they need it and in a form they can use!

28. The tone of this passage can be described as

 a. confused
 b. neutral
 c. mournful
 d. positive

29. Which of the following are part of the soil food web?

  I. bacteria
  II. protozoa
  III. nematodes

a. I only
b. II only
c. I and II only
d. I, II, and III

30. According to the context of the passage, "tilled" means

a. plowed
b. hardened
c. moistened
d. destroyed

31. What benefits do earthworms provide by burrowing in the soil?

a. They provide valuable fertilizer
b. They open pathways for roots to grow in
c. They slow the decomposition rate
d. They allow bacteria into the soil

Questions 32-36 refer to the following passage:

The Missouri territory came to the United States as part of the 1803 Louisiana Purchase, one of the best real estate deals the United States ever made. Before Missouri became the 24th state on August 10, 1821, certain compromises had to be made to keep a balance in the Union between the slave and non-slave states. Those compromises would later turn neighbor against neighbor.

Under the Missouri Compromise of 1820, designed by statesman Henry Clay, Missouri entered the Union as a slave state, and Maine entered as a free state, thus keeping the number of slave and non-slave states equal at 12 each.

John F. Smith recalled in an interview an incident when Jayhawkers, a group opposed to slavery, came to his house in 1861. One of the Jayhawkers threatened to shoot his father, a Missouri slave owner. "... (then) we heard a shout and looked up the road... The man dropped his gun to his side, when Judge Myers rode up, he was shaking his head and his eyes were blazing fire...All the Jayhawkers turned around and sulked off like whipped dogs."

The Civil War continued to divide Missourians. Although the state remained with the Union, some of its citizens chose to fight for the Confederacy. Smith's father and his rescuer, Judge Myers, remained best friends despite their conflicting views on slavery, but the two ended up fighting on opposite sides of the war.

32. This passage would most likely be found in a(n)

a. World history textbook
b. American history textbook
c. Ancient history textbook
d. Art history textbook

33. According to the passage, how did the Missouri Territory become part of the United States?

- a. Through the Missouri Compromise
- b. Through the defeat of the Confederacy
- c. Through the Louisiana Purchase
- d. As a result of a Jayhawkers revolt

34. What can you infer from the statement "Those compromises would later turn neighbor against neighbor" at the end of the first paragraph?

- a. All Missourians wanted a free state
- b. All Missourians wanted a slave state
- c. Missourians disagreed on the issue of slave ownership
- d. Neighbors were arguing over property lines

35. According to the passage, Jayhawkers were

- a. part of the Ku Klux Klan
- b. a slavery opposition group
- c. Confederate soldiers
- d. judges

36. What is the author most likely to discuss next?

- a. Missouri's role in the Civil War
- b. Different judges' rulings on slavery
- c. The biography of Henry Clay
- d. The history of the Jayhawkers

Questions 37-40 refer to the following passage:

Corals in the deep sea? When asked to describe corals, most people think of those that make up tropical, shallow-water reefs like the Great Barrier Reef. However, there are corals that live in much deeper, colder waters where there is no sunlight. Over the past 8 years, my colleagues and I have been studying these deep-sea corals in North Atlantic waters deeper than 1,000 meters.

Between 2003-2005, we visited a previously unexplored group of extinct underwater volcanoes in the western North Atlantic—the New England Seamounts and Corner Rise Seamounts—looking for deep-sea coral communities living between 1,000 and 2,500 meters. Our explorations revealed some spectacular assemblages of bamboo corals, bubblegum corals, black corals, and a variety of other sea fan and sea whip species.

Living amidst the corals were a myriad of animals, including shrimp, crabs, snake stars, sea stars, feather stars, scale worms and many species of deep-sea fish. Most of the species we found were new to science, while others (or their close relatives) were known only from the eastern North Atlantic and were being observed in the western Atlantic for the first time.

As a follow-up to those discoveries, we planned this expedition to explore the deep slopes of the northern Bahamas. In the western North Atlantic, a major deep-sea current flows from north to south along the slope of the continental USA, but as it approaches the tropics, it encounters deep, cold water flowing northward from

Antarctica. Our goal is to determine if the coral species, and their associated fauna, living in the subtropical Bahamas are the same as those on the seamounts to the north, or will we begin to see a different group of species reflecting a southern influence?

37. The best title for this passage is

a. Underwater Volcanoes
b. The Western North Atlantic
c. Bubblegum Coral
d. Coral Reefs in the Deep Sea

38. Deep sea coral reefs are unique because

a. they are less than 1,000 meters deep
b. they survive where there is no sunlight
c. they are found in tropical waters
d. they are composed of shallow water reefs

39. This passage was written in

a. first person
b. second person
c. third person
d. fourth person

40. What is the goal of the next expedition?

a. To reach deep-sea communities at 2,500 meters
b. To visit an unexplored group of extinct underwater volcanoes
c. To determine if the corals living in the Bahamas are the same as those on the seamounts to the north
d. To discover crabs, snake stars, sea stars, feather stars, and scale worms

Verbal

30 minutes, 60 questions

For questions 1-30: Select the synonym. Each question has a word in all capital letters followed by five answer choices in all lower-case letters. Select the answer choice with a definition closest to the capitalized word.

1. ENTHRALL:
- a. extreme
- b. fascinate
- c. devote
- d. bizarre

2. COWARD:
- a. gutless
- b. boor
- c. judge
- d. brave

3. NOVICE:
- a. expert
- b. nurse
- c. beginner
- d. naught

4. TEMPERATE:
- a. extreme
- b. lenient
- c. taut
- d. moderate

5. AUTHENTIC:
- a. genuine
- b. colorful
- c. flimsy
- d. laughable

6. SALVAGE:
- a. bless
- b. slobber
- c. swagger
- d. recover

7. VERNACULAR:
- a. poison
- b. language
- c. veracity
- d. ballad

8. ATTEST:

    a. bewitch

    b. accommodate

    c. vouch

    d. heed

9. DERELICT:

    a. abandoned

    b. corrupted

    c. dispirited

    d. depressed

10. ORDAIN:

    a. arrange

    b. create

    c. command

    d. adorn

11. HAUGHTY:

    a. obscure

    b. arrogant

    c. perilous

    d. bitter

12. LAPSE:

    a. prank

    b. margin

    c. error

    d. award

13. NAUSEATE:

    a. rival

    b. crave

    c. annoy

    d. repulse

14. PALTRY:

    a. cheap

    b. peaceful

    c. severely

    d. lurid

15. REFINED:

    a. aromatic

    b. blatant

    c. cultured

    d. frightened

16. VIRTUAL:

    a. real

    b. visible

    c. potent

    d. simulated

17. LOATHE:

    a. fear

    b. hate

    c. exist

    d. charge

18. MIMIC:

    a. recall

    b. delve

    c. imitate

    d. curtail

19. BRITTLE:

    a. fragile

    b. radical

    c. broad

    d. smooth

20. WRETCHED:

    a. wicked

    b. awry

    c. absorbed

    d. miserable

21. VEHEMENT:

    a. troubled

    b. intense

    c. changeable

    d. obstinate

22. DIATRIBE:

    a. criticism

    b. apology

    c. commend

    d. merit

23. COGITATE:

    a. surprise

    b. endanger

    c. confuse

    d. deliberate

24. INVIDIOUS:
a. offensive
b. pleasant
c. ornate
d. infectious

25. HYPERBOLE:
a. reference
b. amendment
c. exaggeration
d. demarcation

26. INNOCUOUS:
a. harmful
b. innocent
c. scandalous
d. hidden

27. CAPRICIOUS:
a. steady
b. unpredictable
c. pleasant
d. violent

28. INTERMITTENT:
a. occasional
b. intense
c. frequent
d. bursts

29. SOLITARY:
a. single
b. solid
c. sturdy
d. stoic

30. PRECIPITOUS:
a. rugged
b. dangerous
c. steep
d. wet

For questions 31-60: These questions ask you to identify and compare relationships between pairs of words. Select the answer that best completes the comparison.

31. surgeon is to operating room as
a. chiropractor is to doctor
b. novelist is to panel
c. conductor is to symphony hall
d. truck driver is to rest stop

32. opinionated is to indecisive as

    a.   diffident is to shy
    b.   frugal is to spendthrift
    c.   conspicuous is to obvious
    d.   thoughtful is to thought-provoking

33. pleased is to overjoyed as

    a.   dirty is to squalid
    b.   thrilled is to happy
    c.   determined is to decided
    d.   perceptive is to unaware

34. punitive is to punishment as

    a.   spatial is to measurement
    b.   exhausted is to sleep
    c.   perplexed is to answer
    d.   complimentary is to praise

35. considerable is to extensive as

    a.   enormous is to vacant
    b.   diminutive is to microscopic
    c.   outlandish is to undistinguished
    d.   descriptive is to straightforward

36. insipid is to boredom as

    a.   tasty is to craving
    b.   gratuitous is to freedom
    c.   morose is to rebellion
    d.   jovial is to optimistic

37. sedentary is to sit as

    a.   descry is to lampoon
    b.   espoused is to belief
    c.   perseverance is to endurance
    d.   peripatetic is to wander

38. querulous is to amiable as

    a.   sequential is to serial
    b.   ponderous is to insubstantial
    c.   illicit is to forbidden
    d.   pugnacious is to truculent

39. abstemious is to restraint as

    a.   discerning is to awareness
    b.   servile is to aggression
    c.   avowal is to affirm
    d.   exhilarate is to enlivened

40. Motorcycle is to bicycle as speedboat is to:

  a. Motor
  b. Paddleboat
  c. Float
  d. Transportation

41. Apple is to seed as person is to

  a. Parent
  b. Embryo
  c. Nourishment
  d. Cell

42. Fraction is to whole as slice is to

  a. Pie
  b. Cut
  c. Part
  d. Element

43. Temperature is to heat as pound is to

  a. Weight
  b. Height
  c. Measurement
  d. Heavy

44. Bank is to savings as safe is to

  a. Valuables
  b. Combination
  c. Crack
  d. Vault

45. Island is to sea as star is to

  a. Light
  b. Night
  c. Celestial
  d. Space

46. Inattention is to accidents as practice is to

  a. Improvement
  b. Performance
  c. Discipline
  d. Repetition

47. Sight is to sense as gravity is to

  a. Weight
  b. Pounds
  c. Distance
  d. Force

48. Dexterity is to skill as English is to

a. Language
b. Literature
c. Japanese
d. Linguistics

49. Coach is to team as teacher is to

a. Knowledge
b. School
c. Students
d. Principal

50. Article is to magazine as chapter is to

a. Verse
b. Book
c. Number
d. Paragraph

51. House is to neighborhood as tree is to

a. leaf
b. timber
c. forest
d. limb

52. Wallet is to money as envelope is to

a. mail
b. letter
c. address
d. post office

53. German shepherd is to dog as strawberry is to

a. red
b. vine
c. seeds
d. fruit

54. Joyful is to sad as empty is to

a. bare
b. crowded
c. productive
d. vacant

55. Automobile is to garage as dish is to

a. plate
b. food
c. cupboard
d. spoon

56. Doctor is to medicine as teacher is to

    a. student
    b. teaching
    c. education
    d. school

57. Chirp is to tweet as jump is to

    a. leap
    b. rope
    c. high
    d. street

58. Sleeping is to tired as drinking is to

    a. glass
    b. thirsty
    c. swallow
    d. water

59. Four-leaf clover is to luck as arrow is to

    a. bow
    b. Cupid
    c. shoot
    d. direction

60. Question is to answer as problem is to

    a. mathematics
    b. solution
    c. worry
    d. trouble

Quantitative

Read each question, perform the appropriate calculations, and determine the correct answer.

1. André drew a data table that represents the relationship between x and y where $y = 3x$. Which table could NOT be the data table that André drew?

a.

x	1	3	5
y	3	6	8

b.

x	2	4	6
y	6	12	18

c.

x	1.5	2	2.5
y	4.5	6	7.5

d.

x	1	10	50
y	3	30	150

2. Simplify the expression.

$$\frac{(-9 + 3)}{2}$$

a. 6
b. −6
c. 3
d. −3

3. Tavario made 32 t-shirts for his customers and is packaging them in sets of 4. He wants to know how many packages he will have. Which option is NOT a way that Tavario can express this division problem?

a. $4\overline{)32}$
b. $\frac{4}{32}$
c. $32 \div 4$
d. 32 divided by 4

4. Which equation CANNOT be used to find the area of a square?

a. $A = s^2$
b. $A = s \cdot s$
c. $A = s + s + s + s$
d. $A = bh$

5. Which of the following expressions is equivalent to $2(a + 3) + 3a + 4$?

    a. $5a + 10$
    b. $5a + 7$
    c. $4a + 10$
    d. $12a$

6. The table shows the rate a babysitter charges for babysitting services.

Hours	Dollars
3	30
5	50
6	60
8	80

Which best represents the dependent variable in the table?

    a. Hours
    b. Dollars
    c. Dollars per hour
    d. $10 per hour

7. What is the measure of angle A?

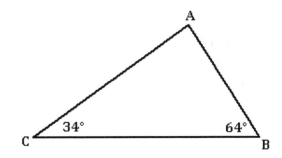

    a. 86°
    b. 82°
    c. 78°
    d. 92°

8. The table shows a relationship between s and t, where s is the independent value.

s	t
1	4
2	8
7	28
9	36

Which equation represents the relationship between s and t?

a. $s = t + 4$
b. $s = 4t$
c. $t = 4s$
d. $t = s + 4$

9. Jordan owns a jewelry business and listed the wire options for their customers below using fraction measurements.

$$\frac{1}{8}, \frac{1}{4}, \frac{3}{8}, \frac{1}{2}$$

Which list correctly lists the wire options in decimal form?

a. 0.12, 0.25, 0.266, 0.5
b. 1.8, 1.4, 3.8, 1.2
c. 0.8, 0.4, 0.38, 0.2
d. 0.125, 0.25, 0.375, 0.5

10. The list below represents a set of data points.

1, 1, 1, 2, 2, 2, 0, 1, 1, 1, 2, 2, 2, 0, 0, 0, 2, 1, 1, 1

What is the mode of the data set?

a. 0
b. 1
c. 1.5
d. 2

11. The length of a classroom is 7.3 meters. Which length is equivalent to 7.3 meters?

a. 0.0073 kilometers
b. 7,300 centimeters
c. 0.073 kilometers
d. 73 millimeters

12. A recipe calls for 5 cups of flour for every 2 cups of sugar. Azah wrote a proportion to find the amount of sugar needed with 8 cups of flour. Which proportion could Azah have written?

a. $\frac{2}{5} = \frac{8}{x}$
b. $\frac{2}{8} = \frac{x}{5}$
c. $\frac{5}{8} = \frac{2}{x}$
d. $\frac{5}{2} = \frac{8}{x}$

13. Nadia is working summer jobs. She earns $5 for every dog she walks, $2 for bringing back a trashcan, $1 for checking the mail, and $5 for watering the flowers. Nadia walks 3 dogs, brings back 5 trashcans, checks the mail for 10 neighbors, and waters the flowers at 6 houses. Which expression can be used to find out how much money Nadia earned?

    a. $2(5) +$6(10) + $1
    b. $10(6) + $1 + $5
    c. $5(3+6) + $2(5) + $1(10)
    d. $15 + $10 + $16

14. The dimensions of a trapezoid are given in centimeters.

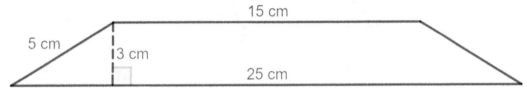

What is the area of the trapezoid?

    a. 100 cm^2
    b. 60 cm^2
    c. 21.5 cm^2
    d. 22.5 cm^2

15. Jason wants to put dry fertilizer on the grass in his front yard. The yard is 20 feet wide and 45 feet long. Each pound of the fertilizer he plans to use is enough for 150 square feet. Which procedure could Jason use to determine the correct amount of fertilizer to use on the entire yard?

    a. Divide 150 by 20 and divide 150 by 45, and then add those quotients together
    b. Add 20 and 45, double that total, and then divide that total by 150
    c. Multiply 20 by 45, and then subtract 150 from that product
    d. Multiply 20 by 45, and then divide that product by 150

16. Which statement is true about the examples below?

Example 1	Example 2
$2x + 4 - x$	$2x - x = -4$

    a. Example 1 is an equation and Example 2 is an equation.
    b. Example 1 is an expression and Example 2 is an expression.
    c. Example 1 is an expression and Example 2 is an equation.
    d. Example 1 is an equation and Example 2 is an expression.

17. Steven has $50 to buy snacks for his party. He plans to spend $10 on soda and the rest on pizza. If each pizza costs $8, which of the following inequalities represent the number (n) of pizzas Steven can buy?

    a. $50n \geq 8n - 10$
    b. $8n + 10 \leq 50$
    c. $10n - 8 \leq 50$
    d. $8n \leq 50 - 10n$

18. What is the volume of this rectangular prism?

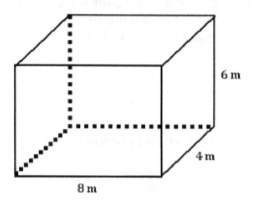

6 m

4 m

8 m

    a. 18 m³
    b. 192 m³
    c. 206 m³
    d. 186 m³

19. Which of the following describes all requirements of similar polygons?

    a. Similar polygons have congruent corresponding angles and proportional corresponding sides
    b. Similar polygons have congruent corresponding angles and congruent corresponding sides
    c. Similar polygons have proportional corresponding sides
    d. Similar polygons have congruent corresponding angles

20. Elyse wrote a list of values.

$$0.23, \frac{20}{100}, 45\%, 0.6, \frac{2}{5}$$

Which list correctly orders the values from greatest to least?

    a. $45\%, \frac{2}{5}, \frac{20}{100}, 0.6, 0.23$
    b. $0.6, 45\%, \frac{2}{5}, 0.23, \frac{20}{100}$
    c. $0.6, 45\%, 0.23, \frac{2}{5}, \frac{20}{100}$
    d. $45\%, 0.6, \frac{2}{5}, 0.23, \frac{20}{100}$

21. In the formula for the volume of the figure shown below, written as $V = B \cdot h$, h represents the height of the prism when it rests one of its bases. What does the B represent?

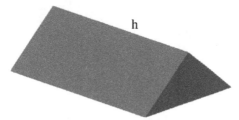

a. $\frac{1}{3}bh$, where b represents the length of the triangle's base and h represents the triangle's height
b. bh, where b represents the length of the triangle's base and h represents the triangle's height
c. $2bh$, where b represents the length of triangle's base and h represents the triangle's height
d. $\frac{1}{2}bh$, where b represents the length of triangle's base and h represents the triangle's height

22. The table shows the portion of bowls of food each puppy ate at a doggy day camp.

Puppy Food Chart	
Puppy Name	**Portion of bowls eaten**
Athena	$\frac{2}{5}$
Buddy	$\frac{7}{8}$
Rufus	80%
Sparky	33%
Spot	$\frac{3}{4}$

Which list shows the puppies in order from greatest to least amount of food eaten?
a. Buddy, Rufus, Spot, Athena, Sparky
b. Sparky, Athena, Spot, Rufus, Buddy
c. Sparky, Athena, Rufus, Buddy, Spot
d. Buddy, Rufus, Athena, Spot, Sparky

23. Which of the following statements is true for this set of similar triangles?

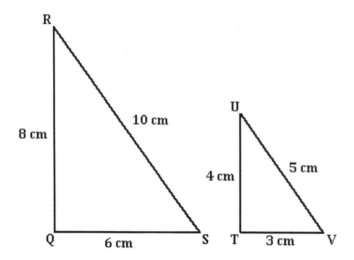

a. $\dfrac{RQ}{RS} = \dfrac{UT}{TV}$

b. $\dfrac{RS}{QS} = \dfrac{UV}{UT}$

c. $\dfrac{QS}{RS} = \dfrac{TV}{UV}$

d. $\dfrac{RQ}{QS} = \dfrac{UT}{UV}$

24. Which of the following statements is true?

a. All triangles are similar.
b. All trapezoids are similar.
c. All polygons are similar.
d. All squares are similar.

25. Bella is limiting her social media time to no more than 420 minutes per week. If she spends the same amount of time on social media each day, which inequality describes all possible numbers of m minutes Bella could spend each day of the week on social media?

a. $60 \geq m$
b. $60 \leq m$
c. $60 < m$
d. $60 > m$

Answer Key and Explanations for Test #3

Quantitative

1. B: This problem focuses on equivalent fractions and percentages. A percentage is a part out of 100, so 148% is equivalent to $\frac{148}{100}$. This fraction can be simplified by dividing the numerator and denominator by the greatest common factor. $\frac{148}{100} = \frac{148 \div 4}{100 \div 4} = \frac{37}{25}$.

2. A: The unit rate is determined by the ratio $\frac{\text{Cost}(\$)}{\text{Number of tickets}}$. Using the data from the first column from the table, the unit rate is $\frac{30}{5}$ or $\frac{6}{1}$. Therefore, choice A is correct.

3. C: To solve this formula, follow the order of operations. First, add what is in the parenthesis, 4 + 2, to get 6. Then, multiply the 6 by 35 to get 210. Last, we should add 20 + 210 + 47 to get 277.

4. C: Since the lengths of Triangle B are related to the lengths of Triangle A by a scale factor of $\frac{1}{4}$, each side length of Triangle A should be multiplied by the factor $\frac{1}{4}$: $12 \times \frac{1}{4} = 3$; $8 \times \frac{1}{4} = 2$; $16 \times \frac{1}{4} = 4$. The side lengths of Triangle B measure 3 cm, 2 cm, and 4 cm, respectively.

5. A: If each package holds 12 cupcakes, the relationship between packages and cupcakes is that the number of cupcakes is 12 times the number of packages. This can be expressed by many equivalent equations: $c = 12p$, $p = \frac{c}{12}$, "and" $\frac{c}{p} = 12$. $12c = p$ would express the reverse relationship, that the number of packages is 12 times the number of cupcakes.

6. B: The equation represented by the algebra tiles is $3x - 8 = 4$. Solving for x gives $3x = 12$, so $x = 4$. The equation can be visually solved by adding 8 green tiles to each side, and using the additive inverse property to isolate the $3x$. The equation can then be written as $3x = 12$. Each x can be mapped to 4 positive integer tiles. Thus, $x = 4$.

7. B: To answer this question, find the total number of bulbs required by multiplying 10 by 3. The number of packages of bulbs required can be found by dividing this total number of bulbs, 30, by 5, to find that 6 packages are needed. Then, multiplying 6 by the cost per package, 8, we find that the total cost for all the bulbs needed was $48.

8. C: Looking at the chart, a pattern can be seen in the relationship between the number of gills and the number of fluid ounces. Each number of gills in the first column, when multiplied by 4, gives the number of fluid ounces in the second column. So, f equals 4 times g, or $f = 4g$.

9. A: Since the scale factor is less than 1, the second rectangle is smaller than the first rectangle. To find the dimensions of the second rectangle, multiply each dimension of the first rectangle by $\frac{1}{2}$ or 0.5. Since (0.5)(3) is 1.5, and (0.5)(6) is 3, the dimensions of the second rectangle are 1.5 meters by 3 meters. Therefore, choice A is correct.

10. A: The equation $x + 2 = 5$ can be solved by subtracting 2 from both sides of the equation. This results in $x = 3$. This is represented by a solid circle at 3 on a number line. Therefore, choice A is correct.

221

11. B: Tommy's age is 4 more than Gianna's age. For example, if Tommy is 13 years old, Gianna is 9 years old. Tommy's age, t, is Gianna's age, g, plus 4. The equation $t + 4 = g$ is the only equation listed that represents the relationship in the story.

12. A: This problem focuses on writing situations to match a graph. There are many strategies that can be used to solve this problem. One strategy is to identify an equation to match the graph and then match the story to the equation. The graph includes the points (0,3), (1,4), (2,5), (3,6), and (4,7) where each y value is 3 more than each x value. The equation that matches the graph is $y = x + 3$. The story that represents the relationship is option A, where Damien is 3 years older than Jackson.

13. D: The box symbol shown at $\angle R$ means that $\angle R$ measures 90°. Since we are told $m\angle S$ is 20° less than $m\angle R$, subtract 90 –20 to get 70. This means that $m\angle S$ = 70°. The sum of $m\angle R$ and $m\angle S$ is found by adding: 90 +70 = 160. The sum of all angles in a triangle always adds up to 180°, so subtracting 180 – 160 results in a difference of 20. So, $m\angle T$ is 20°.

14. B: This problem focuses on interpreting data from a dot plot. Based on the data, the sandwich shop sold 135 sandwiches on two days and sold 124 sandwiches on two days, so the first statement is not supported by the data. The sandwich shop sold more than 129 sandwiches on 5 days, so the second statement is supported by the data. The sandwich shop sold sandwiches for 11 days, so the third statement is not supported by the data. The sandwich shop sold fewer than 130 sandwiches $\frac{6}{11}$ of the times, so the fourth statement is not supported by the data.

15. C: If Kimi makes $10 for each lawn, where x is the number of lawns, then the expression $10x$ describes the number of dollars Kimi makes. If the earbuds Kimi wants cost $195, she needs at least $195 to buy the earbuds. If Kimi needs at least $195, that means that she can make more than $195 to get the earbuds but cannot make less than $195. This means that the number of dollars made, $10x$, must be more than or equal to $195. The expression that represents this is $10x \geq 195$, or $195 \leq 10x$.

16. A: This problem focuses of writing equations that represent a problem. If a grocery store received 250 apples and 14 could not be sold, $250 − 14$ equals the number of apples that can be sold. This means that $a = 250 − 14$. Two equivalent equations to $a = 250 − 14$ are $a + 14 = 250$ and $250 − a = 14$.

17. D: This problem focuses on identifying the ordered pair representation of a point on a coordinate plane. Point T is located 3 units to the right of the origin and 6 units down from the x-axis, so the ordered pair that best represents point T is (3, −6).

18. C: This problem focuses on graphs that represent relationships in a story. If a company creates 75 posts each hour, the equation that represents the story is $y = 75x$, where each y value is 75 times the corresponding x value. This means that after 0 hours, the company would create 0 posts. After 1 hour, the company would create 75 posts. After 2 hours, the company would create 150 posts, and so on. Graph C is the only graph that appropriately represents this relationship.

19. D: This problem can be solved by substituting each option into the inequality: substituting $b = 12$ results in $(30)(12) < 372$, or $360 < 272$, which is a true statement. Alternatively, solve the inequality for b by dividing both sides by 30, which yields $b < 12.4$; of the choices, only 12 is less than 12.4. Therefore, choice D is correct.

20. D: The total cost y includes the constant price of the airline ticket plus the price of the baggage, which varies depending on the number of checked bags. The total cost y can be represented by the equation $y = 406 + 35x$, where x represents the number of checked bags

21. C: The fraction $\frac{4}{5}$ can be converted to a decimal by dividing 4 by 5. Doing so gives 0.80, which is equal to 80%.

22. A: When setting up a proportion, it's important to remember that like quantities must be placed in the numerators, and like quantities must be placed in the denominators. The general idea for a problem like this is $\frac{\text{feet}}{\text{miles}} = \frac{\text{feet}}{\text{miles}}$. The correct proportion is $\frac{5,280}{1} = \frac{26,400}{x}$. Therefore, choice A is correct.

23. A: The following proportion can be used to solve the problem: $\frac{3}{8} = \frac{24}{x}$. Solving for x gives: $3x = 192$, which simplifies to $x = 64$.

24. D: This problem focuses on equivalent ratios. The ratio of green to white paint is $3 : 8$, so solving the equation $3 : 8 = x : 192$ will provide the number of ounces of green paint to 192 ounces of white paint. $8 \cdot 24 = 192$, and $3 \cdot 24 = 72$, so $3 : 8 = 72 : 192$. There are 72 ounces of green paint to every 192 ounces of white paint in the paint mixture that Tanya ordered.

25. C: The ratio of the circumference of a circle to the diameter of the circle is pi. This can be written as $\frac{C}{d} = \pi$. Therefore, choice C is correct.

Reading Comprehension

1. B: As used in this passage, the word "parasite" means an organism that lives on or in another organism, Choice B. Choice A and C are obviously wrong, since the passage mentions nothing of Paris or insects. Choice D is another definition for "parasite," but does not fit the context of the word used in this passage.

2. C: According to the description of Roundworms, they can live in the subcutaneous tissue of humans, Choice C. Choices A, B, and D describe where protozoa live and how they are transmitted.

3. D: According to the first paragraph, protozoa are transmitted through food and water contaminated by fecal matter. It can then be inferred that clean sanitary conditions will prevent the spread of protozoa, Choice D. Choice A is an incorrect inference because the passage discusses both larval and adult forms of parasites that infect humans. Choice B is an incorrect inference, since the first paragraph states that protozoa are transmitted by mosquitoes. Choice C is an incorrect inference because the second paragraph is about worms that infect humans.

4. D: To answer this question, you will need to verify all three statements in the passage. All three of these statements are true and are supported by the passage.

5. C: This passage was written to give the reader the history of the American holiday, the Fourth of July, Choice C. With regard to Choice A, the Declaration of Independence is mentioned in the passage, but the main purpose of the passage does not focus on it. The same is true for Choice B. The passage does talk about movies associated with the Fourth of July, but the main purpose of the passage is not to encourage the reader to watch those movies. In Choice D, the passage does mention that independence from Britain is taken for granted, but the passage does not explain why.

6. A: This passage is primarily about the most popular American holiday, the Fourth of July, Choice A. The passage does relate to some extent to the other choices, but these do not reflect the main idea of the passage.

7. B: This detailed question offers four time periods mentioned in the passage as possible answer choices. Use caution when choosing the answer. Look back at the passage. The end of paragraph one offers the correct choice, Choice B.

8. D: As used in this passage, "berate" means to scold or rebuke, Choice D. Choices A and B are antonyms. Choice C does not fit the meaning.

9. C: The last sentence of the passage gives the best clue to the tone of the passage: "American independence has always been an important concept in our country, and Americans will protect it from any and all challenges facing it." Of the four options given, *admiring* would best describe the tone.

10. C: You could possibly find this passage in a tourist guidebook, Choice A, but you would most likely find the passage in an online encyclopedia, Choice C. Choices B and D can be eliminated, since a history text book and a comic book are the least likely choices.

11. B: The passage explains that nutria have several adaptations to help them in the water. The logical inference is that their eyes, ears, and nostrils are high on their heads to prevent water from entering them while they are swimming, Choice B.

12. A: Use caution when answering this detailed question, since all the choices given are quantitative possibilities used in the passage. According to the third paragraph, nutria reach sexual maturity in four to six months, Choice A.

13. D: Look back to the passage to answer this detailed question. According to the second paragraph, fur farms failed due to the drop in prices of fur and nutrias' failure to reproduce well in captivity, Choice D.

14. C: This passage is about Harry Houdini. In both the first paragraph and the last paragraph, the author refers to Houdini as a master of illusion. The best choice is Choice C. Choices A and D are both mentioned in the passage, but are not the main idea of the passage. Although Choice B seems like a possibility because a whole paragraph focuses on the escape, several other escapes are also described, making this a poor choice.

15. A: This passage gives facts and details about the life of Harry Houdini and was written in order to inform the reader, Choice A. Although the passage could be considered entertaining, its main purpose is to inform. There are no persuasive techniques used in the passage, nor is it humorous, making Choices C and D incorrect.

16. D: According to the first paragraph, Beatrice Houdini was Harry Houdini's stage assistant and wife, Choice D.

17. C: To answer this detail question, look back at the passage. The last paragraph states that "Houdini had created a sensation" with The Vanishing Elephant act, Choice C. Choices A and B are acts discussed in the passage, but they are not described as his most sensational. Choice D is not an actual act discussed in the passage, and therefore, an incorrect choice.

18. A: Choice A, "exploit" is a synonym for "feat." Choice B, "failure," is an antonym. Choices C and D do not fit the context of the sentence. The correct answer is Choice A.

19. A: The first paragraph describes how gaseous emissions from volcanic vents formed the early oceans and atmosphere, Choice A.

20. B: Although all of the answer choices point to the word "crowd," Choice B is the only logical choice based how the word is used in the context of the passage.

21. B: Of the choices given, this passage would most likely be found in a science textbook, Choice B.

22. D: The second paragraph states that erosion and weathering have sculpted "majestic landscapes and formed fertile soils", Choice D.

23. C: The best title for this passage is Choice C. The first paragraph tells the reader that Billie Holiday's nickname was Lady Day. The entire passage focuses on her career as a Jazz singer.

24. C: To answer this question, you will need to find supporting statements in the passage. Only the first two statements are supported by the passage, Choice C.

25. A: The second paragraph describes the racism that blacks were facing in the 1930s. It supports this inference, stating that one of Holiday's songs was a sad "expression of protest against man's inhumanity to man that has ever been made in the form of vocal jazz." There is no support in the passage for the other three answer choices. Choice A is the correct answer.

26. C: The purpose of this passage is to inform the reader. Choice C is the correct answer.

27. B: The answer choices are all dates from the passage. Refer back to the passage to check each date. The first paragraph gives the correct answer, Choice B.

28. D: Scan the passage for words that reveal how the author feels about the subject. The author states that Earthworms have an "important role" and play a "necessary part" in the soil food web. These words have a positive connotation. The last paragraph also exudes a positive feeling towards earthworms. Choice D is the correct answer.

29. D: To answer this question, you will need to verify all three options in the passage. The second paragraph lists all three organisms as members of the soil food web, Choice D.

30. A: To till means to plow or cultivate, Choice A. The other answer choices do not fit the context of the sentence.

31. B: According to the fifth paragraph, burrowing helps nutrients enter the subsoil at a faster rate and opens up pathways for roots to grow into, Choice B.

32. B: Because this passage is about how the Missouri Territory became a part of the United States, the most likely place to find this passage is in an American history textbook, Choice B.

33. C: According to the first paragraph, the Missouri Territory became part of the United States through the 1803 Louisiana Purchase, Choice C.

34. C: First, determine what the compromise was. According to the passage, compromises had to be made to keep a balance in the Union between the slave and non-slave states. An accurate inference would be that Missourians disagreed on the issue of slavery, Choice C.

35. B: According to the third paragraph, Jayhawkers were members of a group opposed to slavery.

36. A: All the answer choices are related to the passage in some way. However, the last paragraph of the passage begins discussing Missourians and the Civil War. The most logical choice, then, would be Choice A, a continued discussion of Missouri's role in the Civil War.

37. D: Although the first three answer choices are mentioned in the passage, the last answer choice is best in summarizing the passage as a whole. The correct answer is choice D.

38. B: All choices, except Choice B, describe shallow water coral reefs. According to the passage, deep sea coral reefs are found where sunlight does not reach, making them unique. The correct answer is Choice B.

39. A: This passage was written in the first-person format. The author refers to himself or herself with the pronouns "we" and "I." A passage written in second person would include the pronouns "you." A passage written in the third person would have a narrator telling the story, but not part of the events. There is no fourth person narrative. The correct answer is Choice A.

40. C: Answer Choices A, B, and D all refer back to the first expedition. The end of the passage clearly states that the next goal is to "determine if the coral species, and their associate fauna, living in the subtropical Bahamas are the same as those on the seamounts to the north." The correct answer is Choice C.

Verbal

1. B: To enthrall is to fascinate or mesmerize.

2. A: A coward is someone who is gutless, or lacks courage when facing danger.

3. C: A novice is someone who is new to the circumstances, or a beginner.

4. D: Temperate means to be moderate or restrained.

5. A: Something authentic is genuine or true.

6. D: To salvage something is to save or recover it from wreckage, destruction or - loss.

7. B: Vernacular is the speech or language of a place.

8. C: To attest is to vouch for or to certify.

9. A: Derelict means to be neglected or abandoned, e.g., "a derelict old home."

10. C: To ordain is to order or command.

11. B: To be haughty is to be proud or arrogant.

12. C: A lapse is an error or mistake, e.g., "a lapse of memory."

13. D: To nauseate is to disgust or repulse.

14. A: Something paltry is cheap, base, or common.

15. C: To be refined is to be cultured and well-bred.

16. D: Virtual means to be simulated, especially as related to computer software.

17. B: To loathe is to hate or abhor.

18. C: When you mimic, you imitate or copy someone or something.

19. A: Something brittle is fragile and easily damaged or destroyed.

20. D: Wretched means miserable or woeful.

21. B: Vehement most closely means the same thing as intense.

22. A: Diatribe most closely means the same thing as criticism.

23. D: Cogitate most closely means the same thing as deliberate.

24. A: Invidious most closely means the same thing as offensive.

25. C: Hyperbole most closely means the same thing as exaggeration.

26. B: Innocuous most closely means the same thing as innocent.

27. B: The word "capricious" means "unpredictable" or "changeable."

28. A: The word "intermittent" also means "occasional" or "discontinuous."

29. A: Solitary can mean a number of different things, but one meaning is single. For example, if you said there was a solitary tree in a yard, you would mean that there was a single tree.

30. C: The word "precipitous" means "steep."

31. C: The relationship sought is one of a professional to the place in which he/she performs his/her professional work. The only answer that has that relationship is that of conductor to symphony hall.

32. B: The relationship sought is that of antonyms. The only answer that has that relationship is that of frugal to spendthrift.

33. A: The relationship sought is one of an adjective to another adjective that is a stronger form of the first word. The only answer that has that relationship is that of dirty to squalid.

34. D: The relationship sought is one of an emotional state to the action taken as a result of being in that state. The only answer that has that relationship is that of complimentary to praise.

35. B: The relationship sought is that of synonyms. The only answer that has that relationship is that of diminutive to microscopic.

36. A: The relationship sought is one of an adjective to the state of mind something modified by that adjective creates. The only answer that has that relationship is that of tasty to craving.

37. D: The relationship sought is one of an adjective to the action which the state of being described by the adjective necessitates. The only answer that has that relationship is that of peripatetic to wander.

38. B: The relationship sought is that of antonyms. The only answer that has that relationship is that of ponderous to insubstantial.

39. A: The relationship sought is that of an adjective and an action or state of being exhibited by one accurately described by that adjective. The only answer that has that relationship is that of discerning to awareness.

40. B: A motorcycle is a motorized bicycle; a speedboat is a motorized paddleboat.

41. B: An apple develops from a seed; a person develops from an embryo.

42. A: A fraction is a part of a whole; a slice is a part of a pie.

43. A: Temperature is used to measure heat; pounds are used to measure weight.

44. A: A bank is a place to keep one's savings; a safe is a place to keep one's valuables.

45. D: An island is surrounded by the sea; a star is surrounded by space.

46. A: Inattention can lead to accidents; practice can lead to improvement.

47. D: Sight is an example of a sense; gravity is an example of a force.

48. A: Dexterity is a kind of skill; English is a kind of language.

49. C: A coach is in charge of a team; a teacher is in charge of students.

50. B: An article is a section of a magazine; a chapter is a section of a book.

51. C: A house is a part of the neighborhood and a tree is a part of the forest.

52. B: A wallet holds money and an envelope holds a letter.

53. D: A German shepherd is a type of dog and a strawberry is a type of fruit.

54. B: Joyful is an opposite of sad and empty is an opposite of crowded.

55. C: An automobile is stored in the garage and a dish is stored in a cupboard.

56. C: A doctor works in the field of medicine and a teacher works in the field of education.

57. A: Chirp is a similar action to tweet and jump is a similar action to leap.

58. B: Sleeping is a solution for being tired and drinking is a solution for being thirsty.

59. D: A four-leaf clover is a symbol of luck and an arrow is a symbol of direction.

60. B: A question requires an answer and a problem requires a solution.

Quantitative

1. A: To solve this problem, the relationship between x and y needs to be identified for each data table. The relationship in data table A is that y is 3 more than x: $y = x + 3$. The relationship in data table B is that y is 3 times as much as x: $y = 3x$. The relationship in data table C is that y is 3 times as much as x: $y = 3x$. The relationship in data table D is that y is 3 times as much as x: $y = 3x$. Data table B, C, and D could be the table that André drew, and A could not be the table that he drew.

2. D: This problem focuses on solving problems with integers and using the order of operations. The first step is to solve the addition problem in the parentheses, so $-9 + 3 = -6$. The next step is to simplify the fraction $\frac{-6}{2}$ using division, so $-6 \div 2 = -3$.

3. B: This problem focuses on the different ways to represent division. In the story given, Tavario has 32 shirts and is packaging them in sets of 4. He can express the division problem in many ways, but no matter the representation, this problem explains that 32 shirts are divided into piles of 4, or 32 divided by 4. Division can be represented using long division, a fraction, the division symbol, and word form. Each representation expresses the division problem from the story except option B, which represents 4 divided by 32 instead of 32 divided by 4.

4. C: This problem focuses on the formula for the area of a square. A square is a type of rectangle where all sides are the same length. Because a square is a rectangle, the formula for the area of a rectangle, $A = bh$, can be used to find the area of a square. Also, because a square has equivalent side lengths, the base and height are equal and can be described as side length, s. This means that the area of a square is $A = s \cdot s$. Also, a value multiplied by itself can be represented as the square of that value, so $A = s \cdot s$ is equivalent to $A = s^2$. The formula $A = s + s + s + s$ would add all the side lengths of a square, which is used not to find the area, but to find the perimeter.

5. A: Applying the distributive property to $2(a + 3) + 3a + 4$ yields $2a + 6 + 3a + 4$. Combining like terms yields $5a + 10$. Therefore, choice A is correct.

6. B: In this table, the x values represent the number of hours and the y values represent the number of dollars. The number of hours is the independent value because the number of dollars is dependent on the number of hours.

7. B: The sum of the angles of a triangle is 180°. The measure of angle A can be found by $180° - (34° + 64°)$, or $180° - 98°$, which is 82°. Therefore, choice B is correct.

8. C: This problem focuses on writing equations from a table. In this table, s is the independent value which means that an operation is being performed on s to get t. In this example, each s value is multiplied by 4 to get the t value, which is expressed by the equation $t = 4s$.

9. D: This problem focuses on converting fractions to decimals. There are a couple strategies that can be used to convert fractions to decimals. One way would be through using division. $\frac{1}{8}$ is equivalent to 0.125, $\frac{1}{4} = 0.25$, $\frac{3}{8} = 0.375$, and $\frac{1}{2} = 0.5$.

10. B: This problem focuses on identifying the mode of a data set. The mode of a data set is the value that appears the most. In this example, the value 0 appears 4 times, the value 1 appears 9 times, and the value 2 appears 7 times. The mode of the data set is 1.

11. A: This problem focuses on converting measurements. The conversion sheet can be used to find that 1 meter is equivalent to 100 centimeters, so 7.3 meters is equivalent to 730 centimeters because $7.3 \cdot 100 = 730$. Also, 1 centimeter is equivalent to 10 millimeters, so 7.3 meters is equivalent to 7300 millimeters because $7.3 \cdot 1,000 = 7,300$. Lastly, 1 kilometer is equivalent to 1,000 meters, so 7.3 meters is equivalent to 0.0073 kilometers because $7.3 \div 1,000 = 0.0073$.

12. D: This problem focuses on using proportions to solve a problem. If a recipe calls for 5 cups of flour for every 2 cups of sugar, the ratio of flour to sugar is $\frac{5}{2}$. If Azah needs to know the number of cups of sugar used for 8 cups of flour, this ratio of flour to sugar can be expressed by $\frac{8}{x}$, where x represents the number of cups of sugar. The ratio of flour to sugar stays proportional, which means that $\frac{5}{2} = \frac{8}{x}$.

13. C: Since she earns \$5 for walking dogs and watering flowers, this term can be combined to simplify the equation. The other terms for bringing back trashcans and checking the mail are straight multiplication.

14. B: This problem focuses on using the area formula to find the area of a trapezoid. The reference sheet can be used to find the formula for the area of a trapezoid, $A = \frac{1}{2}(b_1 + b_2)h$. Based on the diagram, $b_1 = 15$ cm, $b_2 = 25$ cm, and $h = 3$ cm. These values can be inserted into the trapezoid formula, where $A = \frac{1}{2}(15 + 25) \cdot 3 = \frac{1}{2}(40) \cdot 3 = 20 \cdot 3 = 60$.

15. D: This procedure first finds the area to be fertilized, by multiplying the length and width of the rectangular yard. Then, it divides that area by the area each pound of fertilizer will cover.

16. C: This problem focuses on the difference between an equation and an expression. An expression is a number, variable, or group of numbers, variables, and operations. Expressions are often meant to be simplified, can stand alone, and can be found on one side of an equal sign. An equation is a group of expressions separated by an equal sign. Equations are often meant to be solved, usually solving for a variable. In this problem, $2x + 4 - x$ is a group of numbers, variables, and operations that does not include an equal sign, so Example 1 is an expression. $2x - x = -4$ is a set of expressions; $2x - x$ and -4 are both expressions. These expressions are separated by an equal sign, so Example 2 is an equation.

17. B: The total cost of the soda and pizza must be less than or equal to \$50. Since each pizza cost \$8, $8n$ represents the cost of n pizzas, and since Steven plans to spend \$10 on soda, $8n + 10$ represents the cost of the pizza and soda together, which must be less than or equal to \$50. The correct inequality is $8n + 10 \le 50$. Therefore, choice B is correct.

18. B: The volume of the rectangular prism is found by multiplying the area of the base times the height, or Volume = length × width × height. So, $V = (8m)(4m)(6m) = 192$ m³. Therefore, choice B is correct.

19. A: Similar polygons must have congruent corresponding angles and proportional corresponding sides. Both requirements must be fulfilled in order to declare similarity in polygons.

20. B: There are many ways to order the given values. One way is to convert all values to decimals. 0.23 and 0.6 are already in decimal form. $\frac{20}{100}$ is equivalent to 0.2, 45% is equivalent to 0.45, and $\frac{2}{5}$ is equivalent to 0.4. These decimal values listed from greatest to least are 0.6, 0.45, 0.4, 0.23, 0.2.

21. D: The B in the formula $V = Bh$ represents the area of the triangular base. The formula for the area of a triangle is $\frac{1}{2}bh$, where b represents the length of the triangle's base and h represents the triangle's height.

22. A: There are many strategies that can be used to correctly order these values from greatest to least. One way to approach this problem would be to use number sense and conversions. By reviewing the table and using some number sense, identify the largest or smallest values. The largest values in the table are $\frac{7}{8}$ and 80%. To appropriately compare these values to find the greatest value, they should be converted to a similar format, like decimals. The decimal form of $\frac{7}{8}$ can be found using division, where 7 divided by 8 equals 0.875, and 80% is equivalent to 0.8. Based on this comparison $\frac{7}{8}$ is the greatest value, followed by 80%. By understanding fractions, percents, and decimals, it can be identified that $\frac{3}{4}$ is equivalent to 0.75, or 75%, so $\frac{3}{4}$ is the next greatest number. The remaining values are 33% and $\frac{2}{5}$. These values can be converted to decimals. 33% is equivalent to 0.33 and $\frac{2}{5}$ is equivalent to 0.4, so 0.33 is the smallest value. The correct list from greatest to least is represented by option A: $\frac{7}{8}$, 80%, $\frac{3}{4}$, $\frac{2}{5}$, 33%.

23. C: The corresponding sides of similar triangles are proportional. In these triangles, RQ corresponds to UT, QS corresponds to TV, and RS corresponds to UV. Therefore, $\frac{QS}{RS} = \frac{TV}{UV}$.

Choice C is correct.

24. D: Similar figures have the same shape, and corresponding angles of the similar figures are congruent. Since all squares are quadrilaterals with four right angles and four congruent sides, all squares are similar. Not all triangles, trapezoids, or polygons are similar. Therefore, choice D is correct.

25. A: This problem focuses on solutions to inequalities. The story expresses the inequality $420 \geq 7m$ because Bella doesn't want to spend more than 420 minutes on social media during each week, which means that she could spend 420 minutes but cannot go over 420 minutes. This inequality can be simplified by using division. $420 \geq 7m$ is equivalent to $\frac{420}{7} \geq \frac{7m}{7}$, which can be simplified to $60 \geq m$.

How to Overcome Test Anxiety

Just the thought of taking a test is enough to make most people a little nervous. A test is an important event that can have a long-term impact on your future, so it's important to take it seriously and it's natural to feel anxious about performing well. But just because anxiety is normal, that doesn't mean that it's helpful in test taking, or that you should simply accept it as part of your life. Anxiety can have a variety of effects. These effects can be mild, like making you feel slightly nervous, or severe, like blocking your ability to focus or remember even a simple detail.

If you experience test anxiety—whether severe or mild—it's important to know how to beat it. To discover this, first you need to understand what causes test anxiety.

Causes of Test Anxiety

While we often think of anxiety as an uncontrollable emotional state, it can actually be caused by simple, practical things. One of the most common causes of test anxiety is that a person does not feel adequately prepared for their test. This feeling can be the result of many different issues such as poor study habits or lack of organization, but the most common culprit is time management. Starting to study too late, failing to organize your study time to cover all of the material, or being distracted while you study will mean that you're not well prepared for the test. This may lead to cramming the night before, which will cause you to be physically and mentally exhausted for the test. Poor time management also contributes to feelings of stress, fear, and hopelessness as you realize you are not well prepared but don't know what to do about it.

Other times, test anxiety is not related to your preparation for the test but comes from unresolved fear. This may be a past failure on a test, or poor performance on tests in general. It may come from comparing yourself to others who seem to be performing better or from the stress of living up to expectations. Anxiety may be driven by fears of the future—how failure on this test would affect your educational and career goals. These fears are often completely irrational, but they can still negatively impact your test performance.

> **Review Video: 3 Reasons You Have Test Anxiety**
> Visit mometrix.com/academy and enter code: 428468

Elements of Test Anxiety

As mentioned earlier, test anxiety is considered to be an emotional state, but it has physical and mental components as well. Sometimes you may not even realize that you are suffering from test anxiety until you notice the physical symptoms. These can include trembling hands, rapid heartbeat, sweating, nausea, and tense muscles. Extreme anxiety may lead to fainting or vomiting. Obviously, any of these symptoms can have a negative impact on testing. It is important to recognize them as soon as they begin to occur so that you can address the problem before it damages your performance.

> **Review Video: 3 Ways to Tell You Have Test Anxiety**
> Visit mometrix.com/academy and enter code: 927847

The mental components of test anxiety include trouble focusing and inability to remember learned information. During a test, your mind is on high alert, which can help you recall information and stay focused for an extended period of time. However, anxiety interferes with your mind's natural processes, causing you to blank out, even on the questions you know well. The strain of testing during anxiety makes it difficult to stay focused, especially on a test that may take several hours. Extreme anxiety can take a huge mental toll, making it difficult not only to recall test information but even to understand the test questions or pull your thoughts together.

> **Review Video: How Test Anxiety Affects Memory**
> Visit mometrix.com/academy and enter code: 609003

Effects of Test Anxiety

Test anxiety is like a disease—if left untreated, it will get progressively worse. Anxiety leads to poor performance, and this reinforces the feelings of fear and failure, which in turn lead to poor performances on subsequent tests. It can grow from a mild nervousness to a crippling condition. If allowed to progress, test anxiety can have a big impact on your schooling, and consequently on your future.

Test anxiety can spread to other parts of your life. Anxiety on tests can become anxiety in any stressful situation, and blanking on a test can turn into panicking in a job situation. But fortunately, you don't have to let anxiety rule your testing and determine your grades. There are a number of relatively simple steps you can take to move past anxiety and function normally on a test and in the rest of life.

> **Review Video: How Test Anxiety Impacts Your Grades**
> Visit mometrix.com/academy and enter code: 939819

Physical Steps for Beating Test Anxiety

While test anxiety is a serious problem, the good news is that it can be overcome. It doesn't have to control your ability to think and remember information. While it may take time, you can begin taking steps today to beat anxiety.

Just as your first hint that you may be struggling with anxiety comes from the physical symptoms, the first step to treating it is also physical. Rest is crucial for having a clear, strong mind. If you are tired, it is much easier to give in to anxiety. But if you establish good sleep habits, your body and mind will be ready to perform optimally, without the strain of exhaustion. Additionally, sleeping well helps you to retain information better, so you're more likely to recall the answers when you see the test questions.

Getting good sleep means more than going to bed on time. It's important to allow your brain time to relax. Take study breaks from time to time so it doesn't get overworked, and don't study right before bed. Take time to rest your mind before trying to rest your body, or you may find it difficult to fall asleep.

> **Review Video: The Importance of Sleep for Your Brain**
> Visit mometrix.com/academy and enter code: 319338

Along with sleep, other aspects of physical health are important in preparing for a test. Good nutrition is vital for good brain function. Sugary foods and drinks may give a burst of energy but this burst is followed by a crash, both physically and emotionally. Instead, fuel your body with protein and vitamin-rich foods.

Also, drink plenty of water. Dehydration can lead to headaches and exhaustion, especially if your brain is already under stress from the rigors of the test. Particularly if your test is a long one, drink water during the breaks. And if possible, take an energy-boosting snack to eat between sections.

> **Review Video: How Diet Can Affect your Mood**
> Visit mometrix.com/academy and enter code: 624317

Along with sleep and diet, a third important part of physical health is exercise. Maintaining a steady workout schedule is helpful, but even taking 5-minute study breaks to walk can help get your blood pumping faster and clear your head. Exercise also releases endorphins, which contribute to a positive feeling and can help combat test anxiety.

When you nurture your physical health, you are also contributing to your mental health. If your body is healthy, your mind is much more likely to be healthy as well. So take time to rest, nourish your body with healthy food and water, and get moving as much as possible. Taking these physical steps will make you stronger and more able to take the mental steps necessary to overcome test anxiety.

Mental Steps for Beating Test Anxiety

Working on the mental side of test anxiety can be more challenging, but as with the physical side, there are clear steps you can take to overcome it. As mentioned earlier, test anxiety often stems from lack of preparation, so the obvious solution is to prepare for the test. Effective studying may be the most important weapon you have for beating test anxiety, but you can and should employ several other mental tools to combat fear.

First, boost your confidence by reminding yourself of past success—tests or projects that you aced. If you're putting as much effort into preparing for this test as you did for those, there's no reason you should expect to fail here. Work hard to prepare; then trust your preparation.

Second, surround yourself with encouraging people. It can be helpful to find a study group, but be sure that the people you're around will encourage a positive attitude. If you spend time with others who are anxious or cynical, this will only contribute to your own anxiety. Look for others who are motivated to study hard from a desire to succeed, not from a fear of failure.

Third, reward yourself. A test is physically and mentally tiring, even without anxiety, and it can be helpful to have something to look forward to. Plan an activity following the test, regardless of the outcome, such as going to a movie or getting ice cream.

When you are taking the test, if you find yourself beginning to feel anxious, remind yourself that you know the material. Visualize successfully completing the test. Then take a few deep, relaxing breaths and return to it. Work through the questions carefully but with confidence, knowing that you are capable of succeeding.

Developing a healthy mental approach to test taking will also aid in other areas of life. Test anxiety affects more than just the actual test—it can be damaging to your mental health and even contribute to depression. It's important to beat test anxiety before it becomes a problem for more than testing.

Review Video: Test Anxiety and Depression
Visit mometrix.com/academy and enter code: 904704

Study Strategy

Being prepared for the test is necessary to combat anxiety, but what does being prepared look like? You may study for hours on end and still not feel prepared. What you need is a strategy for test prep. The next few pages outline our recommended steps to help you plan out and conquer the challenge of preparation.

STEP 1: SCOPE OUT THE TEST

Learn everything you can about the format (multiple choice, essay, etc.) and what will be on the test. Gather any study materials, course outlines, or sample exams that may be available. Not only will this help you to prepare, but knowing what to expect can help to alleviate test anxiety.

STEP 2: MAP OUT THE MATERIAL

Look through the textbook or study guide and make note of how many chapters or sections it has. Then divide these over the time you have. For example, if a book has 15 chapters and you have five days to study, you need to cover three chapters each day. Even better, if you have the time, leave an extra day at the end for overall review after you have gone through the material in depth.

If time is limited, you may need to prioritize the material. Look through it and make note of which sections you think you already have a good grasp on, and which need review. While you are studying, skim quickly through the familiar sections and take more time on the challenging parts. Write out your plan so you don't get lost as you go. Having a written plan also helps you feel more in control of the study, so anxiety is less likely to arise from feeling overwhelmed at the amount to cover.

STEP 3: GATHER YOUR TOOLS

Decide what study method works best for you. Do you prefer to highlight in the book as you study and then go back over the highlighted portions? Or do you type out notes of the important information? Or is it helpful to make flashcards that you can carry with you? Assemble the pens, index cards, highlighters, post-it notes, and any other materials you may need so you won't be distracted by getting up to find things while you study.

If you're having a hard time retaining the information or organizing your notes, experiment with different methods. For example, try color-coding by subject with colored pens, highlighters, or post-it notes. If you learn better by hearing, try recording yourself reading your notes so you can listen while in the car, working out, or simply sitting at your desk. Ask a friend to quiz you from your flashcards, or try teaching someone the material to solidify it in your mind.

STEP 4: CREATE YOUR ENVIRONMENT

It's important to avoid distractions while you study. This includes both the obvious distractions like visitors and the subtle distractions like an uncomfortable chair (or a too-comfortable couch that makes you want to fall asleep). Set up the best study environment possible: good lighting and a comfortable work area. If background music helps you focus, you may want to turn it on, but otherwise keep the room quiet. If you are using a computer to take notes, be sure you don't have any other windows open, especially applications like social media, games, or anything else that could distract you. Silence your phone and turn off notifications. Be sure to keep water close by so you stay hydrated while you study (but avoid unhealthy drinks and snacks).

Also, take into account the best time of day to study. Are you freshest first thing in the morning? Try to set aside some time then to work through the material. Is your mind clearer in the afternoon or evening? Schedule your study session then. Another method is to study at the same time of day that

237

you will take the test, so that your brain gets used to working on the material at that time and will be ready to focus at test time.

STEP 5: STUDY!

Once you have done all the study preparation, it's time to settle into the actual studying. Sit down, take a few moments to settle your mind so you can focus, and begin to follow your study plan. Don't give in to distractions or let yourself procrastinate. This is your time to prepare so you'll be ready to fearlessly approach the test. Make the most of the time and stay focused.

Of course, you don't want to burn out. If you study too long you may find that you're not retaining the information very well. Take regular study breaks. For example, taking five minutes out of every hour to walk briskly, breathing deeply and swinging your arms, can help your mind stay fresh.

As you get to the end of each chapter or section, it's a good idea to do a quick review. Remind yourself of what you learned and work on any difficult parts. When you feel that you've mastered the material, move on to the next part. At the end of your study session, briefly skim through your notes again.

But while review is helpful, cramming last minute is NOT. If at all possible, work ahead so that you won't need to fit all your study into the last day. Cramming overloads your brain with more information than it can process and retain, and your tired mind may struggle to recall even previously learned information when it is overwhelmed with last-minute study. Also, the urgent nature of cramming and the stress placed on your brain contribute to anxiety. You'll be more likely to go to the test feeling unprepared and having trouble thinking clearly.

So don't cram, and don't stay up late before the test, even just to review your notes at a leisurely pace. Your brain needs rest more than it needs to go over the information again. In fact, plan to finish your studies by noon or early afternoon the day before the test. Give your brain the rest of the day to relax or focus on other things, and get a good night's sleep. Then you will be fresh for the test and better able to recall what you've studied.

STEP 6: TAKE A PRACTICE TEST

Many courses offer sample tests, either online or in the study materials. This is an excellent resource to check whether you have mastered the material, as well as to prepare for the test format and environment.

Check the test format ahead of time: the number of questions, the type (multiple choice, free response, etc.), and the time limit. Then create a plan for working through them. For example, if you have 30 minutes to take a 60-question test, your limit is 30 seconds per question. Spend less time on the questions you know well so that you can take more time on the difficult ones.

If you have time to take several practice tests, take the first one open book, with no time limit. Work through the questions at your own pace and make sure you fully understand them. Gradually work up to taking a test under test conditions: sit at a desk with all study materials put away and set a timer. Pace yourself to make sure you finish the test with time to spare and go back to check your answers if you have time.

After each test, check your answers. On the questions you missed, be sure you understand why you missed them. Did you misread the question (tests can use tricky wording)? Did you forget the information? Or was it something you hadn't learned? Go back and study any shaky areas that the practice tests reveal.

Taking these tests not only helps with your grade, but also aids in combating test anxiety. If you're already used to the test conditions, you're less likely to worry about it, and working through tests until you're scoring well gives you a confidence boost. Go through the practice tests until you feel comfortable, and then you can go into the test knowing that you're ready for it.

Test Tips

On test day, you should be confident, knowing that you've prepared well and are ready to answer the questions. But aside from preparation, there are several test day strategies you can employ to maximize your performance.

First, as stated before, get a good night's sleep the night before the test (and for several nights before that, if possible). Go into the test with a fresh, alert mind rather than staying up late to study.

Try not to change too much about your normal routine on the day of the test. It's important to eat a nutritious breakfast, but if you normally don't eat breakfast at all, consider eating just a protein bar. If you're a coffee drinker, go ahead and have your normal coffee. Just make sure you time it so that the caffeine doesn't wear off right in the middle of your test. Avoid sugary beverages, and drink enough water to stay hydrated but not so much that you need a restroom break 10 minutes into the test. If your test isn't first thing in the morning, consider going for a walk or doing a light workout before the test to get your blood flowing.

Allow yourself enough time to get ready, and leave for the test with plenty of time to spare so you won't have the anxiety of scrambling to arrive in time. Another reason to be early is to select a good seat. It's helpful to sit away from doors and windows, which can be distracting. Find a good seat, get out your supplies, and settle your mind before the test begins.

When the test begins, start by going over the instructions carefully, even if you already know what to expect. Make sure you avoid any careless mistakes by following the directions.

Then begin working through the questions, pacing yourself as you've practiced. If you're not sure on an answer, don't spend too much time on it, and don't let it shake your confidence. Either skip it and come back later, or eliminate as many wrong answers as possible and guess among the remaining ones. Don't dwell on these questions as you continue—put them out of your mind and focus on what lies ahead.

Be sure to read all of the answer choices, even if you're sure the first one is the right answer. Sometimes you'll find a better one if you keep reading. But don't second-guess yourself if you do immediately know the answer. Your gut instinct is usually right. Don't let test anxiety rob you of the information you know.

If you have time at the end of the test (and if the test format allows), go back and review your answers. Be cautious about changing any, since your first instinct tends to be correct, but make sure you didn't misread any of the questions or accidentally mark the wrong answer choice. Look over any you skipped and make an educated guess.

At the end, leave the test feeling confident. You've done your best, so don't waste time worrying about your performance or wishing you could change anything. Instead, celebrate the successful completion of this test. And finally, use this test to learn how to deal with anxiety even better next time.

> **Review Video: 5 Tips to Beat Test Anxiety**
> Visit mometrix.com/academy and enter code: 570656

Important Qualification

Not all anxiety is created equal. If your test anxiety is causing major issues in your life beyond the classroom or testing center, or if you are experiencing troubling physical symptoms related to your anxiety, it may be a sign of a serious physiological or psychological condition. If this sounds like your situation, we strongly encourage you to seek professional help.

Tell Us Your Story

We at Mometrix would like to extend our heartfelt thanks to you for letting us be a part of your journey. It is an honor to serve people from all walks of life, people like you, who are committed to building the best future they can for themselves.

We know that each person's situation is unique. But we also know that, whether you are a young student or a mother of four, you care about working to make your own life and the lives of those around you better.

That's why we want to hear your story.

We want to know why you're taking this test. We want to know about the trials you've gone through to get here. And we want to know about the successes you've experienced after taking and passing your test.

In addition to your story, which can be an inspiration both to us and to others, we value your feedback. We want to know both what you loved about our book and what you think we can improve on.

The team at Mometrix would be absolutely thrilled to hear from you! So please, send us an email at tellusyourstory@mometrix.com or visit us at mometrix.com/tellusyourstory.php and let's stay in touch.

Additional Bonus Material

Due to our efforts to try to keep this book to a manageable length, we've created a link that will give you access to all of your additional bonus material:

mometrix.com/bonus948/ssatmiddle

CPSIA information can be obtained
at www.ICGtesting.com
Printed in the USA
BVHW021441130323
660322BV00013B/592